CHRONICLES OF THE SOUTH
Volume Two

CHRONICLES OF THE SOUTH

Volume Two: In Justice to so Fine a Country

Chronicles Press
Rockford, Illinois
2011

To Harry Teasley, whose generous support made Chronicles of the South *possible.*

All of the pieces in this volume first appeared in *Chronicles: A Magazine of American Culture.* The original dates of publication are listed in *About the Authors* (pp. 287-289).

Cover photo licensed from *www.istockphoto.com/Pgiam*

ISBN 978-0-9843702-4-5

CONTENTS

CHRONICLES OF THE SOUTH
Volume Two

Introduction to Volume Two

Clyde Wilson

THE SOCIOLOGIST and one-time *Chronicles* columnist John Shelton Reed does not regard the South as a Big Problem, but rather as something to be objectively described like any other human phenomenon, and maybe even appreciated a little bit. (And where else but *Chronicles* would you expect to find the only real live sociologist in captivity who can write well and has a sense of humor?)

In *The Enduring South* Reed painstakingly quantified a lot of data about behavior and attitudes to establish that, yes indeed, there are such things as Southerners who can be identified as distinct from the baseline of regular Americans. The difference is not absolute but is statistically significant. Reed found the difference most identifiable in three areas.

Southerners adhere to the basic tenets of orthodox Christian belief more than other Americans, even the general run of Catholics. Indeed, the South is the only Protestant society remaining in the world that is not post-Christian.

Second, Southerners are more family and locally oriented. They are more likely to name their children after Granpaw or somebody else close by than to adopt some trendy name; more interested in their own community than in celebrities or those national and international "issues" which many Americans mistakenly believe they understand and have some control over.

Thirdly, Southerners have a different attitude toward the appropriate uses of violence. Put shortly, this means that in the South you are more likely to be murdered by someone you know, and elsewhere by a stranger. This characteristic also suggests a persistence of old-fashioned sex roles and a bit of chivalry, familiarity with firearms, and a willingness to resort to self-defense before calling in the police.

I can add some other distinctions. The South remains not only the most socially conservative but the most politically conservative region of the United States. It is the only region that has continued for decades to vote congressional majorities against every leftist measure adopted, right up to the Obama administration's healthcare plan. This remains true even though districts have been gerrymandered in favor of minority candidates and constituencies and country-club Republicans have appeared in droves.

Another Southern distinction is of fairly recent origin. The South is the only part of the United States in which a majority of African-Americans say that they feel at home, and the only part with a net in-migration of African-Americans. The significance of this phenomenon will, of course, never be acknowledged by the political class, the media, the educational establishment, or enlightened opinion. They have far too great an investment in self-righteousness, the self-love confirmed by having the South to correct. Old habits die hard, especially if they make you feel superior.

Most certainly the South has changed lately, but it has not yet disappeared, as has so happily, confidently, and frequently been predicted. I give in evidence the talents and allegiances of the writers collected here and the richness of their Southern subject matter. It is true that in recent years not only country-club Republicans from north of the Potomac have moved in, but so have hundreds of thousands of folks from south of the Rio Grande. Even so, the Southern distinctiveness may remain. While the South is being dragged along in the direction of the new multicultural, metrosexual America, the rest of the country is moving that way so fast that the gap may even be widening.

Another way to say this is that more of the original America lives on in the South than elsewhere. That alone ought to justify *Chronicles'* nonconformist and prolific treatment of the South over many years as something to be known rather than condemned. Of course, one must understand, as Thomas Fleming has repeatedly pointed out in the pages of *Chronicles*, that the original America referred to is the one that began at Jamestown, not the one that began at Plymouth Rock and has so long and so zealously been promoted as the one and true and only America.

THE FIRST VOLUME of *Chronicles'* Southern collection concerned literature, religion, the Agrarian tradition, and problems of definition. This one is more concerned with history, politics, and interesting aspects of contemporary Southern life. *Original Intentions* is the title of a book by M.E. Bradford that revivified the Southern constitutional tradition. "The Late Unpleasantness," of course, is a polite, conciliatory name for the unparalleled bloodletting of 1861-65. "The Present Unpleasantness" is a cheerful but less conciliatory title for various writings giving a Southern view on some aspects of contemporary America. *High Times and Hard Times* was the title of a collection of Old South "Sut Lovingood" stories by the Tennessee riverboat captain George Washington Harris. Sut Lovingood is one of the funniest and most ornery characters in American literature, and Harris one of the very few writers that William Faulkner mentioned as a model.

The South won't go away. Not yet. For one reason, there are those of us who love her still. For another, those old Southern constitutionalists and Agrarian critics of "progress" are for many people beyond Mason-Dixon's Line starting to look less like disagreeable relics and more like gifted prophets.

ORIGINAL INTENTIONS

Jefferson or Mussolini?

Thomas Fleming

T HE RIGHT SIDE of the World Wide Web has been aquiver [in late 1998] with reports on Executive Order 13083, otherwise known as Bill Clinton's attempted *coup d'état.* How seriously should we take the Clinton plot to abolish the last vestiges of states' rights? Setting aside the equivocations and dissimulations that mark all of Mr. Clinton's official utterances, one can reduce his executive order on federalism (issued in Birmingham, England, in May) to two points: a very weak restatement of the principle that, under the Constitution of the United States, some powers are reserved to the states; and an aggressive and wide-reaching declaration of the conditions that entail an exception to the Tenth Amendment.

The first two exceptions, which involve interstate relations, are more or less justifiable. The rest are subjective to the point of being capricious. The federal principle is to be suspended when, for example, there is "a need for uniform national standards," when "decentralization increases the costs of government," or when states either have not protected individual rights or have failed to impose regulations from the fear that businesses would relocate. It is hard to conceive of any significant activity of state government that could not be usurped on at least one of these grounds.

Simultaneously with his decree that gives the *coup de grâce* to constitutional federalism, the President also issued Executive Order 13084 on Indian Tribal Governments. On the surface, the executive order appears to establish "regular and meaningful consultation and collaboration with Indian tribal governments in the development of regulatory practices on Federal matters that significantly or uniquely affect their communities," *etc., etc.* In fact, the effect—and purpose—of the order is to circumscribe tribal sovereignties within a ring of federal regulations that will leave them only the name of sovereignty. The penultimate sentence is ominous: "This order shall complement the consultation and waiver provisions in sections 4 and 5 of the Executive order, entitled 'Federalism,' being issued on this day."

Clinton's orders are less alarming and more depressing than they appear at first sight: less alarming because they only confirm a *status quo* that has been established since the 1960's; and more depressing because it probably does not matter what declarations and ultimatums are issued by the President. Real power is in the hands of a permanent establishment whose brains are in the federal judiciary and whose brawn consists of the tens of thousands of armed federal agents who, on mere suspicion, can raid your home, drive a tank through the walls, fill the rooms with toxic gas, and lay down a line of fire to prevent a few stray survivors from making their escape—all to the applause of congressional cheerleaders like Tom Lantos and Charles Schumer. (With Democrats like Lantos, who needs Nazis?)

If mere words meant anything, then Ronald Reagan's beautiful Executive Order 12612 on federalism would have restored the republic. Reagan's order not only reaffirmed the Tenth Amendment but went so far as to proclaim that "the people of the States created the national government when they delegated to it those enumerated powers relating to matters beyond the competence of the individual States." In fact, despite Reagan's best intentions (I think we should grant him that much), the centralization of power proceeded as rapidly in the 1980's as it had in preceding decades.

"True but irrelevant" is the usual response of a sincere American nationalist. As much as he might regret the death of the old republic, the nationalist is a pragmatist who insists upon the recognition of new realities. With a little encouragement, he will go on to explain that this is a diverse nation of over 260 million inhabitants—*citizens* is no longer a relevant concept—and there is no reason that a people who subdued a continent cannot find a way of adapting their ancient Constitution to changing circumstances. "Even if we wanted to restore the states to their original rights and privileges, we would need all the power of a central state to accomplish the task. The real objective today is the reconstruction of the American nation, and while the interests of efficiency and even of justice might be served by a stricter application of the Tenth Amendment, the various devolutionist movements—whether they are calling for states' rights or outright secession—by dividing the patriotic middle classes against each other, stand in the way of the populist uprising that will overturn the entrenched power of the current ruling class and rebuild Euro-American civilization."

The argument makes a great deal of sense, and if there were any real prospect that Middle American Radicals would escape from the pages of Don Warren's books and lead a peasants' march on Washington, my heart (if not my head) would be with them. Unfortunately, a MARS attack on the federal government is about as likely as the restoration of states' rights or an invasion of bug-eyed aliens from the red planet.

SUPPOSING A POPULIST REBELLION did succeed, what sort of America would be restored? Here is the real fly in the imaginary nationalist ointment. States' rights is not simply a part of the American political inheritance: It is the core that has defined us as a nation since 1776, when 13 colonies individually threw off the shackles that bound them to the British Empire. They not only opposed the corrupt regime of 18th-century England but rejected the concept of the modern unitary state.

The usual counterargument—that the incorporation of the "principles of the Declaration" into the Constitution justifies the national government's usurpation of the rights of the states—is the tawdriest sort of propaganda, which is not to say that there is nothing to learn from Mr. Jefferson's "unanimous Declaration of the thirteen united States of America." Consider only the orthography: "States" is capitalized, because they are the sovereign parties to the agreement, while "united" is merely a descriptive adjective. The pattern is repeated in the conclusion, which goes on to spell out the fact that they are "Free and Independent States." Their unity was through the Congress, a body composed of diplomatic representatives of the several states. In November 1777, the specific and limited form of that unity was declared in the Articles of Confederation, whose second article stipulates that "Each state retains its sovereignty, freedom, and independence, and every power, jurisdiction, and right, which is not by this Confederation expressly delegated to the United States in Congress assembled."

In time, some (by no means all) American political leaders came to the conclusion that the Articles had to be modified in the direction of a stronger general government that could act decisively to settle disputes between states and provide a stronger common defense against the infant nation's many enemies, not all of them foreign. It is not easy to determine the exact relationship between the Articles and the Constitution adopted ten years later. In one sense, the Constitution obviously supersedes the Articles, but it is not always easy to understand the provisions of the later document without having some knowledge of the earlier. The Tenth Amendment, for example, is clearly an attempt to declare that the states, in ratifying the Constitution, were not giving up their rights under the Articles except to the extent that certain powers were explicitly delegated to the revised government. Even some of the more general language of the Constitution appears to have been borrowed deliberately from the Articles so as to leave less room for misunderstanding.

James Madison, often called the "father of the Constitution," complained that the general government of the United States was attempting "to enlarge its powers by forced construction of the constitutional charter which defines them," adding that

> indications have appeared of a design to expound certain general phrases . . . so as to destroy the meaning and effect of the particular enumeration which necessarily explains and limits the general phrases; and so as to consolidate the States, by degrees, into one sovereignty, the obvious tendency and inevitable result of which would be to transform the present republican system of the United States into an absolute, or, at best, a mixed monarchy.

In Madison's view, then, republicanism itself depended on the preservation of states' rights, and he opposed the broad construction of general language (in, for example, the Preamble) which, he says, could not possibly be misinterpreted because "having been copied from the very limited grant of powers in the former Articles of Confederation, were the less liable to be misconstrued." So, expressions like "common defense" and "general welfare," as they are used in the Constitution, are to be read in the light of the Articles.

Madison's protest against the centralization of power is not a personal expression in a private letter. It is contained in a set of resolutions passed by the Virginia House of Delegates in December 1798. Almost simultaneously, Kentucky passed an even longer and more explicit declaration of states' rights. The gist is given in the first resolution:

> the several States composing the United States of America are not united on the principle of unlimited submission to their General Government; but that, by a compact under the style and title of a Constitution for the United States . . . they constituted a General Government for special purposes . . . reserving, each State to itself, the residuary mass of right to their own self-government; and that whensoever the General Government assumes undelegated powers, its acts are unauthoritative, void, and of no force; that to this compact each State acceded as a State, and is an integral party, its co-States forming, as to itself, the other party: that the government created by this compact was not made the exclusive or final judge of the extent of the power delegated to itself; since that would have made its discretion, and not the Constitution, the measure of its powers; but that, as in all other cases of compact among powers having no common judge, each party has

an equal right to judge for itself, as well of infractions as of the mode and measure of redress.

This is the strongest possible statement of what became known as the "compact theory," and in the eighth resolution, Kentucky laid her cards on the table—and they were all trumps. Arguing that the unauthorized centralization of power "is not for the peace, happiness or prosperity of these States," it is resolved that "where powers are assumed which have not been delegated, a nullification of the act is the rightful remedy . . . every State has a natural right . . . to nullify of their own authority all assumptions of power by others within their limits . . . "

THE AUTHOR of the Kentucky Resolutions was not a 16-year-old John C. Calhoun but Madison's political chief and then-mentor, Thomas Jefferson. Madison, in drawing up the resolutions that were moved by John Taylor in the Virginia legislature, was acting in concert with (or, rather, under instructions from) Jefferson, who was working feverishly in this period to prevent the breakup of the federal union. A firm stand on states' rights, he thought, would keep Virginia from bolting.

The Virginians were disgusted with the New England administration of John Adams, which (so they believed) was every day assuming monarchical dimensions, and they were infuriated by the Alien and Sedition Acts, designed to punish the Jeffersonians and their immigrant friends. "But if," wrote Jefferson to John Taylor on June 4, 1798, "on a temporary superiority of the one party, the other is to resolve to a scission of the Union, no federal government can ever exist," because the habit of fissioning, once established, would not cease until North Carolina and Virginia would part company. "A little patience," he concluded, "and we shall see the reign of witches pass over, their spells dissolve, and the people recovering their true sight, restore the government to its true principles."

By 1798, Jefferson had quarreled with his old friend and colleague John Adams, and neither of the men (or their supporters) was capable of being fair to the other. The followers of Vice President Jefferson viewed President Adams as "King John," a priggish and conceited despot in embryo and an enemy to republican government. The misnamed Federalists, on the other hand, red-baited Jefferson and his friends as bloodthirsty Jacobins, already sharpening the blades on their guillotines. There was some truth (though not much) in each side's propaganda. John Adams was something of a prig—how could the descendant of Puritans help it?—and he had grown flat-footed, politically, from standing too much upon ceremony.

21

Jefferson, on the other hand, was subject to most of the follies of the 18th century. He believed in progress and enlightenment, viewed inherited rank and status as the enemy of humanity, and believed that the purely moral doctrines of Jesus had been perverted by priests and bigots into a system that oppressed the human mind. As a conventional child of the Enlightenment, Jefferson was a platitudinizing leftist with an ability to turn a phrase, an honest Voltaire, a Tom Paine with roots. But Jefferson did have roots in the soil of Virginia, with runners connecting him with the best families in the Old Dominion. It was not his fashionable radicalism or acquaintance with French intellectuals that made Jefferson distinctive, but the lessons he learned as a Virginian. Jefferson the radical is merely an American *philosophe*; Jefferson the Virginian is the great reactionary of the American political tradition.

Jefferson showed his two sides on virtually every issue, but as he matured, the Virginian slowly overtook the *philosophe* (a reversal of the Jekyll and Hyde story). In his early days, he spoke windily about the need for a new, more progressive education; he ended up both as a militant apologist for the classical tradition and—as Albert Jay Nock pointed out—as a staunch elitist. The authors of *Who Killed Homer?* are aware that Jefferson's University of Virginia had something like an open curriculum. What they do not know is that UVA required graduates "to be able to read the highest classics in the language with ease, thorough understanding, and just quantity." (Jefferson took a keen interest in Greek and English prosody.)

In his political struggle with Hamilton and his allies, Jefferson came to believe that Hamilton was attempting to reinflict the British system of organized corruption upon the American people. The fulfillment of this ambition required a centralization of power that went beyond the limits laid down in the Constitution: a national bank undergirded by a national debt that would make the government dependent upon the commercial interests who, in turn, would support the government; restrictions on the press that would prevent the emergence of a principled opposition; and a crackdown on foreigners that would quarantine Americans against the French political disease.

In protesting against the Alien and Sedition Acts, the Jeffersonians had to move cautiously, to avoid the impression that they were either opposing the ascendant Federalists for purely political motives or defending traitors and foreign agitators. Madison and Jefferson took their stand on the Constitution's reservation of unenumerated powers to the states and to the people. In the Kentucky Resolutions, Jefferson goes to what seems to be the absurd length of insisting that "alien friends are under the jurisdiction and protection of the laws of the State wherein they are: that no power over them has been delegated to the United States, nor prohibited to the individual States, distinct from their power over citizens."

Even the most entrenched advocates of states' rights would probably concede that immigration and naturalization are matters better left to the general government, but Jefferson's position is far from unworkable. In frontier communities, for example, aliens were often allowed to vote in local elections, on the grounds that they were part of the local—if not of the national—community, and it is not too much of a stretch to imagine a federal republic in which Florida might choose to take in an unlimited supply of Cuban exiles who would not be allowed to enter Georgia. Contrariwise, Florida would have been able to reject both the "Marielitos" expelled by Castro and the Haitians whose highly dubious claims to refugee status were acknowledged by the federal government, much to the disgust of the people of Florida and their governor. The whole immigration debate might be depoliticized if border states were able to import seasonal labor without imposing them as welfare claimants and supposititious citizens on the entire nation.

A state-and-local approach would also defuse the abortion debate, the same-sex "marriage" crisis, Mormon polygamy, the war on drugs, and the gun issue. Nationalists will always protest, claiming that guns, drugs, and homosexual couples will find their way from one state to another, but Muslims have no difficulty, apparently, in bringing their harems and high explosives into the United States. Fifty separate (but cooperating) jurisdictions would have to do a better job of putting tourniquets on the spreading poison of drugs and automatic weapons than the manifestly incompetent and brutal murderers who work for the BATF, the FBI, and other agencies that maintain strict compliance with the Americans With Disabilities Act.

STATES' RIGHTS AND FEDERALISM, we know, are relics in the museum of dead ideologies; consolidation of power is inevitable and progressive, the wave of the future. But we live in the future, and it does not work. Perhaps it is time to give the sage of Monticello a second chance. He was, after all, no simplistic ideologue on the subject of states' rights. As Dumas Malone points out, Jefferson had acknowledged the need to strengthen the government set up by the Articles; his criticisms of the Constitution "related, not to the reduction in the powers of the states, but to the lack of safeguards for individuals."

In drafting the Kentucky Resolutions, according to Malone, "Jefferson went further in his emphasis on the rights and powers of the states vis-à-vis the general government than he had ever done before or was ever to do again." This is not entirely accurate. The 1798 Resolutions may represent the high-water mark of his defense of states' rights, but that is partly because the nature of the crisis demanded a strong and principled response. In 1800, Jefferson was in office and could hardly regard his own administration as a threat to Virginia, and his Virginia dynasty lasted through three presidencies for 24 years. However, it was only in his later years that Jefferson fully articulated his vision of decentralized political authority, both in his plan for a localized system of state education in Virginia and in his blueprint for a government of wards, outlined in a series of letters written in the last ten years of his life.

In Jefferson's comprehensive vision, each level of government—national, state, local, and neighborhood—would have sufficient autonomy to manage its own affairs. Each ward (corresponding to a township or neighborhood) would be given "those portions of self-government for which they are best qualified, by confiding to them the care of their poor, their roads, police, elections, the nomination of jurors, administration of justice in small cases, elementary exercises of militia." In short, says Jefferson, these wards will become "little republics . . . for all those concerns which, being under their eye, they would better manage than the larger republics of the county or State."

Ultimately, the principle of devolution works its way down even to the household, to "the administration of every man's farm by himself." This principle, if carried out, would serve as a secure foundation of political liberty: "Where every man is a sharer in the direction of his ward-republic . . . and feels that he is a participator in the government of affairs, not merely at an election one day in the year, but every day; . . . he will let the heart be torn out of his body sooner than his power be wrested from him by a Caesar or a Bonaparte."

It hardly needs to be said that would-be Bonapartes and their lackeys are instinctively revolted by Jefferson's vision. Today, he would he called President Moonbeam, because it is a mark of insanity to believe that a government can be anything but corrupt.

What are the inspirations for Mr. Jefferson's vision? His own experience of managing an estate and working with his neighbors must have been at the back of his mind, but Jefferson also had read enough about the history of ancient Greek and Renaissance Italian city-states to know that political liberty and national creativity are always rooted in local attachments.

24

His radically American dream may have drawn its strength from ancient and medieval sources, but despite the constant opposition of national and state governments, America remained a predominantly Jeffersonian nation through the 19th century. Most so-called public schools were owned and operated by communities as small as one of his wards, and the volunteer-ism that he recommends ("Get them to meet and build a log cabin," he urges Joseph Cabell in describing how a local community can take charge of its own affairs) and that is described by Tocqueville was the spirit that animat-ed the towns and villages that sprang up on the prairies without any "by your leave" from any of the Caesars and Walpoles who had taken up permanent residence on the Potomac.

When honest men ponder the future of the United States, they would do well to consider Jefferson's recommendation that the best defense against dictatorship is the independence of neighborhoods, counties, and states. In a famous pamphlet, Ezra Pound floated the idea of Jefferson and/or Mus-solini. As usual, Ol' Ez was half right, but whatever good points Mussolini had, he was Caesarist. If that is what the nationalists of left and right desire for their country, I wish they would say so. But for my political leader, I shall take Jefferson without any ifs, ands, or buts.

One Nation Divisible

Donald W. Livingston

S OMETHING EXTRAORDINARY has happened over the last decade or so—
something neither the Republican nor Democratic leadership seems to
understand. A large and growing number of Americans are now openly
saying that much of what the central government does is not simply waste-
ful, corrupt, and destructive but illegitimate as well. This year [1998] the
central government will spend about $1.7 trillion, more than it spent (even
adjusting for inflation) from the Revolutionary period through 1940. And
next year it will no doubt spend more than that. But Americans are not just
concerned that the spending of nearly two trillion dollars in one year by
435 "representatives" and 100 senators for an empire of 265 million subjects
would lead to plunder and corruption; they are also concerned about how
the money is spent.

The unprecedented power concentrated in Washington supports a universalist egalitarian ideology that is openly hostile to the inherited moral, religious, and cultural traditions of American society. Largely through the enormous patronage concentrated at the center, this ideology has come to dominate state governments, universities, and the media and has had a corrupting
influence on the mainline churches. Today Americans stand by impotently,
but with smoldering resentment, as they watch their tax money being used to
suppress or extinguish their own cultural inheritance. What is to be done?

A furor was raised over the November 1996 issue of *First Things*, in
which a number of contributors argued that individuals should consider open resistance against the central government (especially the Supreme
Court) in those areas where it had offended Christian conscience and natural law. Now, resistance in the name of conscience is not entirely to be
despised, but it often leads to terrorism. John Brown did some thinking
about natural law, and his conscience told him to murder innocent families in their sleep. He was greatly applauded by New England Transcenden-
talists and by Northern universalist Christians who had lost their trinitari-
an faith, and he is still applauded by their progeny today. Things could get
ugly indeed if this sort of "Christian" began to place his conscience in the
scales against the rule of law.

But there is another form of resistance to federal tyranny not considered by the contributors to *First Things*—and one, moreover, that is constitutional. I have in mind the remedy that Jefferson, in the Kentucky Resolutions, and Madison, in the Virginia Report, called state "interposition." A state, as a sovereign political society that has delegated to the central government only enumerated powers, has the constitutional authority to interpose its authority to protect its citizens from tyrannical actions of the central government. Any genuine federal system that is serious about preserving the distinct moral cultures of its political units must allow some form of state interposition. But state interposition cannot be effective unless it can be enforced, and in a federal system this can only mean the ultimate right of a state to secede from the federation. The Canadian constitution, for example, through its "notwithstanding" clause, allows a province to nullify actions of the central government in the area of civil rights; and it is generally understood that a Canadian province can secede. It was through state interposition that 15 republics of the former Soviet Union were able to secede.

If American states have the constitutional right and, as Jefferson insisted, the constitutional *duty* to interpose their authority to check an unconstitutional act of the central government, why have no states exercised this right over the past 40 years or so, when violations of the reserved powers of the states, especially by the Supreme Court, have been so blatant as to defy belief?

One answer is that the enormous patronage concentrated in the central government has corrupted the states and rendered them administrative units of the center—an effect Hamilton said (and hoped) federal patronage would bring about. This is certainly true, but it is not the whole story. At some point in our history, many Americans came to think that secession of a state is ruled out by the Constitution; and without the right of secession, state interposition loses its force. But is it true that there is a constitutional prohibition to the secession of an American state?

There are two incompatible theories of the Constitution to which Americans have given their allegiance: the compact theory and the nationalist theory. The compact theory was the understanding of the Framers and was first given formal expression by Thomas Jefferson in the Kentucky Resolutions (1798). In this theory, secession is legal, for the Constitution is a compact between sovereign states, which created a central government as their agent and endowed it with only enumerated powers (mainly defense, regulation of interstate commerce, and foreign treaties). No branch of the central government can have the final say over what powers were delegated to the central government and what powers were reserved to the states because the central government is the agent of the compact and the states are the principals. As a sovereign political society, a state may interpose its authority to check an unconstitutional action of the central government and, as the last remedy, may recall those powers it had delegated and secede from the federation. As Jefferson put it in 1816: "If any State in the Union will declare that it prefers separation . . . to a continuance in union . . . , I have no hesitation in saying 'let us separate.'"

The nationalist theory was a late arrival, first appearing in Joseph Story's *Commentaries* in 1833. The nationalist theory holds that the states were never sovereign. Upon breaking with Britain, the people descended into the philosopher's "state of nature." From this nonpolitical state, the American people spontaneously emerged as a sovereign political society. This sovereign people formed the Continental Congress, which authorized the formation of states as administrative units of the general will. Not being sovereign, a state cannot legally secede from the union any more than a county can, on its own, secede from a state. Though an elegant system, Story's jurisprudence was grounded in historical theses that are spectacular absurdities.

THE FORMER COLONIES did not lose their character as political societies by seceding from Britain. The Scottish philosopher David Hume wrote this memo to himself in the 1740's: "The Charter Governments in America are almost entirely independent of England." Each former colony declared sovereignty for itself. These new states formed the Articles of Confederation, and Article II declared that "each State retains its sovereignty, freedom, and independence." During and after the war, states exercised the powers of sovereignty: building navies, raising armies, issuing letters of marque, coining money (Massachusetts coined money as early as 1643), conquering British territory in their own name, and negotiating agreements with foreign powers. After the war each state was recognized by name by the British sovereign as a "free, sovereign, and independent state." States reaffirmed their sovereignty after the war, and New York, Rhode Island, and Virginia asserted their sovereignty in the strongest terms by writing into their ordinances ratifying the Constitution the right to secede. There is no question that if the nationalist theory had been put to these states, and they had been told that they were not and had never been sovereign states, and that once in the union they could not withdraw, there would have been no union.

It is true that Hamilton, Madison, and Wilson had proposed a nationalist constitution with federal control of the states, but they were soundly defeated. Madison's proposal almost wrecked the Philadelphia Convention, and Hamilton's proposal did not even receive a second. Having just seceded from

Britain, the states were not about to consolidate themselves into an American version of a centralized British state.

THIS LEADS TO THE SECOND THESIS of the nationalist theory: that the union is perpetual and cannot be divided. The Supreme Court took up the question of secession in *Texas* v. *White* (1869) and, predictably enough, ruled that the Constitution does not permit the secession of a state. The Court reasserted the absurd nationalist doctrine that "the union created the states." To this it tacked on the statement in the Articles of Confederation that the union is "perpetual" along with the Preamble to the Constitution that declares the intention to build a "more perfect Union," and concluded: "It is difficult to convey the idea of indissoluble unity more clearly than by these words. What can be indissoluble if a perpetual Union, made more perfect, is not?" The force behind this conclusion, however, is more the cheers of a victorious army than the historical coherence of true constitutional reasoning.

If the union were indeed perpetual, as a matter of fundamental law, there must at least have been a solid history of union continuity. But there was no such history. Those who went to the Philadelphia Convention were authorized only to *amend* the Articles of Confederation. Instead, the delegates proposed a new constitution and abandoned the requirement of the Articles that any fundamental change would require the unanimous consent of the states. The new constitution would take effect if only nine states ratified it. Nine states did ratify, leaving North Carolina, Rhode Island, Virginia, and New York free to go it alone. Rhode Island refused to attend the convention, and by its veto made unanimous consent impossible. Rhode Island remained out of the union as an independent state for nearly two years.

That the union had been dissolved and was not perpetual was openly acknowledged. In the *Federalist*, Madison said that if some states refused to ratify, then "no political relation can subsist between the assenting and dissenting states," but he hoped that one day a "re-union" should occur. Many argued that dissolution of the union was justified because states had violated the terms of the Articles on a number of occasions, and as Madison put it: "a breach of any article, by any one party, leaves all the other parties at liberty to consider the whole convention dissolved." This is just the argument that Southern states would later use to secede from the union in 1860-61. Finally, the Preamble claims "to *form* a more perfect Union," and that, of course, is quite different from perfecting an old one.

Nor is the nationalist theory buttressed by the wording of the Constitution. The Preamble, with its reference to "We the People," was tirelessly used by Story, Webster, and Lincoln and in *Texas* v. *White*, and has been used since to support the contention that sovereignty resides in the American people in the aggregate. But the original wording of the Preamble was in the style of the Articles: "We the people of the State of New Hampshire, Massachusetts," *etc.* This wording passed unanimously, but was changed by the committee on style on the grounds that it was not known which states would ratify. The change was considered trivial and brought forth no response, as it would have had it carried the radical meaning with which nationalists later endowed it.

But perhaps nothing shows more clearly the absurdity of the nationalist theory than the manner in which the Constitution was authorized. It was not ratified by majority vote of the American people in the aggregate but by the people of the respective states. Each state ratified the Constitution for itself alone, with no authority to bind the people of another state. The question of whether the new union would be indivisible was not raised at the Philadelphia Convention. The would-be nationalists at the convention had been soundly defeated. And, having just voted to dissolve a union said to be "perpetual," they were in no position to argue that the new union would be indivisible.

From the very beginning, and throughout the antebellum period, the Constitution was regularly described as a compact, the union as a confederation, and, most importantly, as an "experiment," implying that it was divisible. This idiom was publicly established by Washington in his Farewell Address: "Is there any doubt whether a common government can embrace so large a sphere? Let experience solve it." It is, he continued, "well worth a fair and full experiment." In only 60 years, experience would show conclusively that the experiment of the union, having swollen to some ten times the landmass of Washington's "so large a sphere," had failed.

Everyone used the language of the compact theory because it was natural to Americans. Under British rule, each colony negotiated directly with the Crown for its rights and duties. Having become states, each saw its relation to the other in terms of a compact. Would-be nationalists were compelled to speak of the Constitution as a compact between sovereign states. Consider the comforting words Madison had in the *Federalist* for those who feared the states would be swallowed up into a political marriage from which there could be no divorce. Ratification, he said, "is to be given by the people, not as individuals composing one entire nation; but as composing the distinct and independent States to which they respectively belong." Each state "is considered as a sovereign body independent of all others, and only bound by its own voluntary act. In this relation the new Constitution will . . . be a *federal* and not a *national* Constitution."

31

Hamilton explained, in *Federalist* 28, how a state could protect itself from federal tyranny. The people would have the authority "through the medium of their state governments, to take measures for their own defense with all the celerity, regularity, and system of independent nations." Even James Wilson could speak of the people of the states as sovereign: "those who can ordain and establish may certainly repeal or annul the works of the [central] government." These statements, by the most important of the would-be nationalists, speaking the language of the compact theory, contain all the elements necessary for the doctrines of state interposition and secession later developed by Jefferson and Calhoun.

Hamilton understood that these consequences did follow, which is why he called the Constitution a "worthless fabric." But he hoped that a clever administration, by concentrating patronage to the center, could "triumph altogether over the state governments and reduce them to entire subordination." In this he was right, but it would take time and would not be accomplished without violence and the first modern total war directed against a civilian population.

IT IS IMPORTANT to understand that the compact theory was the *only* theory for the first 40 years of the union. There were, of course, criticisms of this or that act of state interposition or threat to secede. But these did not constitute an alternative *theory*; they were typically counsels of prudence or entreaties to give the "experiment" a chance. In fact, Daniel Webster, who became an eloquent defender of the new nationalist theory, began his career as a New England secessionist.

But nothing shows more clearly the deeply established belief in the compact theory than the many acts of nullification and threats of secession in every section of the union throughout the antebellum period. State nullification was asserted in Jefferson's Kentucky Resolutions (1798) and in Madison's Virginia Report (1799). Connecticut and Massachusetts endorsed nullification in 1808 and in 1814. Vermont nullified fugitive slave laws in 1840, 1843, and 1850. Massachusetts did the same in 1843 and 1850, and declared the Mexican War unconstitutional in 1846. In 1859, Wisconsin asserted the supremacy of its supreme court over that of the U.S. Supreme Court. (The latter has jurisdiction only over those powers delegated to the central government by the states.) Northern governors used nullification to block the unconstitutional centralizing policies of Lincoln. And there were many other instances.

Secession was also considered an option available to an American state. The region that most often considered secession was New England: over the Louisiana Purchase in 1803, the embargo in 1808, over war with England in 1814, and over the annexation of Texas in 1843. From the 1830's to 1861, New England Abolitionists argued strongly for secession of the Northern states from the union. Typical was this declaration of the American Anti-Slavery Society: "Resolved, that the abolitionists of this country should make it one of the primary objects of this agitation to dissolve the American Union." It is for this reason that Abolitionists such as Horace Greeley and those who wrote for Frederick Douglass's *Douglass Monthly* could support secession of the first Southern states that formed the Confederacy. Jeffrey Hummel, in *Emancipating Slaves, Enslaving Free Men* (1996), has revived this Abolitionist argument that secession was the best way of dealing with the problem of how to end slavery.

Many of the strongest supporters of secession were Northeastern Federalists who had favored a nationalist constitution. If anyone was a nationalist, Gouverneur Morris of New York was. He was a major figure in the Philadelphia Convention and was disappointed in the Constitution, but he knew it was a compact between sovereign states and that secession was an option. In 1812 he published an essay in the *New York Times* calling for the secession of New York and New England to form a more perfect union. This essay led to the Hartford Convention in 1814 with the object of forming a New England Confederacy.

Federalist William Rawle was head of the Pennsylvania bar and a nationalist who was also disappointed in the Constitution. But he too knew that the Constitution was a compact from which a state could secede. His widely acclaimed *A View of the Constitution of the U.S.A.* (1825) was one of the first commentaries on America's fundamental law. It was the text on constitutional law used at West Point from 1825 until 1840. In it, Rawle outlines the steps necessary for the legal secession of an American state. By 1861 every Southern state had taken those steps.

Foreign writers who had studied the Constitution concluded that a state could secede from the compact. Tocqueville wrote: "If one of the States chose to withdraw from the compact . . . the Federal Government would have no means of maintaining its claims directly either by force or right." Lord Brougham, in his magisterial study of constitutions, published in 1849, taught that the American Constitution was a compact from which a state could secede. He described the union as a "treaty," a "Federacy of states," and as "the Great League."

John Quincy Adams, in his famous speech celebrating the jubilee of the Constitution (1839), went out of his way to argue that a state could secede. What holds "the several states of this confederated nation together," he said, is not "in the right" but "in the heart." Should common affection and interest fail, then "far better will it be for the people of the disunited states to part in friendship from each other, than to be held together by constraint." One must follow the "precedent" (Adams recognized, as *Texas* v. *White* would not, that the union had been dissolved before) "to form again a more perfect Union by dissolving that which could no longer bind, and to leave the separated parts to be reunited by the law of political gravitation to the center." Four years after this speech, the former president, along with other New England leaders, would call for the dissolution of the union over the annexation of Texas.

In the late 1850's, anticipating the secession of South Carolina, there was a movement in the mid-Atlantic states to form a "Central Confederacy." It would include such states as New York, Delaware, New Jersey, Virginia, Tennessee, Maryland, and connected states. Such a confederacy, it was argued, was the conservative and moderate core of the union; it could prevent war and provide a rallying point around which the disaffected states of the Deep South could one day return, should they secede. Here was a splendid case of the Constitution under the compact theory working as it should. The sectional crisis between North and South could only be solved constitutionally by actions of the sovereign states themselves. The movement by prominent leaders to form a Central Confederacy was cut short by Lincoln's decision to send Massachusetts troops into Maryland. Blood was drawn, and states had to choose sides.

Virginia, Tennessee, North Carolina, and Arkansas had voted to *remain* in the union even after the Deep South states had seceded. They reversed themselves only after Lincoln demanded troops to coerce the seceding states back into the union. To these people, it was clear that the constitutional tradition they had inherited prohibited the coercion of a state. Hamilton had argued just this at the New York ratifying convention: "To coerce a state would be one of the maddest projects ever devised. No state would ever suffer itself to be used as the instrument of coercing another." But Massachusetts could and did. A new order of men had entered the world whose souls were shaped by the ideology of the French Revolution and the hubris of the Industrial Revolution, which has everywhere demanded consolidation and centralization.

In none of the enumerated powers granted by the states to Congress in Article I, section 8, is there authority to prohibit secession. The only conceivable power is the authority to "suppress insurrections." And it was this power that Lincoln seized upon to justify coercing the seceding states back into the union. But an insurrection is an attempt to overthrow either the central government or the government of a state. The orderly secession of a state, authorized by the people in convention (the same instrument authorizing entrance into the union) is not an attempt to overthrow either a state government or the central government. It is an act of the people to withdraw those powers delegated to the central government and to govern themselves. This, of course, is a serious matter, but it is not insurrection. It was not prohibited by the Constitution in 1861, and it is not prohibited today.

So deep was this understanding that, when secession of Southern states seemed imminent, no less than three amendments were proposed to the Constitution to make secession illegal. By the Ninth and Tenth Amendments, what is not prohibited to the people of the states by the Constitution is permitted. The attempt to prohibit secession by an amendment is clear proof that secession was permitted by the Constitution.

AMERICANS HAVE YET to come to terms with the stark immorality and barbarism of the invasion of the Southern states to preserve the union. The war was the bloodiest of the 19th century, leaving 1.5 million killed, missing, or wounded. The moral question becomes insistent when considered in light of the peaceful secession of 15 republics from the Soviet Union and other peaceful secessions after 1990. Here in America was a union formed by secession from the Articles of Confederation, itself a union grounded in the secession of 13 self-proclaimed sovereign states from the British Empire; a union in which the constitutional right of state interposition and secession had been acknowledged in every section throughout the antebellum period; a union only 70 years old that had swollen to some ten times its size in only 50 years and by that expansion had rapidly created new majorities, minorities, instability, and conflicts between great sectional interests; a union seeking to deal with a great sectional crisis in the way that was most continuous with its inherited constitutional tradition—namely, by peaceful secession of sovereign states by conventions of the people. Lincoln opposed this with a sophistical "nationalist" theory, not 30 years old, that inverted some 80 years of American constitutional experience with its perverse historical doctrine that the union created the states.

But the violence of war was not sufficient to destroy the federated polity of the Founders; though weakened, it remained intact. The Southern states were now ruled by Southerners loyal to the union; they returned their members to Congress and immediately ratified the 13th Amendment abolishing slavery. But when the 14th Amendment was floated in Congress, they rejected it, as did many non-Southerners, fearing that it would concentrate too much power in the central government. In hopes of getting the amendment ratified, and fearful of being reduced to a minority by a union of Southern and Northern Democrats, the Republican Congress expelled the Southern states, declaring them conquered provinces and placing them under military dictatorship. Nothing had changed in these states; if they had the authority to ratify the 13th Amendment, they also had the authority to vote against the 14th Amendment.

Lincoln had invaded the Southern states on the grounds that a state could not secede from a union that was perpetual, organic, and indivisible: "indestructible states in an indestructible union," as *Texas* v. *White* would put it. This formulation was, of course, nothing but a mask for power, and it ignored the fact that Virginia had been dismembered without its consent and in violation of the Constitution to create the Republican state of West Virginia, and that Congress had dismembered the union itself by expelling the Southern states that in theory had never left the union and had just recently ratified the 13th Amendment.

Although there is no space to argue the point here, it seems clear enough that, even without the Southern states, the 14th Amendment was not legally passed by Congress. But even if it had been, Forrest McDonald has shown that it was not constitutionally ratified by the states. Yet this so-called amendment has been manipulated by the Supreme Court to turn the Constitution on its head through the "incorporation doctrine." This doctrine, through judicial alchemy, has transmuted the Bill of Rights, which was designed to protect the states from the central government, into a grim rod of antinomic liberal individualism used to subvert the independent political societies of the states. The arbitrary use that has been made of the 14th Amendment and the consequent destruction of the social fabric that has resulted from it is, nevertheless, a faithful imprint of the violence and arbitrariness of its birth, and indeed of the birth of the entire nationalist theory.

British philosopher Alasdair MacIntyre has observed that to read current decisions of the Supreme Court is to witness reenactments of Shiloh and Gettysburg. There is today no intellectually coherent American jurisprudence. The Constitution is a grant of authority by sovereign states to a central government endowed with only enumerated powers. Incoherence necessarily arises from trying to read this document as the constitution of a unitary state—as Story, Webster, Lincoln, and the gaggle of judicial activists spawned by the Warren Court have done.

REFORM CAN ONLY COME through reviving the states as the substantial moral communities and constitutional agents they once were. Runaway judicial activism must be countered with the constitutional remedy of state activism. As far as the concentration of power at the center is concerned, it matters little who is president or which party controls Congress. The center will not (and perhaps, cannot) reform itself. Political energy must now be spent in forming a third party devoted to genuinely *federal* principles and in electing *state* representatives and senators endowed with the civic virtue to *reclaim* those powers the states have allowed to drift away and to interpose state authority to check unconstitutional action of the central government.

Such reform would of course overturn a large body of law and judicial precedent. But righting long-standing *constitutional* wrongs is more important than precedent. Nationalist liberals, in pursuit of a unitary state, have never worried about precedent. The Warren Court and the rush of judicial activism that followed it have overturned constitutional practices of more than 150 years. But the oldest of these usurpations is only some 40 years. Surely that is not a sufficient span of time to legitimize a massive corruption of American's fundamental law.

Some would acknowledge that usurpations by the central government have occurred, but would say that they were justified in the name of a "higher law" to eliminate racial and sexual discrimination. In a genuinely federated polity, there will be practices in some political units that will be considered unjust by those in other units; and it is understandable that those believing themselves to suffer injustice will be disposed to look for a remedy from the center. Consequently, there will always be a political market for concentrating power at the center in the name of human rights and for endlessly expanding the definition of human rights. Most of the totalitarian regimes of the modern period, from the Terror of the French Revolution to the Marxist regimes of the 20th century, have claimed to support human rights. What made them totalitarian was the destruction of those independent political societies (states, principalities, regional authorities, the Church) that had hitherto been a means of corporate resistance to tyranny from the center. The people were then free of any injustice these intermediate orders might perpetrate, but they were also bereft of their protection. What has prevented the American polity from becoming totalitarian is not the current liberal notion of an ever-expanding number of individual rights—for that has moved the regime decidedly in a totalitarian direction—but the stubborn survival of its federated character. This bulwark, however, is in disrepair and will not survive unless it is understood, politically acknowledged, and imaginatively cultivated by state governors and legislators.

There is indeed a "higher law" derived from the knowledge of things human and divine. And one of the many things it teaches is that, in a polity of 265 million souls, the moral evils that humans are inclined to pursue can be handled better in a genuinely federated polity of distinct political societies—each pursuing its own vision of the human good and in moral competition with other societies—than in a unitary state. In a regime of continental scale and size, a federation of states that preserve their distinct moral cultures, through interposition and secession, is *morally superior* to consolidation into a one-dimensional and dehumanizing unitary state.

What the Founders Didn't Count On

Clyde Wilson

"I assert that the people of the United States . . . have sufficient patriotism
and intelligence to sit in judgment on every question which has arisen or
which will arise no matter how long our government will endure."
—William Jennings Bryan

As CITIZENS IT IS FITTING that we engage in acts of civic piety while celebrating the bicentennial of the federal Constitution. That celebration acknowledges that in some sense the Constitution is a success. Given the long record of the crimes, follies, and misfortunes of mankind and the perishability of free and popular governments, it is a success in which we can take great satisfaction. But as an historian and even as a conscientious citizen, I cannot put aside a disquieting question: Which Constitution am I being asked to celebrate?

Even if we do not subscribe to an "evolutionary" rendering of the Constitution (as opposed to "original intent"), we are forced to recognize that the Constitution has a history. Besides many lesser scars, it carries on its face the great and bloody gash of Civil War and Reconstruction, an unparalleled social upheaval which was in its essence a question of constitutional interpretation. Even if, carried away by the moment and the warm glow of patriotism (not something to be despised), we can put aside the complications of history, still, we are confronted with a Constitution that means different things to different people—things that are sometimes mutually exclusive.

Opposing the Bork nomination, someone recently wrote to the "Letters" column of *Time* (August 3, 1987): "His reliance on original intent precludes the notion that the Founding Fathers originally intended us to evolve as a people into something better than we were. The nation, and indeed the President's legacy, would be better served by a justice who views the Constitution as a living part of the present rather than a relic from the past."

This passage encapsulates a vast region of mischief and misunderstanding, which includes both the proponents and the opponents of "original intent." A few obviously political points can be made: Would we be a better people by having more abortions? By executing fewer murderers? By having fewer prayers in fewer places? By oppressing more people with reverse discrimination? But it is more interesting that the letter-writer does not reject "original intent." Indeed, logically, no one can. Rather he has supplanted the "original intent" of the written Constitution with an "original intent" of the Founding Fathers, for us to "evolve as a people into something better than we were." Those realistic republicans, the Framers, skeptical of human nature and anxious to construct a power that was both effective and limited, content with compromise, have been converted into a priestly caste who bequeathed to us a secret mission of evolving into better beings.

This appeal to the higher law is legally, logically, and historically an absurdity. It traces back not to the founding but to Transcendentalism, which was a 19th-century vulgarization, by a small but influential group of Americans, of German philosophy. Carlyle took Emerson around the London slums again and again, but he could never make him believe in the reality of the Devil. This letter-writer could be taken around history again and again but could never be convinced that the Framers did not share his aspirations. They were sensibly hopeful men and principled republicans, which is not the same as devotees of national "evolution."

THIS CONFUSION of the Constitution with some sort of subjective higher law, one way or another, is nearly pervasive among both the "liberals" and the "conservatives," though it takes different forms at different times. Though a good deal more clever and circumstantial about it, the faculty of the Harvard Law School (and thus the Supreme Court for the last 40 years) present essentially the same view of the Constitution. They have read into it an intent, or at least a natural tendency, to evolve into meanings that extend the ideological program of social democracy. The Constitution evolves, but only in the direction *they* say. Although evolution is presumably by definition open-ended, it cannot evolve in directions they do not approve of, even if such an evolution is compatible with its letter and history. The Supreme Court is supposed to read the election returns, but only if the returns turn out their way. Once the Court has discovered something in the Constitution, no one else is allowed to discover something that contradicts it—a curiously limited and controlled form of evolution. Thus there is a federal right to prevent the states from *prohibiting* abortions, but there can be no federal right to prevent the states from *allowing* them. In fact, both propositions are nonsense because the real "original intent" of the Constitution (even with the 14th Amendment added) is not a matter in which there is any federal power, nor any judicial power, except in the most limited sense.

The simple truth is that the Constitution of our forefathers is not very compatible with the commercial progressivism by-way-of-federal-power of the "conservatives" and not compatible at all with the programmatic egalitarianism by-way-of-federal-power of the "liberals." Since these have become the foremost American values (at least in effective political terms), the Constitution has had to give. The question is not between "original intent" and interpretation, it is who will interpret; not whether the Constitution will give, but how much and in what direction.

So incompatible is the Constitution with programmatic egalitarianism that we have had to invent a secret history of abolitionism on the part of the Framers (which has been alluded to in every bicentennial statement I have seen, with greater zeal by "conservatives" than by "liberals"). On the flimsiest evidence, against both the letter and the substantive history of the instrument, we have postulated that the Framers intended to do away with slavery but could not quite manage it immediately. It is true that some, not all, had vaguely antislavery sentiments which in general had a lower priority than the interests of the Maine codfish industry, but no one believed—neither the Framers nor the public—that they possessed the power to abolish slavery. (It is one thing to be pleased that the 13th and 14th Amendments did away with slavery three generations after the founding; it is another to attribute false motives and anachronistic powers to the Founders.) Judging from the number of times this false history is alluded to, our self-esteem seems to be bound up with it. Perhaps we have a secret, unacknowledged fear to admit the Founders were really not entirely like us, because we would then have to throw them out completely.

Anyone who has honestly and closely studied the founding years and the period that followed knows how large states' rights loomed in the understanding of the Constitution in those days. Although there was some disagreement, some ambivalence, and even a few cases of disingenuousness among the Founders about the locus of sovereignty, there can be no doubt that most of the Founders and the subsequent two or three generations of statesmen accepted as natural and right the broadest possible idea of states' rights. To most of the founding generation, the Bill of Rights meant primarily a binding of the federal government by the states. To most people of the time, the victory of Jefferson and his friends in 1800 signified primarily the defeat of a too assertive federal power. Throughout the first half of the 19th century, the absolute central principle of the Jeffersonian Party and of the Democratic Party which came along later was states' rights—the belief that the states were the truest representatives of the people's will and the best guardians of the people's liberty. And this belief was matched by democratic sentiment—the more faith one had in the people the more allegiance one gave to states' rights. As recently as 1932 the Democratic Party went on record against the dangers of an overextended federal government.

It is not likely that states' rights will be affirmed during our current bicentennial, even in an historical context. What would the Founders, or indeed anyone before 1932, have made of a situation in which the states have all but disappeared except as administrative units and electoral counters of the federal machinery? And all in the name of freedom and the rights of the individual? Today the federal government, and usually the unelected parts of it, determine the qualifications of the voters and the apportionment of the legislatures of the states. It determines the curriculum and student assignments of their public schools, the rules of proceedings in their criminal courts, the speed limits on their highways, and the number of parking spaces for the handicapped in their public and private buildings. We observe the strange spectacle of legislatures *required* to pass laws according to specifications drawn up by federal judges and federal bureaucrats, which, of course, is not lawmaking at all. The states may have larger budgets and do more things than ever before, but their constitutional authority has never been lower.

In the perspective of American history or of the Founders, this is an absolutely amazing development, a revolution consummated entirely since 1960, which has had less impact on the public consciousness than the Super Bowl or Michael Jackson. (Because, I think, the predominant strain in the national character has become utilitarian—it cares only for ends and does not care how they are accomplished—the idea of principles simply doesn't exist. This may be good or bad, but it is utterly incompatible with the Constitution.)

The appeal to federally guaranteed individual rights as the chief (evolutionary) feature of the Constitution is essentially antidemocratic. It takes the Constitution away from the people, whose Constitution it is, and gives it into the keeping of an elite class that considers itself the master of mysteries that no majority, either state or federal, can tamper with. It is not the dead hand of the past ("a relic from the past") that the advocates of an evolutionary Constitution fear. What they fear is the restraining hand of consensus—that is, of democracy.

AN EVOLUTIONARY CONSTITUTION implies a path of evolution, either inevitable or actively pursued. But who is to discern the path? The Supreme Court of the later 19th century thought the path was illuminated by Herbert Spencer; more recently egalitarian social democracy has been the beacon. In either case we have a guardian class of savants privileged to lead the way.

The status of such men rests not on talents or public services but on claims to special revelation. In other words, they are not republican delegates of the people but priestly oracles—what the Founders would have immediately seen to be clever usurpers, and to us hardly distinguishable from the vanguard of the proletariat.

It is true that majorities can be wrong and that minorities have indefeasible rights enshrined within the spirit of the Constitution. But make no mistake: Our elitist interpreters and molders of the Constitution are not talking about the rights of minorities to be defended and to defend themselves. They are talking about the rights of a minority, themselves, to rule, to be the sovereign, the ultimate authority. And this is not a theory, but a fact.

It is a curious truth that those who claim rationality, the liberals, with their permanent revolution and reliance on the supposedly objective spirit and findings of social science, always resort to the most irrational view of the Constitution—on the one hand, to a mystical and disembodied appeal beyond the letter; and on the other, to the most petty and deceitful manipulations of the plain sense. One of the most obvious results of this is to remove the Constitution from the people and have it perform as a cover for elitism.

But in fact, the Constitution, properly considered, does not give any rights at all. The most essential point of a written constitution is that it is a limitation of government. The people establish institutions and give up to them certain powers, and no more. The government is not presumed to give the people their rights; and indeed the Bill of Rights is cast in a negative form: "The Congress shall make no law ... " That is, our rights are not a grant from the federal government, and the chief duty of the federal government is to refrain from interfering with them and leave to our real communities their day-to-day definition and application. By this analysis, all that the 14th Amendment "intended" was to make the freed men citizens.

There is a certain liberal spirit, genuinely American and legitimately derived from Jefferson, which says that the earth belongs to the living generation, which must be free to make its own arrangements. But our current evolutionists represent the exact opposite of this spirit—they represent not a forthright amendment by popular consent (which can be completely compatible with the spirit of traditions and institutions) but an essentially rigid and disguised manipulation of the existing Constitution.

I HAVE SAID that the appeal over the Constitution to the higher law is pervasive. For example, I have before me a *Reader's Digest* (September 1987) containing the reflections of the ex-chief justice Warren Burger on how our

Constitution should be viewed and celebrated. It is impossible to imagine anything more "mainstream." I set aside the silliness of the title, "The Birth of a True Nation." (Was the United States an "untrue" nation before the Constitution?) I quote the blurb, which is not the language of Burger but is a not-unfair representation of his sentiments expressed on this and other occasions: "Two centuries ago in Philadelphia, one of the most extraordinary events in all human history occurred, and America—and the world— were thereby transformed."

The framing of the Constitution was a remarkable event, but I will have to reflect a little on the invention of the wheel and the appearance of Jesus before conceding "one of the most extraordinary events in all human history." Further, the Constitution was not a unique event but a part of a series of events which ought to be understood not as "a miracle at Philadelphia" (to quote the title of a popular work—one does not know whether the pseudoreligion or the pseudohistory is more odious), but rather as a realistic human achievement. Every clause of the *Digest's* statement is, in fact, either a falsehood or a gross exaggeration.

AMERICA WAS NOT TRANSFORMED *by* the Constitution, except in a limited sense that a new governmental machinery was launched at the highest level. It remained the same society, essentially, as it had the year before. The Constitution did not create republicanism, which had already been created by the people of the states as the first step in the Revolution. It did not create the idea of the written constitution, which also had already been done by the states, which is why John Adams wrote his *A Defence of the Constitutions of the United States.*

But we have here not only America transformed but also the *world*! Now it is true that the Founders sometimes appealed to Mankind. However, they did not deal in emotions, ideologies, and fantasies, but principles. They had a modest hope that by the successful operation of republican principles they might provide an example and inspiration for other peoples. Nothing could have been further from them than the spirit of making the world "safe for democracy." If someone had blathered "global democracy"—the official rhetoric of the chosen intellectuals of the Reagan administration—to General Washington, he would have reached for his sword. (Unfortunately, aside from rhetoric, the actual practice of the administration in foreign policy is in the hands of the same stuffed shirts who have "managed" the State Department since William Jennings Bryan resigned in 1915.) "Global democracy," in specific historical terms, goes back to the 1930's, when it was created as a mélange of Wilsonianism and Soviet popular-front propaganda. Given the propensity of American governments for dropping high explosives on the "enemies of democracy," such propaganda can do nothing in the 1980's but make every intelligent foreigner feel uneasy and render prudent discussion of the national interest nearly impossible. In the past 50 years, a great achievement in the founding of government for Americans becomes a cover for the dreams of "conservative" politicians and intellectuals for world transformation.

I am less offended by the factual license of the ex-chief justice's blurb than I am by its spirit. The *tone* is all wrong, for a bicentennial statement. It smacks of a spoiled child congratulating himself on Daddy's riches. The Framers, I believe, would not want to be worshiped as workers of a miracle. What they would want is the "decent respect" of sensible men for the hard-won achievements of their fathers.

The glorification of the Framers as demigods is a form of mystification that naturally lends itself to elitist rule. If the Constitution is a miracle, then it has to be treated as a holy object and handled only by the priests, not by the common run of humanity. To treat the Philadelphia Convention as a gathering of demigods is worse than foolish and undemocratic; so far it prevents any real appreciation of their achievement.

The members of the Convention, the Framers, were an able lot; some were great. Yet, in the final analysis, they were not omnipotent or omniscient but merely the delegates of the states. Some very able men who were selected by the states refused to go, either because they had more pressing business or were suspicious of the proceedings. Others were quite desultory in attendance, and several of the best men there refused to sign the finished product.

Nor did the Framers establish or proclaim a new Constitution, something they had no authority to do. What they did was draw up a convincing and appealing proposal—convincing and appealing because it tended to meet the occasion and to anticipate the future—a proposal that, after a considerable amount of explanation and qualification and amendments promised, was approved eventually by an effective majority of the people in each of the states—that is, by the people of the United States as already defined by existing political communities. Those who ratified the Constitution are its real founders (as opposed to its framers). It is wrong, therefore, to cite the debates in Philadelphia as definitive of "original intent," as useful and illuminating as they may be in a subsidiary sense. It is the powers that ratified it that determine, in the final analysis, what the "intention" of the Constitution is. Fortunately, to declare this is merely to declare the validity of democracy and of federalism.

How far we fall short of their achievement. In truth, in the Framers' Constitution, one of the things they took for granted (that we have lost) was an adequate supply of intelligence and honor. Reflect on that magical period in the history of self-government during the last decade when we had Gerald Ford for president, Nelson Rockefeller for vice president, Warren Burger for chief justice, and Tip O'Neill for speaker of the House. At the time of the Framers the justices of the peace of any small county in Virginia or the selectmen of any town in Connecticut could have mustered more intelligence (I leave aside less measurable virtues) than the whole of the government today.

By intelligence I mean learning, wisdom, foresight, digested experience, detachment, ethics. Not shrewdness in self-promotion, conceit, visionary schemes, and vague good intentions. The Founding Fathers did not anticipate the ravages of the two-party system and its ability to deter the best from public life and foist vocal mediocrities on the public. The Constitution presupposed an inexhaustible supply of able and honorable and *independent* public men (whose ambitions needed to be watched). Almost all of our leaders are now the creatures of political parties (what percentage of the people believe the Democrats and Republicans are part of the Constitution?), which means that *ipso facto* they are more adept at winning offices than at filling them, at manipulation and self-promotion than at statesmanship.

The replacement of the independent gentleman by the professional politician beginning in the 19th century, a reflection of changes in society and of the capacity of clever men to manipulate even wisely constructed institutions to their advantage, provided as serious a distortion of the Constitution as did the concomitant rise of lawyers. It would astound our politicians today to learn that at the time of the Founders and even long after, people held public office for the honor and that, in most cases, rather than filling their own snouts at the public trough (except for a few securities speculators), they actually made a sacrifice of their private interests to serve in public office. The Constitution presupposed an aristocratic rather than a bourgeois class of officeholders and aspirants, members of Congress, and Presidential Electors, who would always be capable of independent judgment. That is, the operation of the Constitution rested in part on something that has ceased to exist. The essence of republican government was that the will of the people prevailed but that it was formulated by able and independent delegates. When we say "the will of the people," we have to avoid the mystical and high-flying references to something strongly akin to the General Will, which we all know is not the will of the people but the will of the vanguard of the proletariat on behalf of the people—what the people would want if they were as smart as their masters. This too easily merges over into "all mankind," so that everyone in the world becomes by extension an American citizen—something which if taken too literally constitutes a grave threat both to the United States and mankind. The will of the people under the Constitution can only mean the deliberate sense of the political communities—that is, the states—that make up the United States, expressed through the republican mechanisms that are established. This suggests that judicial review must be relegated to a subsidiary role.

ORIGINAL INTENT, properly speaking, is a legal and not a constitutional idea. The original intent of a piece of legislation may be juridically determined by reference to its legislative history (though given the trickery and evasiveness of recent Congresses this is not as simple as it might be). However, the "original intent" of the Constitution is not similarly determinable because the intent was given to the Constitution by the people who ratified it. An appeal to the Philadelphia Convention, known chiefly through the partial notes of Madison, is not strictly analogous to an appeal to legislative history. The Constitution can be finally interpreted only historically, not juridically. It is also important to note that the "original intent" of a particular provision of the Constitution and the "original intent" of the Constitution in the large sense are different questions.

I have often heard members of Congress and other public officers answer a constitutional question with the quip that they are not constitutional lawyers. Nonsense! Members of Congress, the president, and, more importantly, the people and officials of the states have just as much standing in interpreting the Constitution as any panel of lawyers or law professors, whether or not the latter have yet been appointed to the federal bench. The Founders never intended that the high *political* questions of constitutional interpretation would be at the mercy of lawyers' tricks.

The Federalist justices of the early 19th century—Marshall, Story, *etc.*— were legalists and devotees of the British common law. In one of the most misguided feats in American history, they infused judicial review into the constitutional fabric, believing they were providing a check to unruly popular passions and lending stability to the institutions of self-government. But while they did inject a type of stability that was useful in the progressive commercial sense, the law had a pragmatic and centralizing tendency that carried the emphasis away from the historical rights of the states and from the consent of the people. It is not difficult to understand why Jefferson feared the judiciary as the greatest of all enemies of republican government.

There is a piece of erroneous folklore, again dating to 19th-century distortions of the founding, that the Constitution is in the special keeping of lawyers. In fact relatively few of the Framers were practicing lawyers. Primarily they occupied their time as owners of plantations or other large estates or as merchants (that is, not counter-jumpers but traders on a large scale). They were also clergymen and educators, among other represented professions. It is true that a good many were trained in law. Law was considered a useful study which enhanced one's ability to manage one's own interests and to participate in public life because it was a storehouse of English traditions of order and liberty. However, it was not considered, except by a few of the Framers who were not the most trustworthy, that a decent man would devote his primary attention to the daily practice of law.

The Founders recognized no aristocracies except those of talent, service, and social weight. They would regard the Constitution today as the tools of an aristocracy of federal judges, drawn from a class of lawyers and law professors whose study is not of noble traditions of liberty and order but of the defense of large vested interests, whether of big business or the established left-wing causes of the New Class. It would be difficult to imagine any group, taken as a group, more dissimilar to the great landowners and republican gentlemen of the founding than the choice legal scholars of late-20th-century America. The former were representatives of their communities and the bearers of wisdom and vision. The latter are the representatives of vested interests and of arcane manipulations.

We have here more than the elitist tendencies of 20th-century liberalism or "guardian democracy." We are going to have to go back a lot further than the Warren Court or the New Deal to remedy the ill. An evolutionary captivity of the Constitution was inevitable once the Constitution was given over largely into the hands of lawyers and treated primarily as a legal document, the understanding of which was to rest on the reasonings of judges.

This was a major mistake that the Framers, for the most part, did not expect. The Constitution was not intended to be, except in a subsidiary sense, a legal document. It was not expected that it would be interpreted by lawyers (people who argue cases for pay), much less by law professors (people who teach others how to argue for pay). The Constitution is a political document. Lawyers and judges are qualified to deal with legal matters. Study of the law *per se*, or pursuance of legal procedures *per se*, will never yield an accurate or lasting interpretation of the Constitution in the large sense. Justice Sandra Day O'Connor recently observed that every Supreme Court decision becomes, at the hands of clever lawyers, raw material for a hundred new cases.

This would be no great problem if we were merely dealing with *legal* questions brought on by the complications of modern society. But through the 14th Amendment and the usurpations of all three branches of the federal government, every conceivable legal question has also been made into a *constitutional* question. And even if this process yields a workable rendering of particular clauses of the Constitution, it should not be allowed cumulatively to determine the meaning of the Constitution itself.

WE KNOW that the Constitution has changed and continues to do so. If we look into what Constitution deserves our respect, we find two current views. One view, put forth by recent Supreme Courts and their defenders, says that the Constitution is an evolutionary document whose great virtue lies in its adaptability. According to this, it follows that it is the right or even the duty of the Supreme Court from time to time to bring the Constitution "up to date."

We can hardly deny that the Constitution has changed and evolved. It has a history. However, from the observation that the Constitution must be viewed historically, it does not necessarily follow that the Supreme Court should be the arbiter of that change. In fact, this would not have been accepted by the main body of Founders.

The other view of the Constitution current today is that we are bound by its "intent" unless we want to amend it in the proper way. The Founders, at least that majority who were not overinvolved in a specific agenda, would not have demurred from this proposition. But is it not obviously true that the *intent of the Constitution is an historical question*? That is to say, questions of "original intent" are most properly answered, not by legal reasoning and legal tradition, nor by abstract speculation on democratic philosophy or individual "rights," but by reference to the historical record.

In emphasizing the historical record there are two things I am not saying. I am not suggesting, in the manner of Charles Beard, that there is some secret dirty story to be ferreted out by historians. Nor am I saying that only professional historians can be allowed to put the Constitution in context, for any intelligent person may make a valid historical observation.

If we do not rely on legal interpretation to discern the intent of the Constitution nor on the specialist knowledge of historians nor on philosophical speculation (however relevant any of these may be in a subordinate sense), what do we rely on? We rely on history, and history, if it is not a specialist's but a people's history, is exactly what we mean by tradition—a widely shared understanding handed down from generation to generation.

A people's history may well embody some mythological elements (like the Founders' abolitionism) and some evolutionary developments (like reinterpretation of some basic points in the Civil War) because popular traditions are never precisely accurate in the specialist's sense. But after all, the Constitution rests upon the consent of the people. And it is therefore, in the final analysis, the people who have a right to determine its intent. If we argue that this is a perilous or unworkable doctrine, then we are merely declaring that democracy and federalism are unacceptable.

Of course, if we accept this proposition, our problems are only beginning (I can hear the cries of "simplistic!"), for we are still faced with the task of translating the people's understanding, which is a tacit thing, into the established mechanisms of government. This would seem to require the services of a statesman who, in Andrew Lytle's definition, has the mission of clarifying for a given people their alternatives. Since we have no statesmen, then perhaps the best we can do is get the best judges we can find and trust them. This, indeed, has been the position of most of those who have thought of themselves as conservatives through this century, though it cannot be considered a resoundingly successful strategy.

The defenders of "original intent" argue with ability and earnestness and morality and sense. But the Constitution they defend is not the federal republican instrument ratified in 1787-88. It is the one invented and refounded in the middle of the 19th century by democratic nationalists to accompany and foster the development of a commercial republic, a Constitution under which lawyers formed an aristocracy, an impulse which Tocqueville observed at work in its early stages. As the world goes, that Constitution, compared to the one invented by the Supreme Court in the middle of the 20th century, will serve us just fine if (a big "if") we can get it back. Unlike our current model, it did not violate the essential principles of republicanism and federalism.

I am inclined to think that the Framers, men of another age, would be profoundly uncomfortable with the state of our society today. But, being creative realists, and observing the ill fit between the Constitution and our society and the misuses to which the Constitution has been put, they might well conclude that we ought to follow their example and make a new constitution, more in keeping with our aspirations, even though they would doubt that we had the wisdom and virtue to build as well as they.

Plessy v. Ferguson—One Hundred Years Later

William J. Watkins, Jr.

ONE HUNDRED YEARS AGO this May, *Plessy* v. *Ferguson* was decided. The Supreme Court's 1896 decision upheld Louisiana's law that required all passenger railways operating within the state to have "equal but separate accommodations for the white and colored races." Over the years, the import of the decision and public perceptions of such state regulations have been misunderstood and at times purposely distorted. Scholars have described the decision as the incarceration of blacks in "the *Plessy* prison." The real prison, however, holds all Americans and was built on an unwillingness to examine objectively this important period in American history.

Though *Plessy* receives enormous attention today in classrooms and in discussions of race relations (especially Justice John Marshall Harlan's dissenting opinion invoking the concept of a color-blind Constitution), the decision was largely ignored for many years. The newspapers of the day that did not disregard the Court's pronouncement gave it but scant attention. The *New York Times*, for instance, barely mentioned *Plessy* in its weekly column on railway news.

Routine affirmations of state regulations were hardly newsworthy in the 1890's. The War Between the States did change the nature of state and national relations, but the majority of citizens still accepted that the states were sovereign within their proper sphere.

Separate accommodations, rather than being vehicles for white supremacy, were viewed in a different light than they are today. Several black legislators involved in earlier Reconstruction governments actually sought to enact legislation for separate-but-equal accommodations. Robert Smalls, a black congressman from South Carolina, declared in 1884 that he had "no objection to riding in a separate car when the car is of the same character as that provided for white people to ride in." Booker T. Washington applauded Alabama's railroad commissioners for instituting separate-but-equal accommodations just one year before *Plessy* and made it clear that "it is not the separation that we complain of, but the unequality of accommodation." Blacks, who purchased first-class tickets and were subjected to the filth of the smoking car or other substandard accommodations, had good reason to remonstrate. Long trips in such conditions were not just uncomfortable but hazardous to one's health.

In spite of a justice system that was frequently hostile to them, blacks turned to the courts to demand equal accommodations. It was quite elementary for them to prove that a seat in the baggage or smoking car was not equal to that of first or second class. The success of black plaintiffs enshrined separate-but-equal in common law. The Supreme Court recognized this in 1878 when it upheld separate-but-equal in the common law of common carriers in *Hall* v. *Decuir*.

Clearly, *Plessy* was not the bombshell that it has been so recently billed. State and federal courts had consistently upheld separate-but-equal for years. Lower courts had even declared that separate-but-equal did not conflict with the Civil Rights Act of 1875, which prohibited racial discrimination in access to public accommodations (and was declared unconstitutional in 1883).

MODERN ACCOUNTS OF *PLESSY* seldom mention that blacks often fought for separate-but-equal in legislatures and courts. Because scholars find it difficult to explain the acceptance of such segregation, they normally conclude that conditions were so bad for blacks that almost anything was considered an improvement. In many cases this was no doubt true. The freedmen faced much hostility and very difficult circumstances.

However, such an explanation ignores, in the words of Eugene D. Genovese, "that black nationalism represents an authentic tendency within black America, rather than a pathological response to oppression." A nation, united by common folkways and culture, must, to some extent, separate itself from the cultures of rival nations to remain intact. This has been extremely challenging for black Americans, considering the subjugation and the alien culture forced upon them in slavery. And though separate accommodations certainly are not necessary for the preservation of culture, the acceptance of the need of some type of separation to preserve a culture explains why it was tolerated.

Black attitudes at the time are much easier to understand if one remembers that much of the black intellectual environment in the years before and after *Plessy* favored some sort of separation. Many blacks, for instance, were involved in various "back to Africa" movements. Before the War Between the States, the Friendly Society for the Emigration of Free Negroes, founded by a free black shipowner, took a number of families back to Africa. Martin R. Delany, coeditor with Frederick Douglass of the *North Star*, explored the region of the Niger River and signed agreements with several African kings for a settlement of emigrants from America. More noteworthy were the activities of Bishop Henry McNeal Turner and his calls for black emigration in the years between the War Between the States and World War I.

Certainly not all blacks favored emigration. Most only wanted to be left in peace in America to farm and raise their children. But among those who desired to remain in North America, there was still an element of separatism in their thinking. Booker T. Washington, the undisputed leader of the black community at the time, declared that the races could be "as separate as the fingers" in a system that accorded blacks equal treatment in their legal relations in the private economy.

Other blacks and white progressives tried to supplant separatist tendency in the black community. W.E.B. Dubois and the NAACP provided virulent criticism of Washington's emphasis on economic freedom rather than social equality. After Washington's death in 1915, Dubois and his cohorts set their sights on Marcus Garvey and his Universal Negro Improvement Association's calls for black autonomy and economic self-reliance.

Today, despite the post-*Brown* push for forced integration *vis-à-vis* judicial activism and broad legislation, black nationalism is just as strong as it was in the days of Booker T. Washington and the Garvey movement. The total failure of integration to improve the quality of life for the majority of black Americans is no doubt responsible for the resurgence of nationalism within the black community.

THE ACCEPTANCE OF LOUIS FARRAKHAN by the black community during the Million Man March underscores black nationalist aspirations today. The Nation of Islam itself, of course, was founded by Elijah Muhammad to build a separate black nation paid for by white reparations for slavery. Though Farrakhan avoids blatant calls for total black separation, he nonetheless declares that blacks cannot "integrate into white supremacy and hold our dignity as human beings." And since Farrakhan sees white supremacy as "the idea that undergirds the setup of the Western world," he is in reality saying that blacks cannot integrate into American society, which is a branch of Western civilization.

The popularity of Islam among blacks (not necessarily the Nation of Islam) is emblematic of this rejection of Western culture. Many blacks see Christianity as a "slave religion" and seek a substitute. By the year 2000, Islam is expected to become the second-largest religion in the United States as a result of black converts and immigrants. Black Christian nationalism, with a black Madonna and Christ, is also an alternative for many blacks to mainstream Christianity. A main tenet of black Christian nationalism is to teach "the necessity for separatism," along with the path to eternal salvation.

Other calls for some degree of racial separation are just as loud as that of the separatist religious element. Interracial adoption, for example, is most ardently opposed by black social workers. The National Association of Black Social Workers unabashedly declares that "black children belong to black parents." They rightly fear that interracial adoptees will lose contact with their heritage and not develop culturally and psychologically as they would in a black family.

The strongest front on the integration backlash is, fittingly, school desegregation. Across the nation, black parents are demanding a return to neighborhood schools no matter what their racial composition. In Cleveland, the local NAACP has met strong opposition from within the black community to its attempts to force cross-district busing. "I did not give the civil rights attorneys permission to holocaust my children and get paid for it," says black parent and busing opponent Genevieve Mitchell. Blacks like Mitchell are rejecting the notion that black children need the company of white children to learn. Recent studies show that black academic performance is the last reason why anyone should favor policies of integration.

THIS CHANGE OF ATTITUDE in the black community, according to Aaron Gray, the black president of Denver's school board, is because "pre-1954 was separate and unequal. The difference is today that you can step into an African-American school and you can see the same amount of resources that are provided to a majority Anglo school." Even Supreme Court Justice Clarence Thomas has defended black schools: "Because of their distinctive histories and traditions, black schools can function as the center and symbol of black communities, and provide examples of *independent* black leadership, success, and achievement."

Gray's and Thomas's words contest the Warren Court's assertions in *Brown* and the 40 years of judicially sponsored social engineering that followed the Court's 1954 decision. They signify black abandonment of the opiate of integration that has caused so much damage to American society.

The 100th anniversary of *Plessy* v. *Ferguson* is a proper time to recognize the existence of healthy black nationalist tendencies. Though *Plessy* was at most a footnote in history for many years, it has now unfortunately become a symbol of the need for complete integration. Justice Harlan's calls for a color-blind Constitution have animated universalists to instigate an all-out push for a utopian society.

Such good intentions drive the likes of the Institute for Justice, as they and their kindred organizations litigate to end the use of race as a criterion in state adoption decisions. Good intentions drive civil-rights lawyers as they attempt to force more busing and court supervision of local schools. Fortunately for blacks, these good intentions to undo perceived past wrongs are meeting with stiff resistance from within their own community.

Only when black tendencies for various degrees of separation along with the same tendencies found in white America are accepted and respected can we free ourselves from the fetters of the modern era. By ignoring the needs of both whites and blacks to preserve their unique cultures, policymakers threaten both groups. Blacks, however, will stand up and defend their institutions, while whites sit passively by.

One hundred years after the much-maligned *Plessy* decision, black nationalism is as strong as ever. Whites, on the other hand, when given the opportunity to defend their culture, do little more than mumble platitudes about a nation dedicated to a proposition. It does not take much guesswork to figure out which of the two nations will survive another 100 years.

Reviving Self-Rule:
Ward Government in the South

Don Anderson

A S A GENERAL RULE, democracy does not grow with time. It usually comes into being as the result of some general uprising, and it is supported by the broader and more general popular will. But, with time, and because the larger population does not usually continually watch for the encroachment of smaller groups, the course is reversed. Special interests find the more general rule to be inconvenient. Decisions by the wider population are feared, and factions scheme day and night to limit the acts of the majority that might threaten their own cause.

And so, from generation to generation, a countermovement sets in. What was the substance of democracy becomes form only. Democratic safeguards become ceremony. Eventually the same evils that provoked the multitude to act to protect their liberties again prevail. What begins as the rule of the many becomes, by the mandate of history, the rule of the few. For this reason the people must, from time to time, renew their rights.

Great changes have taken place since the moment when America committed herself to democracy. Although the United States has continually made adjustments to her institutions, the question remains as to whether our politicians have rendered the constant attention necessary to make democracy not simply a remote and guiding idea, but an actual practice. As one generation passed away and another took over, as foreigners became citizens and became the majority, have we varied our techniques and habits to make certain that the people continue to have a strong voice in decisionmaking?

Every schoolboy has been taught the ideas that this nation set out to fulfill. But our experience with the United States Constitution as a source of democracy must convince us that such a government cannot come about merely by assuming the *form* prescribed by the Constitution. Government by the few is not prevented by having courts, a legislature, and a national executive. Political activity on the part of masses of people is not assured by the existence of political parties. In fact, concentrating on the superb form of the government created by the Constitution really obscures how far short we have fallen of the political plan outlined by the Founding Fathers.

If we chose to define democracy after the manner in which Americans deal with public concerns, we would have to define it as a political activity in which neither the people nor any democratic institution makes the initial—and therefore the important—decision as to who will represent a given constituency in the national legislature; one that has no national institution in which the people may participate in the formulation of policy; and one in which special interests, each representing a tiny fraction of the electorate, have a great influence on the national legislature. As a practical matter many of us support special interests, which have replaced the political parties as a means of carrying on our political activity. Anyone, even a small minority, may have a good idea. But these special interests, whether the Sierra Club, the American Medical Association, Texaco, or the National Wildlife Federation, never represent more than a tiny fraction of the population, and they are pressing hard for their own advantage.

Government by special interests is objectionable not simply because it is politics carried on as a purely empirical activity, politics governed by the passion of the moment, but because it is a government of unelected decisionmakers who are not accountable to any democratic institutions. It matters little that the majority ultimately acquiesce in or even support these programs (support, that is, as measured by the polls—the people seldom get to vote on them). It is politics in which no one can be sure that the activity is necessarily advancing the *priorities* of the people.

In the United States there is no popular institution that has the capacity to initiate policy. The fountainhead for initiating policy for the American government is a political entity dominated by one person—the executive branch. Within it there is no mechanism for discovering those matters that are of greatest concern to the people. Most other modern governments reach decisions through collective decisionmaking and on the basis of committee or collective responsibility. But in the United States it is the president alone who will select what problems will be addressed. In theory the national legislature *can* initiate policy. In practice, it seldom does.

Great powers had over the years accumulated in the office of the speaker of the House, but because of the tyrannical fashion in which Speaker Howard Cannon exercised those powers, the House deprived the office of most of them. That act, in effect, deprived the House of its leadership and of any unifying force. Eventually, power accumulated in committee chairmen, who never acted as a group and who, because of their age and conservatism, used that power to thwart legislative initiative. As Congressman Everett Burkhalter said in 1964, upon announcing his retirement after serving one term in the House: "I could see I wasn't going to get anywhere. Nobody listens to what you have to say until you've been in here ten to twelve years. These old men have got everything tied down so you can't do anything. There are only about 40 out of 435 members who call the shots. They're all committee chairmen or ranking members, and they're all around 70 or 80."

In the 1960's even the power of committee chairmen was curbed, and with this development, power was further diffused. Thus, during this century, the Congress has lost its capacity to act in most cases as the initiators of policy for the problems that affect the nation.

It would seem that the legislative branch of government would be the most appropriate to propose legislation because it represents the diverse parts of the country. The Constitution agrees, and Article I states: "*All* legislative Powers herein granted shall be vested in a Congress of the United States, which shall consist of a Senate and a House of Representatives." Yet today it is the president who proposes most major legislation, who points out most of the problems to be dealt with, and who proposes solutions.

AN OPPORTUNITY for the participation by the people in the formulation of programs and policies that concern them was provided by the institution of the political party. To be such a vehicle for democracy, however, would require that the party represent entire counties and cities in its machinery, and that the party machinery be devoted in part to decisionmaking. It would mean that the structure of the party organization assure that the masses of people entered into the formulation of policy, either directly or by representation, and that the instrumentality of the party could assure that its elected representatives would adhere to party policy in the affairs of the government.

But, unlike most modern nations, there is no uniform party structure in the United States. And unlike most countries, no national political parties exist in the United States. What are commonly referred to as "national" parties (Democratic and Republican) are composed of 50 state parties each, and these state parties have surrendered no authority or power to the national body. These entities act as a whole only four or five days out of every four years, when their sole task is to choose a candidate for president. There is no chain of command in either direction, no national hierarchy that reaches down to the local level. The powers that matter reside in the state or local parties. Even the platforms reached at the national conventions are binding on no one. Hence political parties in the United States are not a means for the people to enter into decisionmaking.

Nor do the people have any real influence on what policies the president will eventually propose. In electioneering, promises are given, general attitudes hinted at, and commitments made to certain interests. But once the election is over, the president is bound to no commitment and makes the choices of what he will propose freely, without reference to and usually without consultation with any elected body. Although he will have a myriad of (unelected) advisors, all final decisions about what legislation to propose are made by one man.

This is not the manner in which the Framers of the Constitution intended the government to work. James Madison, writing in the *Federalist*, warned, "It is agreed on all sides that the powers properly belonging to one of the departments ought not to be directly and completely administered by either of the other departments." And he alludes to Virginia as "a State which, as we have seen, has expressly declared in its Constitution that the three great departments ought not to be intermixed."

In the early history of our government under the Constitution, for a president to propose legislation was regarded by some as an impeachable offense. President Theodore Roosevelt was the first to propose legislation to the Congress, and during [the 20th] century this practice grew and flourished, especially under Franklin Roosevelt. Today it is widely accepted—accepted perhaps without the realization that it is a practice that is relatively recent, that it is not the manner in which the creators of the Constitution intended the government to work, and without the clear understanding of the implication of the assumption of these powers by the executive branch of government. As Jefferson wrote in his *Notes on the State of Virginia*, "An elective despotism was not the government we fought for."

STILL, THERE IS MUCH VIRTUE in our government. America is a nation in which the people have substantial freedom. But is America governed by the will of the people? Or is ours a society in which every device is invented, every form of hoax is created to make the people believe that democracy exists when it does not? Is it a form of government in which people are mere spectators, where the society itself is just one huge tribal audience gathered around a television set, observing events but not giving rise to them; where individuals who believe they have gained the attention of their legislators are not aware that while we are sleeping, computers are at work typing out "personalized letters" designed to appear to give individual attention; where presidents are sold like potato chips in two-minute ads, and politics itself has become a science, a technique for the control of the public mind?

Is democracy even a possibility? It may be a simple matter to conduct communal activity on the part of ten or twenty or even a hundred people; but when the numbers get into hundreds or thousands, is it possible to get that many people to engage in a common undertaking or collective decisionmaking? How can residents of a whole city, county, or state govern themselves?

Such considerations were ones in which I personally was involved when helping to draft the Economic Opportunity Act in 1964. I worked on the legislative side and later became the general counsel of the subcommittee of the House of Representatives that drafted and monitored the operation of the legislation. While the act implied self-help for large numbers of people, it did not go far enough in the direction of democracy. It lost faith in its ability to organize large numbers of people, and thus organized only a fraction of the targeted population, crippling the anti-poverty effort and causing it to fall short of its objectives.

This happened despite the fact that the concept of "self-help" was essential to the success of the anti-poverty effort, for two reasons. First, it is generally recognized that simply giving builds up a dependency on the giver. Second, without considerable voluntary efforts on the part of the recipients, comprehensive efforts for an entire community may be prohibitively expensive and ineffective. I realized that in an attempt to eliminate poverty a practical application of democracy was vital, because of the necessity to engage large numbers of people in a voluntary activity of self-help.

In this my own view to the problem of poverty differed from others that I knew. Most antipoverty efforts deal with a single aspect of the problem— housing the homeless, acquiring medical facilities, combating drug activities or teenage pregnancy. Yet concentrating on a single aspect of poverty does not eliminate poverty itself from any given neighborhood. Addressing pieces of the problem is in fact addressing the symptoms—that is, the consequences—of poverty, rather than its causes. Such help may ease the horror of impoverishment, but in most cases only a small percentage of the poor community is affected.

In a poor community, so many aspects of the lives of the people require attention that enormous efforts are needed to deal with them all. What is needed is an ongoing and comprehensive antipoverty activity, dealing with the myriad individual problems that present themselves from day to day, as well as with the major problems that confront an entire community. In poor communities, institutions do not normally exist that can deal with problems. A system that could encourage a large number of volunteers who would carry on these multifaceted activities would greatly reduce the costs of any project, and would also make it more effective. If properly organized, the poor themselves could do much of the volunteering.

But how does one instill a self-help initiative in a large number of people?

Structures of organization must be created, ones that reach extensively into poor communities, and their design must enable large numbers of people to engage in decisionmaking and contribute to self-help efforts voluntarily. With individuals it is different, but with large numbers of people there is no self-help without organization.

In most cities and counties of the United States today the population at large does not have a sense of community. Where those involved are not poor or where they are not confronted with overwhelming problems, the creation of community is less urgent. However, where poverty has caused a need for self-help, there must be some structure through which it may occur.

In attempting to solve the problem of how to organize, I followed the advice Thomas Jefferson gave the Virginia legislators 150 years ago. "Just as Cato ended every speech with 'Carthage must be destroyed,'" he said, "so do I end every opinion with the injunction: divide the counties into wards." And again,

> Among other improvements, I hope they will adopt the subdivision of our counties into Wards. Each Ward could thus be a small Republic within itself, and every man in the state would thus become an acting member of the common government, transacting in person a great portion of its rights and duties, subordinate indeed, but important, and entirely within its competence. The wit of man cannot devise a more solid base for a free, durable, and well administered republic.

A county or city divided into manageable atomic groups, each of which is represented in a central decisionmaking body, has established a channel of communication between the leadership and the people to be served so that decisions may be made on matters that affect them. By mere arrangement, by a logical structure of organization, the habits and even the whole way of life of a community can be changed.

In the 1960's I worked on the staff of Adam Clayton Powell, who was then chairman of the Committee on Education and Labor of the House of Representatives. When the House stripped him of his chairmanship and excluded him from Congress, I left the Congress. I was determined to implement Jefferson's idea of the ward republics, and my adaptation of that idea is now called the idea of the Assembly. In 1964 a wealthy realtor from Virginia advanced the first funds for the implementation of that idea, and I went to southern Virginia to try it out in several areas. To date it has been implemented in 40 municipalities in Virginia, North Carolina, and Georgia, and it has had an impact on thousands of lives and entire counties and cities.

Twenty years ago in the Virginia county of Surry whites, except for six students, abandoned the school system, which was then allowed to deteriorate. There were no medical or recreational facilities for blacks. Much of their housing was tinned roof shacks, 60 percent of which had no running water, and blacks could not get loans at the local banks.

After the establishment of the Assembly, hundreds of new houses were introduced into the county, and 300 homes were winterized. The local bank was induced to make loans to blacks, and blacks were hired in local businesses. The Assembly raised $1 million in funds for a medical clinic and medical personnel and also established, through the county government, a $450,000 recreation center. A $4.6 million high school was constructed, and a $3 million elementary school. The teaching staff was integrated and upgraded, SRA scores rose from the 37th percentile to the 63rd percentile, and those going on to further education rose from 25 percent to 70 percent. Today there is no drug problem in the county, and so little crime that the jail has been closed. Ninety-two percent of the eligible voters have been registered.

THESE WERE THE ACCOMPLISHMENTS of the voluntary efforts of the poor themselves. Other counties and cities had similar successes, marshaling millions of dollars of private and public resources for the poor. Individual success stories are no less spectacular. In 1981 we held a music competition in which the Assemblies participated, the prize being a scholarship to the Shenandoah Conservatory of Music. The competition was won by an 18-year-old manual laborer who was unable to raise sufficient funds for college. He made his debut at the Kennedy Center in 1986, and signed with the Metropolitan Opera last April [1989].

An Assembly is a means of organizing an entire county or city so that the people involved can come to decisions on matters that affect them. Assemblies have been established in the most impoverished areas of the South where, for social and economic reasons and for reasons involving the history of this country, a large black population in 258 counties and several cities exists at a level of deprivation equal to that of some places in the Third World. These people live in a transitional, post-slavery condition. Their poverty is reflected in their housing, their health, their minimal education, and their attitude, one of complete failure.

Assemblies have been created to change these conditions and attitudes. The idea of the Assembly is premised on the principle that all long-term planning is done through institutions. Organization means making a whole of interdependent parts. Our experience has taught us that greater partic- ipation is brought about by breaking down the county or city into units of organization and, since the county or city is usually too large for all people to participate directly, by representing those units in a central decisionmak- ing body. The units of organization are called Conferences. Since dissim- ilar units do not cohere, all Conferences are composed of 50 persons each. The ongoing services provided by the Assemblies prevent both them and the Conferences from isolating themselves.

There is a certain relationship that people of a county or city must have in order to do anything collectively. The Assembly creates that relationship, creating a community where before none existed.

Initiative in a community usually takes place when directed by a smaller group of people, called the leadership. But in order for such initiative to be effective, the leadership must have a means of reaching the larger commu- nity. Under the Assembly method, the leadership reaches the larger com- munity through the representatives from Conferences.

The efficiency of this channel of communication is best understood by observing the internal structure of a Conference. Each Representative is in touch with his or her 50 members through seven Committeemen, who in turn communicate with the members of the Conference. Thus, the Assem- bly enables united action by counties and cities, first, by unifying isolated church communities; then, by creating countywide and citywide leadership; finally, by authorizing that leadership to act on behalf of the larger commu- nity. The Assembly brings together the poor, who then begin solving the problems of their own poverty.

The conventional antipoverty technique is to establish a program, regard- ed by experts or so-called representatives of the poor as being of priority, and to introduce it to a given community. Such an approach rarely works, and for two reasons. First of all, "representatives" of the poor are representatives in the taxonomic sense only. They have the attributes of the poor but are not necessarily chosen by them. Often, therefore, their views do not reflect the views of the larger community. Secondly, programs alone rarely stimulate common action. Unless there is community involvement in the program design, the programs are not likely to be successful in inducing a response from the community. The chances are high that these programs will not be regarded as relevant to the problems that confront the people they are sup- posed to serve. Such efforts also actively discourage self-help initiatives because the programs are necessarily conceived of by persons outside of the community. This is because the communities as a whole are not yet struc- tured to give support and direction to such initiatives.

Yet the only programs that will work are those which have community support, those programs that issue from the poor themselves, unmonitored and uninfluenced by others. These programs do not need to be financed by anyone. They are voluntary efforts by the poor, steps taken in their own self-interest.

Under the Assembly program the leadership is divided into functions. There is an officer for housing, an officer for education, an officer for health (among others)—in other words, a person to deal with all of the categories of problems. Thus the voluntary activity is channeled toward the problems, and a great deal is often accomplished without calling upon public or private resources.

Among the many thousands of the most unsophisticated people of the nation, the Assemblies have converted dejection to hope—a hope that is all the more remarkable in a period of American history that has experienced a decay in the institutions of genuine self-government.

Outgrowing the Past:
Eminent Domain Down South

Tom Landess

WHEN THE U.S. SUPREME COURT ruled in the case of *Kelo* v. *City of New London*, a chill wind blew across the South. The Court upheld the decision of the city fathers of New London, Connecticut, to grant a private development corporation the right to condemn a middle-income residential neighborhood; evict the property owners; and construct a marina, high-rise office buildings, and upscale residential housing.

Thoughtful Southerners found *Kelo* particularly disturbing because, in their region, the developer is king—more admired and accommodated than football players or country-music singers. To pig-eyed mayors and councilmen, he is Moses, sent by the gods of getting-and-spending to lead the region out of Egypt. No candidate for local office has ever been elected by saying, "I don't want this place to grow. And if the bigwigs at General Motors try to move their headquarters and production plants down here, they'll do it over my dead body." Big is better. Small is embarrassing.

Mega-cities such as Atlanta and Memphis and Dallas aren't the only places where this ideology prevails. You can find it in the most out-of-the-way rural town. Take, for example, Blackville, South Carolina. According to the U.S. Census Bureau, in the year 2000, Blackville had a population of 2,973. The Census Bureau estimated the 2004 population at 2,935, a loss of 38 people, or 1.3 percent. However, a website maintained by Blackville realtors insists—against all evidence and reason—that the population is 5,149. It isn't a lie so much as a fond hope.

If you drive through the heart of that town, you will see a weather-ravaged building with a sign that urges tourists to stop and visit "Three Flags Over Blackville." You can be certain that the Devil is sitting inside, leaning back in his swivel chair, picking his teeth.

Over in the next county lies a town buried under coils of blackberry vines, kudzu, pine needles, fallen trees, rotten branches, oaks, and innumerable varieties of weeds. If you go there—and few people are allowed behind the high fences—you can see the remains of curbs, some wide places that used to be driveways, and one or two small bridges. The rest of the town exists only in memory. Today, it is called the Savannah River Nuclear Plant. Once it was called Ellenton.

IN 1951, the U.S. government, using its powers of eminent domain, condemned Ellenton and at least four other communities that lay along the Savannah River—Dunbarton, Meyers Mill, Hawthorne, and Robbins. President Truman announced that the action was taken in the interest of national defense. The word spread quickly: The feds intended to build a plant to manufacture heavy water for use in a hydrogen bomb. The government could have chosen a thousand other sites, but this was a town the politicians were willing to waste.

The residents were stunned, but they were too patriotic, too committed to the Cold War, to protest.

Most of the families lived on working farms. A few ran businesses: "the Long Store," so named because of its shape; Brinkley's grocery; and the Blue Goose, a tavern where, for generations, the men had congregated to forget quarrels with their wives, squalling children, and the boll weevil. Most Ellentonians regarded the condemnation as cataclysmic.

Administration spokesmen and South Carolina politicians maintained that, far from being a tragedy, the "taking" was actually the best thing that had ever happened to Ellenton. People would be paid handsomely for the land. They would move to nearby cities. They would get better jobs. It was the same pitch the city of New London made to Susette Kelo.

Newsweek parroted this argument in a brief article on the subject. The reporter and a photographer swooped into town, located the village idiot (every town has one) and his female counterpart, posed them in front of an abandoned farmhouse, and presented them to the nation as Ellenton gentry. Readers could see at a glance that these vacant-faced trolls would be much better off in Spartanburg or Greenville, working in a textile mill, making enough money to keep them in Moon Pies for the rest of their days.

The federal appraiser offered $20 per acre for the land and varying amounts for the buildings, some of which were good, sturdy farmhouses, several of which were antebellum showplaces. A case in point: For their spacious, five-bedroom clapboard farmhouse, the Dunbar family was offered $5,000. Combined with 800 acres of farmland—a good portion of it covered with timber almost ready to harvest—they received $21,000, just enough to build a three-bedroom, two-bath house in nearby Barnwell and for Otis Dunbar to buy his wife a half-carat diamond ring, a long-postponed engagement present. It was small compensation for land originally given to

William Dunbar by a grateful King James II and farmed by Dunbar descendants until the federal government drove them off.

For decades after they left, the town lived on in the imagination of the dispossessed, lit by memory. But as the years passed, the lights went out one by one, as the older folks died. Today children who, 50 years ago, were snatched out of one world and plopped into another have grown old and forgetful. They have lost touch with one another and consequently with their shared past.

SOME ANECDOTES SURVIVE to commemorate that small, irretrievable world. Here are a few.

One late-fall evening, long, long ago, three of their great-grandfathers came back from a hunting trip, ready for a hot meal. To warm themselves as they rode along on horseback, they had passed a jug of whiskey back and forth. When they reached the first house, servants told them that children from all three families had contracted bronchitis and that the women were congregated in one house to share the responsibilities of administering aspirin, reading stories, and applying mustard plasters. When the men came to the house much too late, the women and children had gone to bed. Only one gaslight burned feebly in a downstairs parlor. Full of spirits, they rode their horses up the steps and into the hallway.

The host dismounted and walked unsteadily into the dining room, where he found a bare table. He peered into the kitchen and saw two pots boiling on the stove. Both contained mustard plasters. Starved, the three tethered their horses on the hall tree, sat down at the kitchen table, and ate the mustard plasters.

No one could have made up that story, and it could never have survived the years in New York or Chicago or even Greenville. Southern literature has its origins in places like Ellenton. In just such a small town, William Faulkner sat on a bench and listened carefully as old-timers swapped tales.

Hollywood, terrified of rural America, typically depicts its inhabitants as cruel and insensitive to the suffering of others. Even in the worst of times, people in Ellenton took care of those who needed help, in part because, in a small town, the needy were so easy to identify. Sometimes it happened quite by accident.

Miss Mary Bush decided that she could no longer carry logs to the house from the woodpile, so she went into the field where her husband, Major, was working with several of the hands and called him aside. She told him she needed a boy to tote wood for her—not a child, but not a grown-up either. He thought for a minute and then said, "I know just the boy. That fellow that's living with the Ashleys. I'll send somebody to fetch him right now."

An hour or so later, Henry Todd showed up, the trace of a smile on his face. He was around 16 at the time, and he had a strong back. However, when you looked into his dull eyes, you could see he was "slow." But he worked hard, and he seemed pleased to be there. So instead of returning him to the Ashleys, with their permission the Bushes put him in a back room of the huge house, and he stayed with the family for some 60 years.

Everyone in Ellenton knew the Ashleys had been "hiding" him, though no one could say how he got there or precisely when he came. The talk was that they weren't hiding him *from* somebody but *for* somebody, a family that didn't want to acknowledge the existence of a retarded member, people with a public reputation to maintain. The Bushes may have extracted the truth from the Ashleys. Or they may have gained crucial knowledge from the boy himself, who was a moron, but not an idiot.

Whatever the means, at some point they learned that Todd was only his middle name. His last name—which his mortified family would not allow him to use—was Lincoln. According to what the Bushes found out, he was the unacknowledged son of Robert Todd Lincoln. Robert was the only child of Abraham Lincoln who lived to adulthood. So Henry Todd was the 16th president's grandson.

After he had lived with the Bushes a while, they made contact with a member of the Lincoln family—Mary Lincoln Beckwith, who was then living at Robert Todd Lincoln's estate house, Hildene, located in Vermont. Mary Beckwith acknowledged the family connection and from time to time contributed money toward Henry Todd's keep.

When he reached adulthood, he grew a beard, and his resemblance to his grandfather was striking. He was not tall, but he had the same dark hair, a long, brooding face, and sunken cheeks. People in Ellenton noted the resemblance.

No one called him "Henry," but always "Henry Todd." "Hey Henry Todd, how are you?" "Fine, how are you?" He said little more than that, perhaps because he couldn't articulate complicated ideas.

Indeed, he never grew up. When one of the Bushes would return from town, a middle-aged Henry Todd would run out to the car to see if they had brought him ice cream. When they hadn't, he would sit down in the middle of the driveway and weep uncontrollably.

When the federal government ordered them to leave Ellenton, the whole family moved to Walterboro—including Henry Todd. There they bought a restaurant and a motel, and Henry Todd did a little work for his keep; but by then he had grown old. Up in his 70's, he walked to town one day, perhaps to get some ice cream, and, in his usual daze, stepped in front of an automobile and was killed instantly.

THOMAS DUNBAR, who served as magistrate in Ellenton during antebellum times, appointed one of his slaves as his bailiff. Since the slave was illiterate, Judge Dunbar would read him the upcoming docket the night before, and the slave would memorize it and call out the names and cases flawlessly the next day.

During Reconstruction, Republicans saw to it that blacks took over many state and municipal offices in South Carolina. For Ellenton, the predominately black legislature appointed Judge Dunbar's bailiff, now a freeman, as magistrate. The new judge immediately appointed his former master as his bailiff, and the two served in those roles for a decade, as if nothing much had changed.

A magistrate's court hears cases involving petty theft, simple assault, criminal domestic violence, public intoxication, and any other misdemeanor that carries a penalty of up to 30 days. Such arrangements could not have occurred in a full-blown city, North or South, since they depended not only on an infinitely subtle bond between two men of different races who knew and trusted each other, but on whole-hearted acceptance by the entire community, both white and black. That acceptance could only have come about because people knew precisely with whom they were dealing.

The idea that a C is "a gentleman's grade" has been much misconstrued. Most academics believe it is a hangover from an earlier age when the stupid or lazy sons of landowners were given C's instead of F's because of who they were. The men of Ellenton knew better. Gentlemen got C's on purpose, to show they weren't bedazzled by the honors of this world. Tom Dunbar, namesake of the antebellum judge, was a brilliant scholar at the Citadel. He knew the answers to all questions, but he purposely answered only 7 of 10, to show he didn't care.

This attitude dates back to the Renaissance, and was part of the character of great courtiers, such as Sir Philip Sidney, who wrote *Astrophel and Stella*, one of the great Elizabethan sonnet sequences; defeated all comers at jousting; and was a world-class diplomat. He did it all with a studied carelessness called *sprezzatura*.

One fall semester, a young Dunbar made the dean's list at the Citadel. When the family gathered at Christmas time, several of the older men took him outside and, with angry faces, explained the rules to him. As a matter of propriety, Dunbars didn't make the dean's list. It never happened again.

FOR MANY YEARS, the all-male Ellenton Agriculture Club had convened once a month at its own two-story wooden clubhouse, where members ate barbecued pork, hash, rice, slaw, potatoes, peas, light bread, and pickles. (The menu was prescribed by the club's constitution.) At these meetings, held every fourth Saturday, attendees heard a 30-minute speech on farming. If the speaker ran over the allotted time, chairs would scrape the floor, and members would begin clearing their throats.

Eminent domain signaled the end of farming for most Ellentonians. Yet they couldn't completely surrender a way of life they had known for generations. So to maintain some sense of continuity with their past, members voted to move the clubhouse to Barnwell, where many of them intended to settle. They also moved Ethel, the black woman who prepared the barbecue, and provided her and her family with a place to live and an adequate income.

In Barnwell, they continued to hold monthly meetings, listen to talks on agriculture, and eat barbecued pork, hash, rice, slaw, potatoes, peas, light bread, and pickles. No one ever discovered a penumbra in the constitution that justified serving something new, like Lobster Newberg on rusks. In an ever-changing world, constitutions ought to mean what they say.

Out of respect for the long dead—and because it's difficult to break an old habit—the club still meets every fourth Saturday in Barnwell.

UNLIKE ATLANTA or New London or Blackville, Ellenton never tried to grow. It was content to let nature take care of the population. If, at the end of a year, more citizens were born than died, the population increased slightly. If more folks died than were born, the population decreased slightly. A few people moved away, and a few moved in. The last thing the town worried about was importing industry and growing to the size of Babylon, whose citizens—as Aristotle noted—didn't know they had been conquered for three full days.

Then industry came to Ellenton unbidden, and the town ceased to exist. On former Dunbar land, the nuclear reactor, which today looks as stark and majestic as one of the pyramids, is no longer in operation. It stands like a tombstone over the dead and anonymous dreams of an almost-extinct people.

As an exercise of its sovereignty, the government insisted on moving all the graves that lay inside the condemned area. However, at least one remained and remains to this day—that of William Dunbar, who died in 1735. Though ordered to do so by government officials, his descendants refused to reveal the location of his remains. Today, he lies there in the shade of bearded oaks, blanketed by tall weeds and snarled vines, a lone holdout against America's proud and irresistible impulse to outgrow her own britches.

As his descendants were leaving Ellenton, trailers and trucks piled with sleigh beds, high-backed sofas, winged chairs, pianos, wood stoves, and all the detritus left behind by vanished generations, someone attached a square piece of wood to the town-limits sign. On it he scrawled this message: "It is hard to understand why our town must be destroyed to make a bomb that will destroy someone else's town that they love as much as we love ours. But we feel that they picked not just the best spot in the US, but in the world."

America—dressed in a three-piece suit, driving a fishtail Cadillac—flashed past that homemade sign without so much as a glance, rushing head-long toward empire and the wars that empire inevitably breeds. In our time, everything happens so fast. It took the Roman Empire centuries to fall to pieces. It took the British Empire decades. If we try hard enough, we can probably accomplish the same thing over a Labor Day weekend. We are certainly doing our damnedest.

This is happening in part because we have forgotten that towns like Ellenton—once scattered across the American landscape like so many stars—provided our people with a paradigm of truth, virtue, and beauty, insofar as such things can exist in a fallen world. The particularities of such communities are more difficult to preserve than the whooping crane or spotted owl—plowing with mules, hand-drawn wells, ten-row movie houses, dressing up to shop in the city, wooden churches, gas lamps, playing Go-In-and-Out-the-Window and Sling-the-Biscuit, hog-killing time, family cemeteries. Only the dead could possibly remember these things.

As for the quick—at least those of us who understand what has been lost—we mustn't take our decline and fall too seriously. We're not the first civilization to destroy itself in a fit of pride, nor will we be the last. To counterbalance the perennial recurrence of human catastrophe, we have it on the best authority that the Church will triumph, come what may, and that the Lamb will feed us, and lead us to the living fountains of waters: and God will wipe away all our tears.

Calhoun and Community

Clyde Wilson

I N ANY DISCUSSION of the Old Federalism—at least among that minority whose substantive knowledge of American principles and ideals precedes the beginning of the Kennedy dynasty—the name of John C. Calhoun and his idea of the concurrent majority is likely to come up.

Calhoun's reputation as a political thinker has had its ups and downs. Widely praised in his own time and after, by no means solely by defenders of slavery and states' rights, he was dismissed as a narrow reactionary fanatic during the intellectual rationalization of the victory in the Civil War. That victory, among other things, implied the triumph of the programmatically implemented will of the majority, in which ideas of constitutional limitations and minority rights had only token place. In the 1950's, however, in biographies and commentaries from surprisingly diverse quarters, Calhoun was rediscovered and elevated. The burden of this rediscovery is conveyed by the title of one of many scholarly articles of the time, Peter Drucker's "Calhoun's Pluralism: A Key to American Politics." Calhoun was celebrated as the philosopher and prophet of minority rights. His idea of the concurrent majority, implying the necessity to secure the assent of significant minorities for major political decisions, was thought of as having described the way American pluralism actually worked.

During the Civil Rights Revolution, Calhoun was again relegated to a minor and negative role. Recently [in 1985], as a part of the broad movement of conservatism, he has once more been receiving favorable attention. He has been so treated in Italian and Japanese scholarly journals. In American books and journals he has been called upon to provide solutions for the problems of the United Nations, Northern Ireland, and South Africa, and his ideas have been invoked to support Supreme Court decisions favoring minority representation on local governing bodies and even as a potential resource for black Americans.

There is some merit and usefulness in these formulations. However, they slight and distort the real burden of Calhoun's thinking on American government. For these formulations only incompletely grasp what Calhoun had to say, and, in my opinion, they sometimes embody a Pollyannaish and inaccurate notion of the way our government works. The formulations, which Calhoun's realism would have scorned, in fact represent the tendency of current thinkers to transcribe into mechanical and ideological terms ideas that are basically moral. Calhoun is better viewed as the last of the great republican thinkers who reached their peak with the Founding Fathers rather than as a prophet of modern pluralism, as a philosopher of democratic consent rather than as an architect of minority rights.

Calhoun's thought, embodied in 40 years of congressional speeches and public papers and in his two treatises, *A Disquisition on Government* and *A Discourse on the Constitution and Government of the United States*, constitutes a remarkable body of commentary on the American system—its political economy, finance, international affairs, and many other matters, as well as constitutional principles. Calhoun was the last active American statesman who was philosophical rather than empirical. To fully elucidate this would take several books. Here I wish to do no more than point to the opening pages of *A Disquisition on Government*. Properly understood, they contain a wealth of insight pertinent to the recovery of the Old Federalism.

A DISQUISITION ON GOVERNMENT, a slim 100 pages, is the most considered of Calhoun's works, to which he devoted his leisure in the last five years of his life. He said that he hoped by it "to lay a solid foundation for political science." Simple and clear in style, the work is complex enough in implications to have provoked many different interpretations. It would be an accurate, though not a complete, description to say that it is a study of the nature of the consent of the governed in a government of people.

A reading of the *Disquisition* afresh should convince anyone that Calhoun's concurrent majority was not, in the first instance, structural. It was not, except incidentally, a series of devices to protect minority rights, though such devices, given a constitutional system that already relied on checks and balances, had some relevance. What Calhoun was interested in was the nature of *consent*. All agreed that American government rested upon the consent of the governed, that this was the starting point for a democratic society. But what was this consent? How was it to be expressed, measured, and preserved? This, to Calhoun, related less to cheeks and balances and the mechanical features of government than to the old republican question of the virtue of the people. It is here that Calhoun has his real relevance. He was attempting to purify and clarify the republican idea of the consent of the governed, to move it to higher ground where it would be safe from the pressures of the 19th century that were silently turning it upside down. In this he failed, but nonetheless is still instructive.

In the *Disquisition*, Calhoun not only argues for his own views, but also recapitulates the implicit assumptions of the Founders of the American Constitution-making period:

> I assume, as an incontestable fact, that man is so constituted as to be a social being. His inclinations and wants, physical and moral, irresistibly impel him to associate with his kind; and he has, accordingly, never been found, in any age or country, in any state other than the social. In no other, indeed, could he exist; and in no other—were it possible for him to exist—could he attain to a full development of his moral and intellectual faculties, or raise himself, in the scale of being, much above the level of brute creation.
>
> I next assume, also, as a fact not less incontestable, that, while man is so constituted as to make the social state necessary to his existence and the full development of his faculties, this state itself cannot exist without government. This assumption rests on universal experience. In no age or country has any society or community ever been found, whether enlightened or savage, without government of some description.
>
> But government, although intended to protect and preserve society, has itself a strong tendency to disorder and abuse its powers, as all experience and almost every page of history testify. . . . The powers which it is necessary for government to possess, in order to repress violence and preserve order, cannot execute themselves. They must be administered by men in whom, like others, the individual are stronger than the social feelings. And hence, the powers vested in them to prevent injustice and oppression on the part of others, will, if left unguarded, be by them converted into instruments to oppress the rest of the community. That, by which this is prevented, by whatever name called, is what is meant by CONSTITUTION, in its most comprehensive sense, when applied to GOVERNMENT. . . . Constitution stands to government, as government stands to society; and, as the end for which society is ordained would be defeated without government, so that for which government is ordained would, in a great measure, be defeated without Constitution.

We like to think of our democracy as having sprung naturally from the political wisdom of the philosophical revolutionists and Constitution-makers of our founding period. We, like they, believe that government rests properly on the consent of the governed, the will of the people. However, when we contemplate modern ideas of the relationship between the democratic state and the people with the degree of historical perspective provided by Calhoun's *Disquisition*, we confront at once an innovative assumption that has crept into our thinking and turned the understanding of the Fathers on its head.

As EXPOUNDED in the 20th century, the theory of democracy is that the rule of the people is the sum of individual wills and inclinations. The democratic man casts his vote, along with all the other citizens, and the numerical majority of these votes determines the will of the people. By this scheme the chief locus of social value is in the democratic process itself—the right of participation and the possibility of the minority becoming a majority at the next election, all of which is together often summed up and celebrated as "the open society." This description seems to me to represent fairly the theory of American politics as it has been described in the last half-century or so by the predominant academic political scientists and popular spokesmen.

Under this dispensation, a great deal that was assumed as basic in the republican philosophy of the Founding Fathers gets lost. What is to be decided by the will of the people, directly or by representatives, for instance, is usually seen as programmatic and empirical. The public good has no independent existence but is the sum of trade-offs between the union member, the manufacturer, the public-school teacher, the welfare client, and all the other participants in the process. The will of the people thus becomes a balance of interests, a sharing of the pie. Not only is the idea of the public good, taken for granted by the Founders and by Calhoun, missing here, but also missing is the idea of the independent citizen whose strenuous virtue is the foundation of the public good.

By this scheme, the citizen is defined and exists by virtue of his participation in the democratic collectivity. In fact, only in its emphasis on "openness" does this idea of the democratic society differ from modern totalitarian theory. In both, the state and the individual confront each other starkly, and the individual, in the final analysis, is defined by the state. But for the Founding Fathers, the bedrock of republicanism was not the egalitarian political participation of the abstract individual so dear to modern democratic theory. Rather, republicanism (government of the people) was defined by the freedom and self-determination of communities of men, preexisting historically in all the complexity and differentiation of their social bonds. The history of American democracy is, until this century, the history of community.

Self-government was the expression, not of the individual, but of communities. Missing from the modern formulation is the assumption with which Calhoun began—preexistent society itself.

For the Founders, liberty was not the right of the rootless individual to do as he pleased or to participate in a process of head-counting leading to majority rule. It was, rather, the right of natural communities to be free from the depredations of the state. The definition of tyranny in the republican philosophy (inherited from the English "country party," amplified by American experience and thought, and underlying the American Revolutionary response) was the overreaching by the state of its legitimate bounds to tamper with or exploit the communities of men. The point of Constitution was not that it guaranteed a process of democratic decisionmaking. It was, rather, that society (the people) created and delimited an authority for its protection. In theory and practice, we have moved from a condition in which majority rule was a device for protecting society from the state, to one in which society is the raw material to be exploited and reconstructed by the state, acting in the name of a "majority."

It was this which Calhoun foresaw when he spoke with contempt of the "mere numerical majority." Here, I submit, is an insight of great importance. For Calhoun was not simply advocating a veto power for a numerical minority within a political system governed by a numerical majority. His point was much more basic. It was that the "numerical majority" or the "mere majority" did not represent the consent of the governed, that the political will of the people properly involved not head-counting but something higher and more intangible, a process of *consent* by society. But here is the key point. The elements of this consent were the organic parts of society, preexistent to government. These elements, being the product of society, and not of the state, ought to be inviolate. It was these elements that deserved the protection of the veto power implicit in the concurrent majority. Throughout Calhoun's discussion is the recognition of the superiority of the natural social elements, those that have come into existence spontaneously by the force of history and the necessities of man's nature, over those artificially created or enhanced by government action. The latter are precisely seen as one of the dangerous byproducts of an unqualified and abstract majority.

IN ANY PROPER THEORY of democratic government, society must precede the state. It is with this observation that Calhoun begins. Society was man as he was found—in family, in custom, in ethnic, territorial, religious, and occupational communities. For Calhoun, and here he was simply restating the assumptions of the Founders, the locus of value was not in the democratic process; it was in society. The democratic process was merely the best means to protect and preserve society. That society is hierarchical and antiegalitarian in both structure and values does not contradict the fact that communities should largely govern themselves and give the law to the state. And there is no protection implied for minorities which seek to come into being or power by state action. No ground is laid here for a pluralism marked by claims to veto power on the part of minorities who wish to disrupt natural society or assert an inviolate right to the earnings of others by state action (*e.g.*, the advocates of "gay rights" and of "welfare rights").

It was Calhoun's assumption, rather, that such artificial minorities threatened the consensual basis of the government of the people. He decried particularly in his own time manufacturers (by virtue of logrolling, a numerical majority) who wished to force industry into prosperity through protective tariffs that preyed upon the earnings of other parts of the community and political spoilsmen who sought the profits and power of office rather than the public good. In the latter connection he spoke again and again on the corruption of democratic consent represented by empty party slogans (like the Whigs' "Tippecanoe and Tyler, too" of 1840) and by the rise of oily equivocators like Martin Van Buren, who sought to mute and obscure issues, to rest their appeal on the broadest and least controversial ground possible, and thus to achieve power as an end in itself rather than as a means to reach fundamental decisions for the public good.

One might argue, as Daniel Boorstin has, that this muting of issues was a pragmatic and constructive avoidance of dangerous antagonisms. This is a kind of evasive pragmatism that would have been anathema to both Jefferson and Hamilton. The effect of this blandness, Calhoun maintained, was to undermine that free deliberation *within and among* communities that was a necessity for achieving the genuine consent of the people. The end result was to suppress disagreements that might be honorably adjusted, force them into other channels, and postpone and increase the explosion. Thus Calhoun predicted that the evasions of party men would lead to civil war, and those historians who have characterized the Civil War as a failure of democracy must concur.

Put another way, the consent of the governed was not to be viewed primarily as a process of counting heads, even when conditioned by technical safeguards for the minority. The consent of the governed was primarily a high moral matter—a process of political deliberation and social assent. The minority veto was not a device to block decision, but an effort to provoke further deliberation and a higher consensus. It trusted in the consent of the governed—that is, in the people—to find the right answers, provided the action of a mere majority, which might be a temporary manifestation of selfish combinations, could be suspended long enough to bring into play the higher consensus of communities.

Reflect upon the degree to which democracy depends upon the spirit of parliamentary institutions—the agreement that opponents are to be heard, to be dealt with civilly, and not to be overridden ruthlessly; that all are bound by decisions made after a proper hearing; and that all are pledged to remain a community even in disagreement. This entire proceeding relates less to the theory of majority rule, head-counting, than it does to the moral heritage of feudal chivalry—tolerance and respect for the opponent as bound within a common system of honor. There is nothing about it that is modern, utilitarian, or efficient or compatible with the "open society" theory. If the consensus is to be maintained, there are things the mere numerical majority must not do, even when it has the power. The majority must look for an answer that is inclusive and morally satisfactory rather than expedient, the morally satisfactory answer being, in the long run, also the most practical if genuine consent of the governed is to be maintained.

HERE, THEN, IS THE LESSON. The community must be the master of the state rather than its raw material. This is indeed a logical necessity in any viable theory of self-government, as well as a constitutional and moral truth. It is also, I believe, an historical truth. Calhoun's postulate that society precedes government is not, like the state of nature, merely a convenient theoretical starting point. It actually describes the origins of American government and provides the element that distinguishes America from Old World societies. In a speech of 1841, Calhoun referred to an historical contingency which "through the mysterious dispensation of Providence" had had a decisive effect on "the prosperity and greatness of our country." This contingency was that British America was not settled by an armed government, but

> by hardy and enterprising emigrants, inspired, in some instances, with a holy zeal to preserve their religious faith in its purity; in others, by the love of adventure and gain; and in all, with a devotion to liberty. It is to settlements formed by individuals so influenced, and thrown, from the beginning, on their own resources almost exclusively, that we owe our enterprise, energy, love of liberty, and capacity for self-government.

When Calhoun premised that society preceded government, he was merely recalling American experience. His own family was part of a kith of

85

Scotch-Irishmen who had come into the upcountry of South Carolina before the Revolution when it was empty of all but hostile Indians, tied together not by the state but by blood, religion, necessity, and the desire to make a new life. They carried some cultural baggage, and there was a distant Crown that was in theory sovereign. But the settlers were in fact virtually self-governing and self-reliant communities in economic, political, ecclesiastical, and military affairs. There was a real sense in which they participated in the creation of their own governments and constitutions by communal acts of consent.

The county in which I now live was occupied at the beginning of the American Revolution by interconnected families of prosperous German farmers. They had been settled for half a century and had no particular quarrel with the king in Great Britain. When confronted with the Revolution they did not appeal to the rights of individual man or to the "open society." The heads of households gathered under the trees, talked for two days, and decided that the interest of their community would best be served by allegiance to the American cause, which they thereafter supported loyally, often at the cost of property and life. If this seems an exaggerated or eccentric statement of historical precedence of society over government in this continent, reflect upon the self-governing congregations of Puritans who settled Massachusetts Bay, on the self-governing wagon trains and mining camps of the West, and on the later communities of immigrants of many sorts. Nowhere does the individual constitute only an abstract integer in a numerical majority.

There is a sense, of course, in which the subjugation of society to government, the reversal of the master-servant relationship between the community and the state apparatus, was an ineluctable product of "modernization." But there is also a sense in which it was a conscious decision, and therefore reversible. For, at an identifiable point in our history, we *decided* that the state ought to become master. This happened at the end of the 19th century, when a progressive elite declared that the conditions of modernity required it to take a guardian role through the federal government and discard previous notions of what constituted American principles. I can illustrate this turning point by a typical assertion of that time that I happen to have conveniently at hand. It is from the founding statement of the American Economic Association in 1885: "We regard the state as an agency whose positive assistance is one of the indispensable conditions of human progress." That is, the community is no longer able to govern itself, but must be guided by a class of experts wielding the power of the state. But the complexity of modern society did not necessarily call for a shift to the state. It called for new instruments of consensus formation. Empowering the state to solve all our problems does not make the state the instrument of the people. It makes the state—and this was Calhoun's point about the "numerical majority"—the instrument of the strongest interests and reduces democracy to an endless game of pie-sharing and the citizen to an abstraction.

If we are to be true to the American inheritance, society must precede government; the community must take precedence over the state. This simple declaration, I realize, does not grapple fully with the complexities of modern life, with the thrust of the predominant strain of the national character, and with the burdens, including the international role, that history has piled upon us. However, I am talking about philosophical starting points, not final solutions.

If it is indeed true that man is capable of self-government, then it is true that his mistakes are to some degree reversible. Much could be accomplished toward the preservation and reordering of self-government if we could reorder our thinking to give society precedence over government and make our communities the master of the state rather than its raw material.

THE LATE UNPLEASANTNESS

Mr. Lincoln's War:
An Irrepressible Conflict?

Patrick J. Buchanan

> *"[T]he contest is really for empire on the side of the North, and for independence on that of the South, and in this respect we recognize an exact analogy, between the North and the Government of George III, and the South and the Thirteen Revolted Provinces. These opinions . . . are the general opinions of the English nation."*
> —The *Times* of London (November 7, 1861)

> *"The preservation of the union is the supreme law."*
> —Andrew Jackson (December 2, 1832)

THE CIVIL WAR was the greatest tragedy ever to befall the American nation. Brother slew brother. Six hundred thousand of America's best and bravest died of shot, shell, and disease. The South was bled to death, invaded, ravaged by Union armies, occupied for a dozen years. Under federal bayonets, her social and political order was uprooted, and the 11 states that had fought to be free of the Union were "reconstructed" by that Union. America's South would need a century to recover.

Thirteen decades after Appomattox the questions remain: Was it "an irrepressible conflict"? Was it a necessary war? Was it, as Churchill wrote, "the noblest and least avoidable of all the great mass-conflicts of which till then there was record"? Was it a just war? What became of the great tariff issue that had divided and convulsed the nation equally with slavery in the decades before the war? Are there lessons for us in this most terrible of tragedies where all of the dead were Americans?

After any such war, it is the victors who write the history. That has surely been true of the Civil War. Among the great myths taught to American schoolchildren has been that the "Great Emancipator," Abraham Lincoln, was elected to free the slaves from bondage, that America's "Civil War" was fought to end slavery in the United States.

This is fable. Even the name given this terrible war is wrong. A civil war is a struggle for power inside a nation like the War of the Roses, or the horrible war between Bolsheviks and czarists in Russia, "Reds" and

"Whites," after Lenin's October Revolution. The combatants from 1861-65 were not fighting over who would govern the United States. The South had never contested Lincoln's election. The South wanted only to be free of the Union.

The war was not over who would rule in Washington, but who would rule in South Carolina, Georgia, and the five Gulf states that had seceded by the time of Fort Sumter. From the standpoint of the North, this was a War of Southern Secession, a War to Preserve the Union. To the South, this was the War for Southern Independence.

The Birth of a Myth

AT THE DEDICATION of Gettysburg Battlefield on November 19, 1863, three years after Lincoln's election, the Great Myth was born. There, Abraham Lincoln declared that the war had been, all along, about equality.

> Four score and seven years ago our fathers brought forth on this continent, a new nation, conceived in Liberty, and dedicated to the proposition that all men are created equal.
>
> Now we are engaged in a great civil war, testing whether that nation, or any nation so conceived and so dedicated, can long endure.

But four score and seven years before Lincoln spoke was 1776. The "new nation" may have been "conceived" in 1776, but it was not born until 1788 after the ninth state had ratified the Constitution. In that Constitution, freemen, black and white, were equal. But slavery, the antithesis of equality, was protected. By Benjamin Franklin's compromise, slaves were to be considered as three fifths of a person for purposes of representation in the House. Painful to concede, it is more truthful to say that slavery, the essence of inequality, was embedded in the Constitution of the new nation.

Moreover, in reaching back to 1776, Lincoln had invoked, in defense of a war to crush a rebellion, the most powerful brief ever written on behalf of rebellion. The Declaration of Independence is not about preserving a union. It is a declaration of secession, of separation; it is about the "Right of the People to alter or to abolish" one form of government "and to institute new Government, laying its Foundation on such Principles, and organizing its Powers in such Form, as to them shall seem most likely to effect their Safety and Happiness." It is about a people's right "to dissolve the political bands which have connected them with another, and to assume among the Powers of the

Earth, the separate and equal Station to which the Laws of Nature and of Nature's God entitle them."

Lincoln's words, eloquent as they are, are the sheerest audacity. As Garry Wills writes approvingly, Lincoln, at Gettysburg,

> performed one of the most daring acts of open-air sleight-of-hand ever witnessed by the unsuspecting. Everyone in that vast throng of thousands was having his or her intellectual pocket picked. The crowd departed with a new thing in its ideological luggage, that new constitution Lincoln had substituted for the one they brought there with them. They walked off, from those curving graves on the hillside, under a changed sky, into a different America. Lincoln had revolutionized the Revolution, giving people a new past to live with that would change their future indefinitely.

On reading Lincoln's address, many, North and South, were astounded. In suggesting the terrible war had all along been about equality, what was the President talking about? Quoting the Constitution back to the President, the *Chicago Times* charged Lincoln with betraying both that sacred document he had taken an oath to defend and the men who had died for it: "It was to uphold this constitution, and the Union created by it, that our officers and soldiers gave their lives at Gettysburg. How dare he, then, standing on their graves, misstate the cause for which they died, and libel the statesmen who founded the government?"

Even as Lincoln spoke, slavery was still legal in Washington, D.C., the seat of government, as well as in Maryland, Missouri, Kentucky, West Virginia, Delaware, and the areas of Tennessee that had remained loyal.

The Emancipation Proclamation of January 1, 1863, freed only the slaves in those states that were still in rebellion. All other slaves remained the protected property of their masters. British Prime Minister Palmerston noted in amusement that Lincoln had undertaken to abolish slavery where he had no power to do so, while protecting slavery where he had the power to destroy it. Indeed, when issuing the proclamation, Lincoln confided to his secretary that he had done so only as a "military necessity" after the defeats of First and Second Manassas, Jackson's Valley Campaign, the Seven Days battle, Chancellorsville, Fredericksburg, and the stalemate at Antietam: "Things had gone on from bad to worse, until I felt that we had reached the end of our rope on the plan of operation we had been pursuing; that we had about played out our last card, and must change our tactics, or lose the game. I now determined upon the adoption of the emancipation policy."

Far from universal celebration, the Emancipation Proclamation was regarded by many, even in abolitionist England, as a cynical and awful weapon of war, settled upon by Lincoln in desperation. As Sheldon Vanauken points out in *The Glittering Illusion: English Sympathy for the Southern Confederacy* (1989):

> [T]he Confederate states were winning the war. Only a few days before, Lee had smashed Burnside at Fredericksburg. The Proclamation freed all the slaves *within* the Confederate lines. . . .
> These slaves were grouped on the isolated plantations, controlled for the most part by the women since their gentlemen were off to the wars. The only possible effect of the Proclamation would be the dreaded servile insurrection (that which John Brown was hanged for inciting). *Either a slave rising—or nothing.* So Englishmen saw it. Lincoln's insincerity was regarded as proven by two things: his earlier denial of any lawful right or wish to free the slaves; and, especially, his *not* freeing the slaves in "loyal" Kentucky and other United States areas or even in Confederate areas occupied by United States troops, such as New Orleans. It should be remembered that [in England] the horrors of the Indian mutiny, as well as the slave uprising in St. Domingo, were in every memory.

The effect of the proclamation upon many in the Union ranks was the same. They had gone to war not to free the slaves but to preserve the nation! As James McPherson writes in *What They Fought For, 1861-1865*, "plenty of soldiers believed that the proclamation had changed the purpose of the war. They professed to feel betrayed. They were willing to risk their lives for the Union, they said, but not for black freedom. . . . Desertion rates rose alarmingly. Many soldiers blamed the Emancipation Proclamation."

Closing his address, Lincoln spoke of the duty imposed on Americans by those who had fallen on the great battlefield. We "here highly resolve," he said, in his immortal words, "that these dead shall not have died in vain—that this nation, under God, shall have a new birth of freedom—and that government of the people, by the people, for the people, shall not perish from the earth." If Southerners found this incredible, it is understandable.

The Confederates had never sought to cause the Government of the United States to "perish from the earth." It was the Union that was seeking to cause the Confederacy and the governments of the 11 Southern states to "perish." Had the South wanted the government to "perish from the earth," the Confederate army could have marched into Lincoln's capital after the First Battle of Bull Run in June 1861, when the Union army had been sent up the road to Washington in wild retreat. The South did not want this; the South only wanted to be free.

While Lincoln surely knew his eloquent words would be noted and remembered, he could not have known his brief remarks would become the most famous address in American history. Nor is there evidence that Lincoln, at this moment, deliberately enlarged the war aims of the Union. But at Gettysburg, the war aims of the Union were enlarged, dramatically. In that address, they go beyond anything Lincoln enunciated before the war began. Indeed, if racial equality was now Lincoln's and the Union's goal, then Lincoln himself was a changed man. For the Abraham Lincoln of 1861 was no champion of political or social equality.

"We Cannot Make Them Equals"

THE LINCOLN AMERICANS KNOW, the father figure with the wise and wonderful wit, who came out of Illinois to free the slaves, and believed in racial equality—who would have marched with Martin Luther King, Jr.—would be unrecognizable to his contemporaries. While Lincoln as early as 1854 had condemned slavery as a "monstrous injustice" and bravely took the antislavery side in senatorial campaign debates with Stephen A. Douglas, here is the Republican candidate for the United States Senate on the stump, in Charleston, Illinois, on September 18, 1858, after he had been baited by the "Little Giant" to explain where he stood on marriage between the races, and on social and political equality:

> I will say then that I am not, nor ever have been in favor of bringing about in any way the social and political equality of the white and black races,—that I am not nor ever have been in favor of making voters or jurors of negroes, nor of qualifying them to hold office, nor to intermarry with white people; and I will say in addition to this that there is a physical difference between the white and black races which I believe will for ever forbid the two races living together on terms of social and political equality. And inasmuch as they cannot so live, while they do remain together there must be the position of superior and inferior, and I as much as any other man am in favor of having the superior position assigned to the white race.

Four years before, at Peoria, on October 16, 1854, Lincoln confessed to his ambivalence as to what should be done about slavery, and with the freed black men and women were slavery abolished:

> If all earthly power were given me, I should not know what to do, as to the existing institution. My first impulse would be to free all the slaves, and send them to Liberia,—to their own native land. . . . [But free] them, and make them politically and socially, our equals? My own feelings will not admit of this; and if mine would, we well know that those of the great mass of white people will not. . . . A universal feeling, whether well or ill-founded can not be safely disregarded. We can not, then, make them equals.

Three years later, in June of 1857, in Springfield, Lincoln was still entertaining the idea of repatriating the freed slaves back to their native continent: "Such separation, if ever effected at all, must be effected by colonization; . . . what colonization most needs is a hearty will. . . . Let us be brought to believe it is morally right . . . to transfer the African to his native clime, and we shall find a way to do it, however great the task may be."

In urging colonization Lincoln was echoing men of far greater learning and higher station, such as Jefferson and Madison. In 1829, the author of the Constitution became president of the American Colonization Society—founded by John Randolph and Henry Clay after the War of 1812— "in the belief that its plan to return slaves to Africa represented the most sensible way out of that long-festering crisis." Clay, Lincoln's idol, advocated returning the slaves to Africa throughout his public career. In eulogizing Clay in Springfield on July 6, 1852, Lincoln celebrated his hero's lifelong association with the American Colonization Society, and quoted Clay's 1827 address to that society: "There is a moral fitness in the idea of returning to Africa her children, whose ancestors have been torn from her by the ruthless hand of fraud and violence. Transplanted in a foreign land, they will carry back to their native soil the rich fruits of religion, civilization, law and liberty."

In hearty approval of Clay's words, Lincoln declared: "This suggestion of the possible ultimate redemption of the African race and African continent was made twenty-five years ago. Every succeeding year has added strength to the hope of its realization. May it indeed be realized!"

Gradual repatriation and return of all the slaves to Africa, said Lincoln in the closing words of his long eulogy, would be a "glorious consummation"— Henry Clay's greatest contribution to his country.

Lincoln's words in the decade before his presidency are jolting to the modern ear. But all they tell us is this: On racial equality, Lincoln in 1858 was a man of his time and place. Like almost all white males of his age, he believed the races should remain separate. This is confirmed by his ardent admirer, Gen. Donn Piatt, who thought Lincoln "the greatest figure looming up in our history." After meeting with the president-elect in Springfield, Piatt wrote on the eve of Lincoln's departure for Washington: "Expressing no sympathy for the slave, [Lincoln] laughed at the Abolitionists. . . . We were not at a loss to get at the fact, and the reason for it, in the man before us. Descended from the poor whites of a slave State, through many generations, he inherited the contempt, if not the hatred, held by that class for the negro."

A man must be measured against his time. As Lincoln himself said in his Second Inaugural: "judge not that we be not judged." Lincoln's position on slavery—that it was evil, that he would have no part of it—was that of a principled politician of courage. As for his views on racial equality, they were the views of almost all of his countrymen. But if Lincoln did not go to war to make men equal, did he go to war to "make men free"—to end the evil of slavery? For to answer the question, "Was this a just war?" we have to understand why both sides fought.

Lincoln's Concessions to the South

UNLIKE THE LINCOLN of Gettysburg battlefield in 1863, the Lincoln who slipped into Washington in disguise in the dead of night in the winter of 1861 did not have the least intention of freeing any slaves. Nor did the South have reason to fear Lincoln would, or could, abolish slavery. The Supreme Court was Southern-dominated, led by Chief Justice Roger Taney of the 1857 Dred Scott decision. There was no threat to slavery from that quarter. And, during the campaign of 1860, Lincoln repeatedly assured the South he was no abolitionist. In the first paragraphs of his Inaugural Address, Lincoln repeated his assurances that he would make no attempt to abolish slavery:

> Apprehension seems to exist among the people of the Southern States, that by the accession of a Republican Administration, their property, and their peace, and personal security, are to be endangered. There has never been any reasonable cause for such apprehension. Indeed, the most ample evidence to the contrary has all the while existed, and been open to their inspection. It is found in nearly all the published speeches of him who now addresses

you. I do but quote from one of those speeches when I declare that "I have no purpose, directly or indirectly, to interfere with the institution of slavery in the States where it exists. I believe I have no lawful right to do so, and I have no intention to do so." Those who nominated and elected me did so with full knowledge that I have made this, and many similar declarations, and had never recanted them.

His party's platform, said Lincoln, endorsed the "inviolate" right of each state to "control its own domestic institutions." In excoriation of John Brown's raid, Lincoln noted in his Inaugural that, in their 1860 platform, Republicans "denounce the lawless invasion by armed force of the soil of any State or Territory, no matter under what pretext, as among the gravest of crimes."

South Carolina had seceded on the grounds that the United States was failing to uphold the fugitive slave provision of the Constitution. But Lincoln assured Southerners their escaped slaves would be returned:

There is much controversy about the delivering up of fugitives from service or labor. The clause I now read is as plainly written in the Constitution as any other of its provisions: "No person held to service or labor in one State, under the laws thereof, escaping into another, shall, in consequence of any law or regulation therein, be discharged from such service or labor, but shall be delivered up on claim of the party to whom such service or labor may be due."

It is scarcely questioned that this provision was intended by those who made it, for the reclaiming of what we call fugitive slaves; and the intention of the law-giver is the law. All members of Congress swear their support to the whole Constitution—to this provision as much as to any other. To the proposition, then, that slaves whose cases come within the terms of this clause, "shall be delivered up," their oaths are unanimous. *Now, if they would make the effort in good temper, could they not, with nearly equal unanimity, frame and pass a law, by means of which to keep good that unanimous oath?* [Emphasis added.]

Lincoln is calling here for a new federal fugitive slave law to reinforce Congress's constitutional obligation that escaped slaves "shall be delivered up" to their masters. In capturing and returning fugitive slaves, said Lincoln, some observers favor state authority, others federal authority. But, he asked, what is the difference? "If the slave is to be surrendered, it can be of but little consequence to him, or to others, by which authority it is done."

The issue on which Republicans were united was that the extension of slavery to new states should be halted. Lincoln did not back down from this position in his Inaugural Address. But he did offer a guarantee to the South that where slavery existed, it could be made a permanent institution, by a *new* constitutional amendment:

> One section of our country believes slavery is *right*, and ought to be extended, while the other believes it is *wrong*, and ought not to be extended. This is the only substantial dispute. . . . I understand a proposed amendment to the Constitution . . . has passed Congress, to the effect that the federal government, shall never interfere with the domestic institutions of the States, including that of persons held to service. To avoid misconstruction of what I have said, I depart from my purpose not to speak of particular amendments, so far as to say that, holding such a provision to now be implied constitutional law, I have no objection to its being made express, and irrevocable.

Thus, in this final concession, Lincoln says he would not oppose a constitutional amendment to make slavery permanent in the 15 states where it then existed. The first 13th Amendment to the Constitution Abraham Lincoln endorsed, then, did not end chattel slavery, but would have authorized chattel slavery forever. No true Abolitionist could have been other than horrified by Lincoln's First Inaugural Address.

Is there a moral defense of Lincoln's offer to make permanent an institution that all now agree was odious and evil? Only this: If it was not wrong for the Founding Fathers to accept slavery as the price of a constitution to establish the United States, it cannot be wrong for Lincoln to reaffirm the Founding Fathers' concession—to repair and restore his fractured country. In appeasing the South on slavery, Lincoln was being faithful to the Constitution he had sworn to protect and defend, and to his duty as president to unite his divided nation. He was also being true to his belief that, if slavery were restricted to where it existed, it would wither and die.

At the dedication of the Freedmen's Monument in Washington in 1876— a sculpture depicting a slave on his knees looking up in gratitude into the benevolent face of the Great Emancipator—Frederick Douglass stunned an audience including President Ulysses S. Grant by calling Lincoln "the white man's President, entirely devoted to the welfare of white men." "Viewed from the genuine abolition ground," Frederick Douglass went on, "Mr. Lincoln seemed tardy, cold, dull, and indifferent; but measuring him by the sentiment of his country . . . he was swift, zealous, radical, and determined." A not unfair assessment.

Did slavery cause the war? In 1927, historians Charles and Mary Beard produced their famous and first in-depth study of American history, *The Rise of American Civilization*. It captivated scholars and laymen alike. After carefully examining the facts concerning slavery and the Civil War, they concluded:

> Since, therefore, the abolition of slavery never appeared in the
> platform of any great political party, since the only appeal ever
> made to the electorate on that issue was scornfully repulsed,
> since the spokesman of the Republicans [Lincoln] emphatically
> declared that his party never intended to interfere with slavery
> in the states in any shape or form, it seems reasonable to assume
> that the institution of slavery was not the fundamental issue during the epoch preceding the bombardment of Fort Sumter.

To those who yet contend that Lincoln and the Union went to war "to make men free," how do they respond to the fact that when the war began, with the firing on Fort Sumter, there were more slave states *inside* the Union (eight) than in the Confederacy (seven)? Four Southern states—Virginia, North Carolina, Tennessee, and Arkansas—had remained loyal. They did not wish to secede; they did so only after Lincoln put out a call for 75,000 volunteers for an army to invade and subjugate the Deep South. That army would have to pass through the Upper South, which would have to join a war against its kinfolk. This the Upper South would not do. It was Lincoln's call to war against the already seceded states of the Deep South that caused Virginia, North Carolina, Tennessee, and Arkansas to leave a Union in which they had hoped to remain. Jeffrey Hummel notes in *Emancipating Slaves, Enslaving Free Men* (1996):

> Previously unwilling to secede over the issue of slavery, these four
> states were now ready to fight for the ideal of a voluntary Union.
> Out in the western territory . . . the sedentary Indian tribes—
> Cherokees, Choctaws, Chickasaws, Creeks, and Seminoles—also
> joined the rebellion. . . . Lincoln [by calling up the militia] had
> more than doubled the Confederacy's white population and material resources.

Before Fort Sumter, the Confederacy sent emissaries to Washington to discuss a compromise. Lincoln refused to meet with them, lest a presidential meeting confer legitimacy on a secession he refused to recognize. Against the advice of army chief Gen. Winfield Scott, Secretary of State William H. Seward, Secretary of War Simon Cameron, and Secretary of the Navy Gideon Welles, all of whom advocated evacuating Fort Sumter, he sent the *Star of the Sea* to resupply the fort. Viewing this as a provocation, the Southerners fired on the fort, and the American flag, and the great war was on.

And Southerners were perhaps not mistaken in their belief that Lincoln had provoked the conflict. As the President wrote with quiet satisfaction to Assistant Secretary of the Navy Gustavus Fox, commander of the expedition to Fort Sumter, on May 1, 1861: "You and I both anticipated that the cause of the country would be advanced by making the attempt to provision Fort-Sumpter [*sic*], even if it should fail; and it is no small consolation now to feel that our anticipation is justified by the result."

Like Polk before him, and Wilson and Franklin Roosevelt after him, Lincoln had maneuvered his enemy into firing the first shot.

Did the South Have a Right to Secede?

IN THE MODERN ERA, one reads more and more that the great Southern leaders were "traitors." Robert E. Lee, Thomas J. "Stonewall" Jackson, and Jefferson Davis, all heroes of the Mexican War, however, were no more and no less traitors than Washington, Adams, and Jefferson were traitors to Great Britain. At West Point, which George E. Pickett, Stonewall Jackson, and Joe Johnston attended, the constitutional law book that all three Confederate generals had studied, *A View of the Constitution of the United States* by William Rawle—a Philadelphia abolitionist and Supreme Court justice—taught that states had a right to secede: "To deny this right would be inconsistent with the principle on which all our political systems are founded, which is, that the people have in all cases, a right to determine how they will be governed."

Union officers had studied Rawle as well. Indeed, the idea of state supremacy, of states' rights to nullify federal law, and of a right to secede if the issue were truly grave, had a long, distinguished history in America. In the Kentucky and Virginia Resolutions of 1798 and 1799, Jefferson and Madison, authors respectively of the Declaration of Independence and the Constitution—enraged at the jailing of editors under the Alien and Sedition Acts—argued that states had a right to nullify patently unconstitutional federal law.

Between 1800 and 1815, three serious attempts were made by New England Federalists to secede—at the time of the Louisiana Purchase in 1803, Jefferson's Embargo Act of 1807, and Madison's War of 1812. The secessionist leader was a Revolutionary War hero and a member of Washington's Cabinet, Massachusetts Sen. Timothy Pickering. The Federalist causes mirrored South Carolina's causes: what they saw as an intolerable regime, interference with trade, incompatibility with alien peoples (Germans and Scotch-Irish), and a conviction the Union was being run for the benefit of the South. Said Pickering in 1803: "I will rather anticipate a new confederacy, exempt from the corrupt and corrupting influence and oppression of the aristocratic Democrats of the South."

By a twist of fate, Jefferson's rival, Alexander Hamilton, who had made Jefferson president in 1801 by persuading his allies to abandon Aaron Burr in the House of Representatives in the tie election of 1800, probably saved the Union. Federalists had conspired with Burr in 1804 to support him for governor, if Burr would lead New York into a New England Confederacy. But the revilement of Burr by Hamilton, as venal, corrupt, dictatorial, and dangerous, persuaded New Yorkers, by 7,000 votes, to reject him. Burr challenged Hamilton to a duel and killed him. Revulsion at the death of the patriot-statesman aborted the Federalists' plot.

In anticipation of John C. Calhoun's nullification, Massachusetts' legislature in 1807 denounced Jefferson's embargo, demanded that Congress repeal it, and declared the Enforcement Act "not legally binding." Many merchants ignored the law; and the New England authorities looked the other way. At the Hartford Convention of 1814, New Englanders, enraged by Madison's war with England when the Mother Country was in a death struggle against the dictator Napoleon, and by the interruption of their trade, threatened to secede and reassociate with Great Britain.

In 1832 South Carolina "nullified" a tariff law it believed was bleeding the South to death and asserted a right to secede. In 1843, when Tyler was driving for annexation of Texas, a vast territory that might be broken into five states, tilting the political balance of power in favor of the slave states, John Quincy Adams thundered that the annexation of Texas would justify Northern secession. And, in 1848, a freshman congressman critic of the Mexican War spoke of the inherent right of states to secede:

Any people anywhere, being inclined and having the power, have the *right* to rise up, and shake off the existing government, and form a new one that suits them better. This is a most valuable,— a most sacred right—a right, which we hope and believe, is to liberate the world. Nor is this right confined to cases in which the whole people of an existing government, may choose to exercise it. Any portion of such people, that *can, may* revolutionize, and make their own, of so much of the territory as they inhabit. . . . It is a quality of revolutions not to go by *old* lines, or *old* laws; but to break up both, and make new ones.

These are the words of Abraham Lincoln on January 12, 1848.

Why Did the South Secede?

IF LINCOLN DID NOT THREATEN slavery, why, then, did the Deep South secede? Answer: By 1861, America had become two nations and two peoples. The South had evolved into a separate civilization and wished to be a separate country. While moderates like Lee wanted to remain in the Union, Southern militants had concluded that, with the election of Lincoln, the North had won the great struggle for control of the national destiny.

The South had given the Union most of her presidents, her Supreme Court justices, her speakers of the House. But the South would never again determine the nation's direction. This first Republican president had not received a single electoral vote in a Southern state; in ten Southern states he had not received a *single vote*. Lincoln owed the South nothing; but he owed everything to her enemies, to the admirers of John Brown, to the Northern industrialists who had Lincoln's commitment to a protective tariff that the South believed threatened its ruin.

After decades of a troubled, unhappy marriage, for the Deep South Lincoln's election was the final blow. They had decided, irrevocably, on divorce. Thus, six weeks after Lincoln's election, on December 20, 1860, South Carolina seceded. By February 1, a month before Lincoln's inauguration, South Carolina had been followed out of the Union by Georgia, Florida, Alabama, Mississippi, Louisiana, and Texas. In these states, federal forts, post offices, customs houses, and military posts had been occupied. Federal employees and troops had been sent packing. Yet, by the day of Lincoln's inauguration, four months after his election, there was no war. Why not?

Because President James Buchanan did not believe the federal government had the right to use military force to compel states to remain within the Union. If the Union was not voluntary, it was not a true Union. To our 15th president, coercion was unconstitutional. As Prof. Woodrow Wilson wrote in *Division and Reunion*, Buchanan "believed and declared that secession was illegal; but he agreed with his Attorney General that there was no constitutional means or warrant for coercing a State to do her duty under the law. Such, indeed, for the time, seemed to be the general opinion of the country." Most Northern newspapers agreed.

As early as November 13, 1860, the *Daily Union* in Bangor, Maine, defended the South's right to secede, asserting that a true Union "depends for its continuance on the free consent and will of the sovereign people" of each state. "[W]hen that consent and will is withdrawn on either part, their Union is gone." If military force is used, then a state can only be held "as a subject province," and can never be a "co-equal member of the American Union."

Horace Greeley wrote in the *New York Daily Tribune*, on December 17, 1860, "the great principle embodied by Jefferson in the Declaration is that governments derive their just power from the consent of the governed." If the Southern states wished to depart, "they have a clear right to do so." And if tyrannical government justified the Revolution of 1776, "we do not see why it would not justify the secession of Five Million of Southrons from the Federal Union in 1861."

Many Northerners and abolitionists were delighted to see the Deep South states gone. Abolitionist editor William Lloyd Garrison had spoken for many when he wrote that the original Constitution, protecting slavery, had been a "covenant with Death" and an "agreement with Hell." In April 1861, Greeley wrote that "nine out of ten of the people of the North were opposed" to using force to return South Carolina to the Union. General Scott, hero of the Mexican War and commander of the U.S. Army, said of the "wayward sisters . . . let them go in peace." Ironically, the "wayward sisters" were like fugitive slaves. They were trying to break free of Father Abraham's house, but he would not let them go.

Absent Abraham Lincoln, there might have been no war. But, without Lincoln, there might also be no United States today. Unlike Buchanan, the new president would accept war, raise an army of a million men, and fight the bloodiest struggle ever on the American continent, rather than let the South go. The Confederate firing on Fort Sumter may have been the spark that ignited the conflagration, but the real cause of the war was the iron will of Abraham Lincoln, as resolute a Unionist as was Andrew Jackson, who also would have accepted war rather than let South Carolina secede. Thus, as the Mexican War had been "Jimmy Polk's War," this was "Mr. Lincoln's War."

To win it, the President would assume dictatorial power, suspend the constitutional right of *habeas corpus*, overthrow elected state legislatures, arrest and hold without trial thousands of political prisoners, shut down opposition newspapers, and order army after army into the South to give his nation a new "birth of freedom," and a new baptism of blood and fire.

When mobs rioted against the draft in July 1863, looting and pillaging New York City, lynching blacks they saw as threats to their jobs and the cause of the war, Lincoln ordered units detached from Meade's army. When the veterans of Little Round Top and Cemetery Ridge entered the city, a witness described the action:

> streets were swept again and again by grape [shot], houses were stormed at the point of a bayonet, rioters were picked off by sharpshooters as they fired on the troops from housetops; men were hurled, dying or dead, into the streets by the thoroughly enraged soldiery; until at last, sullen and cowed and thoroughly whipped and beaten, the miserable wretches gave way at every point and confessed the power of the law.

Estimates of the dead ranged from 300 to 1,000.

Lincoln meant to enforce the draft law. There are no reports of commissions established to investigate the "root causes" of "urban disorder." Though he has come down to us as a kind and courtly homespun, backwoods humorist, there is truth in the depiction of Lincoln in Gore Vidal's novel, where the President is seen through the eyes of a marveling secretary of state: "For the first time, Seward understood the nature of Lincoln's political genius. He had been able to make himself absolute dictator without ever letting anyone suspect that he was anything more than a joking, timid backwoods lawyer . . ."

No tougher, more resolute man ever occupied the White House. As the historians Samuel Eliot Morison and Henry Steele Commager have written, Abraham Lincoln was

> a dictator from the standpoint of American constitutional law and practice; and even the safety of the Republic cannot justify certain acts committed under his authority. . . . A loyal mayor of Baltimore, suspected of Southern sympathies, was arrested and confined in a fortress for over a year; a Maryland judge who had charged a grand jury to inquire into illegal acts of government officials was set upon by soldiers . . . beaten and dragged bleeding from his bench, and imprisoned . . .

To this Lincoln pled military necessity, the imperative of preserving the Union: "Are all the laws but one to go unexecuted, and the government itself go to pieces, lest that one be violated?" To those who denounced him as a tyrant for ignoring due process in crushing sedition, Lincoln made no apology: "Must I shoot a simple-minded boy who deserts, while I must not touch a hair of the wily agitator who induces him to desert?"

The First Emancipation Proclamation

THAT PRESERVING THE UNION, not ending slavery, was Lincoln's agenda is evident from the first year of the war. In the summer of 1861 Gen. John C. Frémont, Republican candidate for president in 1856, was in command in Missouri. In a daring move, Frémont drew a line across the state, separating the pro-Confederacy region from the Union side, and issued an order: Any civilian caught carrying a weapon north of the line would be shot. Any man aiding the secessionist cause was to have all his slaves instantly emancipated.

An instant national hero to abolitionists and Freesoilers in the United States and Great Britain, the general sent his order to the President for approval. But Lincoln, desperate to keep pro-slavery Kentucky in the Union, told Frémont to withdraw it. Frémont refused, insisting he would not comply unless Lincoln issued a direct order. Lincoln issued the order.

The general's wife, impulsive and high-strung Jessie Benton Frémont, daughter of the great Missourian Thomas Hart Benton, who had married the dashing Lieutenant Frémont when she was 16, undertook a journey to Washington, carrying a written plea from her husband. When she arrived in the capital, exhausted after days of day-and-night travel in a dirty coach over rough roads, she sent a brief note to the White House—where she had played as a girl in the days of Andrew Jackson—to set up an appointment to deliver the letter. A response came back that very night: "Now, at once, A. Lincoln."

When Lincoln received her in the Red Room, Jessie Frémont lectured the President on the difficulty of conquering the South with arms alone. She urged Lincoln to appeal to the British nation and the world by declaring emancipation to be the Union's cause.

"You are quite a female politician," an irritated Lincoln responded.

Mrs. Frémont walked out of the White House and wrote in her diary: "I explained that the general wished so much to have his attention to the letter sent, that I had brought it to make sure it would reach him. He [Lincoln] answered, not to that, but to the subject his own mind was upon, that 'It was a war for a great national idea, the Union, and that General Frémont should not have dragged the negro into it . . .'"

Jessie Frémont had clearly upset Lincoln. When a confidant of the President saw the general's wife the next day, he was irate. "Look what you have done for Frémont; you have made the President his enemy!"

The *Chicago Tribune* denounced Lincoln for reversing General Frémont's emancipation proclamation. Lincoln's action takes away the penalty for rebellion, charged the *Tribune* on September 16. "How many times," asked James Russell Lowell, "are we to save Kentucky and lose our self-respect?" In Connecticut, indignation had risen to fury. Sen. Ben Wade of Ohio wrote "in bitter execration": "The President don't object to Genl Frémont's taking the life of the owners of slaves, when found in rebellion, but to confiscate their property and emancipate their slaves he thinks monstrous."

But Lincoln's policy was not emancipation. It was to return the South to the Union, even if it meant appeasing the South on slavery. As Lincoln wrote Greeley in his famous letter of August 22, 1862, "My paramount object in this struggle is to save the Union, and is *not* either to save or destroy slavery. If I could save the Union without freeing *any* slave I would do it."

Lincoln, however, had already settled on his decision to issue the Emancipation Proclamation, and had so informed his Cabinet.

Did Tariffs Cause the War?

IN *FOR GOOD AND EVIL: The Impact of Taxes Upon the Course of Civilization*, historian Charles Adams refers back to John C. Calhoun's 1832 warning about the great sectional division Calhoun had seen on the horizon:

> Federal import tax laws were, in Calhoun's view, class legislation against the South. Heavy taxation on the South raised funds that were spent in the North. This was unfair. Calhoun argued further that high import taxes forced Southerners to pay either excessive prices for Northern goods or excessive taxes. Competition from Europe was crushed, thereby giving Northerners a monopoly over Southern markets. Federal taxation had the economic effect of shifting wealth from the South to the North—not unlike what the OPEC nations have been doing to the oil-consuming nations since 1973.

After Lincoln's election, South Carolina, Georgia, Florida, Alabama, Mississippi, Louisiana, and Texas did not wait to see how he would govern. All seceded before his inauguration. They knew what lay ahead. For even before Lincoln took his oath in early March, the first of the Morrill tariffs had been passed and signed by Buchanan, raising tariff rates to levels not seen in decades.

Consider the situation of the South: As the South purchased two thirds of the nation's imports, and tariffs were the prime source of tax revenue, the South was already carrying a hugely disproportionate share of the federal tax load. By raising tariffs, Congress, in Southern eyes, was looting the South. Southern imports would cost more, while the rising tariff revenue would be sent north to be spent by Republicans who reviled the South. The South's alternative: Buy Northern manufactures instead of British. Either way, more of the South's wealth was headed north.

Dixie was unwilling to sit by and watch Lincoln's customs officers haul their fattening satchels of duty revenue out of Southern ports, up to Washington, to be spent somewhere else, by a president who had not won a single Southern electoral vote. As the historian Adams writes,

> The Morrill Tariff . . . was the highest tariff in U.S. history. It doubled the rates of the 1857 tariff to about 47 percent of the value of the imported products. This was Lincoln's big victory. His supporters were jubilant. He had fulfilled his campaign and IOUs to the Northern industrialists. By this act he had closed the door for any reconciliation with the South. In his inaugural address he had also committed himself to collect customs in the South even if there were a secession. With slavery, he was conciliatory; with the import taxes he was threatening. Fort Sumter was at the entrance to the Charleston Harbor, filled with federal troops to support U.S. Customs officers. It wasn't too difficult for angry South Carolinians to fire the first shot.

Believing itself an exploited region in a country where the newly empowered Republicans despised it, Dixie decided to leave. But there was a powerful reason the industrialized North could not let it go. The free-trade Confederacy had written into its Constitution a permanent prohibition against all protective tariffs: "nor shall any duties or taxes on importations from foreign nations be laid to promote or foster any branch of industry."

To Northern manufacturers a free-trade South spelled ruin. Imports would be diverted from Baltimore, New York, and Boston, where they faced the Morrill Tariff, to Charleston, Savannah, and New Orleans, where they would enter duty-free. Western states would use tariff-free Southern ports to bring in goods from Europe. So would many Northerners. On the very eve of war, March 18, 1861, the *Boston Transcript* wrote:

> If the Southern Confederation is allowed to carry out a policy
> by which only a nominal duty is laid upon imports, no doubt

the business of the chief Northern cities will be seriously injured thereby.

The difference is so great between the tariff of the Union and that of the Confederate States, that the entire Northwest must find it to their advantage to purchase their imported goods at New Orleans rather than New York. In addition to this, the man-ufacturing interest of the country will suffer from the increased importations resulting from low duties.... The ... [government] would be false to all its obligations, if this state of things were not provided against.

Adams describes the political and economic crisis the North would have confronted, living side-by-side with a free-trade Confederacy:

This would compel the North to set up a chain of customs stations and border patrols from the Atlantic Ocean to the Missouri River, and then some. Northerners would clamor to buy duty-free goods from the South. This would spell disaster for Northern industrial-ists. Secession offered the South not only freedom from Northern tax bondage but also an opportunity to turn from the oppressed into the oppressor. The Yankees were going to squirm now!

Nor was Lincoln unaware of the dread prospect. In his First Inaugural Address, where he had been a portrait in compromise on slavery, promising "no bloodshed or violence" against seceding states, be had made an excep-tion: "The power confided to me, will be used to hold, occupy, and possess the property, and places belonging to the government, and *to collect the duties and imposts; but beyond what may be necessary for these objects, there will be no invasion*—no using of force against, or among the people any-where" (emphasis added).

Message to the Confederacy from Abraham Lincoln: You may keep your slaves, but you cannot keep your duty-free ports! British intellectual John Stuart Mill blithely declared, "Slavery the one cause of the Civil War." But, as Adams writes, others in Britain put the cause elsewhere:

In the British House of Commons in 1862, William Forster said he believed it was generally recognized that slavery was the cause of the U.S. Civil War. He was answered from the House with cries, "No, no!" and "The tariff!" It is quite probable the British commercial interests, which dominated the House of Commons, were more in tune with the economics of the Civil War than were the intellectuals and writers.

The tariff was "a prime cause of the civil war," writes historian John Steele Gordon, author of *Hamilton's Blessing*.

But, while tariffs were a cause of sectional rancor and division and one of the reasons for secession, Lincoln never discussed the tariff in depth after his speech in Pittsburgh before the inauguration. Henry Carey, the great protectionist, never forgave Lincoln, whom he had supported to the hilt, for the omission. And given Lincoln's devotion to the Union—the cause to which he subordinated all others—it would seem that, for him as for Andrew Jackson, the tariff was not the end, but the means to the end: a greater, more glorious Union. Murray Rothbard was not too far off when he wrote that Abraham Lincoln "made a god out of the Union."

The South's Fatal Dependency

THOUGH THE ABOLITION of slavery was not why Lincoln went to war, slavery and the South's dependence on trade for the necessities of national life were the South's undoing in that war. Slavery had kept the South in mercantilist bondage. Eighty years after Yorktown, the South was still shipping raw materials to Britain for manufactured goods. Had slavery been abolished, the Deep South would have been forced off her dependence on cotton, tobacco, and rice. Given her natural resources, the capacities of her people, black and white, the South would have developed alongside the North and West. Instead, it was in the North where 90 percent of the manufacturing was done, where warships were built, cannons were forged, locomotives were constructed, and most of the railways laid. From the war's outset, the position of the South to the North was like that of the colonies to Great Britain in the Revolution.

With its fleets, the North quickly imposed a naval blockade, and sliced the Confederacy in two at the Mississippi. Dependent on trade, the South saw her cotton and tobacco rot in warehouses, and her trade dry up. The South's slaves, unlike Northern immigrant labor, could not be used to produce weapons of war. Slavery and the agrarian character of the South tied them to the land. There may be truth in what Henry Carey wrote: "Had the policy advocated by Mr. Clay, as embodied in the tariff of 1842, been maintained, there could have been no secession, and for the reason, that the southern mineral region would long since have obtained control of the planting one." Without slavery, the South's statesmen would not have been forced to use their brilliance defending an institution the South's greatest men—Washington, Jefferson, Madison, Jackson, Lee—knew could not be reconciled with the ideals in which they believed.

Southerners were bound to a system they inherited at birth. Because that system depended on three-and-a-half million slaves, the South had to submit to abuse from moral posturers from the North who ignored the exploitation of immigrant labor and could not care less about the plight of slaves. Eventually the South had to leave a Union their fathers helped create, and fight to their defeat and ruin in an independence struggle made almost impossible of victory because they had relied so long on the land and neglected the "work bench" Jefferson and Randolph had so detested.

One cannot read the story of that four-year struggle without coming away with boundless admiration for the bravery of Southern soldiers, the perseverance of her people, the brilliance of her generals. From Bull Run to Antietam, Gettysburg to Appomattox, the men in gray wrote a chapter in glory that will bring tears to men's eyes as long as they have hearts.

And Mr. Lincoln? Unquestionably, the war changed the man. The president-elect who arrived in Washington anxious to appease Southern slaveowners, that ambivalent man of whom Richard Hofstadter wrote that his mind on the Negro was a "house divided against itself," seemed, by the war's end, to have become a remorseless abolitionist. At Gettysburg, whether he had intended it or not, Lincoln had succeeded for all time in "ennobling" the Northern cause and immortalizing himself. In those brief, haunting, and memorable words, Lincoln had proclaimed that the war, all along, had been about the equality of man.

Antietam, the Battle of the Wilderness, the March to the Sea had hardened Lincoln. Unlike the conciliatory rhetoric of his First Inaugural, his second rings like the final warning of impending judgment from an Old Testament prophet. In that Second Inaugural, the armies of Sherman and Grant have become instruments of God's will. This Inaugural could have been delivered by John Brown:

> Fondly do we hope—fervently do we pray—that this mighty scourge of war may speedily pass away. Yet, if God wills that it continue, until all the wealth piled by the bond-man's two hundred and fifty years of unrequited toil shall be sunk, and until every drop of blood drawn with the lash, shall be paid by another drawn with the sword, as was said three thousand years ago, so still it must be said, "the judgments of the Lord, are true and righteous altogether."

The war had not been about slavery when it began. But, by its end, Abraham Lincoln had declared it to be so. And so it was. And the terrible and tragic manner of his death affirmed it forever.

Was the Cause Just?

WAS THE GREAT WAR A JUST WAR? For the South, the issue comes down to a single question: Did the South have the right to secede from the Union? For if the South had a right to secede—as the colonies had a moral and legal right to break away from the British Empire—then the South had the right to fight for that independence, and to resist a Union invasion and forcible return at the point of Union bayonets.

On that first question, the South in 1861 had at least as strong a case for secession as the Federalists of the Hartford Convention, or ex-president John Quincy Adams, who threatened President John Tyler with secession if Texas were admitted to the Union. By the Jeffersonian test that, to be legitimate, a government must rest upon the consent of the governed, the Confederacy had legitimacy by the time of Fort Sumter. What the Union took back in 1865 was not free men and free states, but defeated rebels and conquered provinces.

In 1861 it had been an open question whether a state had a right to secede. The question was submitted to the arbitrament of the sword and settled only at Appomattox. But, of all the wars America ever fought, "vital interests" were at risk in the Civil War. Had South Carolina, Georgia, and the Gulf states broken away, British and French would have moved in to exploit the Southern free-trade zone to undermine Northern industries and wean the West away from the Union. Indeed, during the war, Napoleon III installed a puppet regime in Mexico in violation of the Monroe Doctrine, and the British were moving troops into Canada. The first secession would not have been the last. Fragmentation of the nation was at hand. As a private in the 70th Ohio wrote home in 1863: "Admit the right of the seceding states to break up the Union at pleasure . . . and how long will it be before the new confederacies created by the first disruption shall be resolved into still smaller fragments and the continent become a vast theater of civil war, military license, anarchy and despotism. Better settle it at whatever cost and settle it forever."

With the Deep South gone, the United States would have lost a fourth of her territory, her window on the Caribbean and the Gulf, her border with Mexico, and her port of New Orleans—the outlet to the sea for the goods of Missouri, Illinois, Iowa, and the Middle West. The South would have begun to compete for the allegiance of New Mexico and Arizona; indeed, rebellions arose in both areas and had to be put down by Union troops.

To Lincoln, secession meant an amputation of his country that would have destroyed its élan and morale. Disunion was intolerable. Where Jackson said it directly, "Disunion is Treason," and "Preservation of the Union . . . the highest law," Lincoln used his rhetorical powers to elevate the cause to one of universal values. But his goal was the same as Jackson's.

Lincoln was the indispensable man who saved the Union. He accepted war and may have provoked war to restore that Union. In the end, that war freed the slaves. "At last after the smoke of the battlefield had cleared away the horrid shape which had cast its shadow over the whole continent had vanished and was gone for ever," wrote England's John Bright. But was war necessary to free the slaves, when every other nation in the hemisphere, save Haiti, freed its slaves peacefully, without the "total war" Lincoln's generals like Sherman and Sheridan unleashed on the South? To Lincoln, then, belongs the credit of all the good the war did, and full responsibility for all the war cost.

While the men of government had one set of reasons for going to war, the men who marched into the guns had another: patriotism, love of country. They fought, as Macaulay said, for the reasons that men always fight, "for the ashes of their fathers and the temples of their gods."

We are fighting against "traitors who sought to tear down and break into fragments the glorious temple that our fathers reared with blood and tears," a Michigan private wrote to his younger brother. A month before he fell at Gettysburg, a Minnesota boy wrote home that he was willing to give his life "for the purpose of crushing this g--d--- rebellion and to support the best government on God's footstool."

In the war's last days, a Union soldier captured a wounded rebel and was astonished by the man's ferocity. "Why do you keep fighting like this?" he demanded. "Because you're here!" the dying rebel replied.

Showdown at Gettysburg

J.O. Tate

Sitting through a showing of the recent [1993] film *Gettysburg* in a multiplex theater amid the abstract sprawl of suburban Yankeedom was somehow an unnerving experience. I don't mean to say that the movie itself was off-putting or unsuccessful, though come to think of it, there were a few awkward moments here and there. No, the hard part was being in the presence of other Americans as the movie was shown. There seemed to be more at stake in that representation of history than the field where it was fought and filmed.

Gettysburg is a good movie as such, and as a movie about the Civil War, one of the best ever made, if not the best. It represents the contribution of many hundreds of reenactors; it is in effect a sort of pageant, a filmed reenactment. The figure of $30 million has been cited as Ted Turner's investment in the project, and as you might expect, the footage (even longer than the four-plus hours of the theatrical release) is supposed to become a cable TV extravaganza and video release later on. It's fine with me if Ted Turner gets his money back. After all, *Gettysburg* is no ignoble undertaking, especially when compared with 90 percent of the trash that's released today. It's graphically striking and well worth seeing.

Jeff Daniels has been widely praised for his portrayal of Joshua Lawrence Chamberlain, "the Hero of Little Round Top," and rightly so. The heroic presentation of such a man, however, suggests numerous contemporary ironies that are part of the problematic "success" of the film. Moreover, the emphasis on Chamberlain and on the extreme left of the Union position skews our perspective of the battle. I suppose that Chamberlain is to a degree overemphasized for dramatic reasons, as a counterweight to the striking personalities of the Confederate brass; that problem is presented to us as much by history as by the screenplay. Still, much more could have been done with Winfield Scott Hancock, and nothing was made of Dan Sickles and his famous blunder, or the consequential loss of his leg.

The dominant presence in the film is a passive one: Tom Berenger as James Longstreet spends a lot of screen time dragging on a cigar and listening to the expostulations of others. His hair and beard are so false and heavy that he looks like a transgalactic alien from *Star Trek: The Next Generation*, and his immaculate uniform seems to say, "General Lee, I've come straight from the dry cleaner's." Though the battle was fought in the heat of early July, this Longstreet never removes a jacket, opens a collar button, or loosens a tie in that blistering sunlight. The thought of just how much antiperspirant Longstreet used at Gettysburg had never crossed my mind before (a great deal, apparently), but then we all have much to learn from the reenactors.

As Robert E. Lee, Martin Sheen is an effective surprise. He conveys Lee's achieved simplicity and intimidating perfection of manner, a composure somehow innate, willed, mild, severe, aristocratic, military, and Virginian all at once. My complaint about Sheen is his lack not only of a waist but also of much else needed to evoke Lee's physical grace. Perhaps elevator shoes and fewer peanuts with those Heinekens would have helped.

BUT I DON'T REALLY MEAN TO CARP. *Gettysburg* is good enough so that its flaws—an unbalanced screenplay, little blood, no sweat, few tears—are actually apparent. I suppose that it just doesn't matter much whether I or anyone else particularly liked the representation, say, of J.E.B. Stuart or A.P. Hill or John Bell Hood or Lewis Armistead or Richard Garnett or George Pickett. No indeed, because apart from its quite considerable cinematic virtues, *Gettysburg* is significant not as a movie but as a rather astounding phenomenon on the cultural scene. We behold Lee and Longstreet at Gettysburg, but outside that focus there's the mind-numbing juxtaposition with all that has replaced them in the national consciousness, such as Senators Kennedy and Biden, Beavis and Butt-Head, and what have you. So the representation of the Civil War as something very like "the last war fought between gentlemen" is surprising in our ahistorical, absurdist context. Nineteenth-century eloquence is all the more striking for the implied contrast with the dumbed-down discourse of the contemporary standard, whether in the multiplex or on cable. It is actually shocking to see the Civil War represented in historically sound language, ideas, and motives, rather than in some rigidly ideological reduction. Precious little in American culture since the 60's has prepared us for the incredible truths presented by *Gettysburg*—a vision that comes as a slap in the face and a wake-up call to the national memory. Thanks, director Ronald F. Maxwell—we needed that.

Maxwell's screenplay was developed from Michael Shaara's novel *The Killer Angels,* and it is both appropriate and necessary to say here that Shaara's vision was developed from history. What shock is there for us in thinking that Longstreet might have been more right than Lee 130 years ago? The shock of *Gettysburg* is not the rehash of strategy or the experience of the battle—it is the reminder of a lost world and a betrayed culture. It is a measure of what we have lost, of what too many of us have never known we had, of the price we pay for induced amnesia, and of the alienation and mendacity required to maintain the present regime of inversion.

Not all of us needed such a reminder, of course. Some are like Elvis Presley in one of his early songs: We forgot to remember to forget. Civil War buffs, muzzleloading enthusiasts, and historically minded people are some of those who, in various ways, remember and commemorate authentic America. But by and large, a cultural hegemony preoccupied with radically restructuring the nation's laws and lobotomizing our treasury of memory by promulgating a repotted history; a masscult obsessed with extracting money from consumers who are habituated to pornographic and other fantasies accompanied by the druggy shake, rattle, and roll of electronic "music"; and enforcers of politically correct substitutes for knowledge and thought who police the academic world—none of these have prepared us for the experience of a film that in 1993 largely deals with Confederate anxieties and presents without irony extollments of the virtues of the families of Virginia.

The seeming novelty of such assertions, and the sight of so many freshly laundered Confederate battle flags (no bullet holes or bloodstains on those banners), seems incongruous in a larger context so distorted that only just this past summer, the U.S. Senate actually voted to refuse a patent to the United Daughters of the Confederacy, endorsing the view of Sen. Carol Moseley Braun of Illinois that the sight of that same flag was "painful." The Senate joined her in "putting a stake through the heart of this Dracula"—the something that kept rising from the grave that apparently is American history itself. Mrs. Moseley Braun's ineptly rehearsed hissy fit was so stultifying in its moronism that no one thought to ask whether the Stars and Stripes might also evoke painful memories, since it denoted (among other painful things) a slaveholding nation for many more years than the Confederate flag represented anything. Neither was anyone heard to inquire whether a painful memory for some justified a rule of censorship for others; for if it did, then perhaps even the Cross—whether painfully representing for some the crucifixion of the perfect Man or painfully constituting for others an object of resentment—might also be rejected by our sensitive senators. (One implication of the movie *Gettysburg* is to remind us that men, even senators in some cases, used to be made of sterner stuff.)

Well, no sooner was the tantrum concluded than Senators Boxer and Feinstein of California, Metzenbaum of Ohio, and Heflin of Alabama were with improbable spontaneity hugging the senator from Illinois in front of the television cameras, congratulating her for her historic contribution, which was—they got quite worked up on this point—one only a woman could have made. Strictly speaking, of course, that was a remarkable thing to say about a deliberate insult to a ladies' service organization—one that had been respected by the Senate for nearly a century.

Perhaps some senator should not only view *Gettysburg* but also study the extent of national, not sectional, involvement in commemorating the virtues of certain Confederates, if not the "Rebellion" itself. Such a leader might also examine how Jefferson Davis (who declared "Sovereigns never rebel") and Robert E. Lee got their citizenship back during the Carter administration—the late Robert Penn Warren wrote a good study of Davis as an American. That solon should note the names of the U.S.S. *Robert E. Lee*, the U.S.S. *Stonewall Jackson*, Fort Bragg, Fort Hood, Fort A.P. Hill, etc., as well as certain U.S. stamps and coins like the old Stone Mountain half-dollar, and so on. Such a lawgiver might then understand that such acknowledgments were more than political payoffs—they were recognitions of notable American soldiers, West Point graduates all, some veterans of the Mexican War (of painful memory, the NAFTA and the immigration policy of its day), who somehow served in the grim period before the Army's appalling sexism and homophobia were chastened. And the flag that these men fought for was, during the War Between the States, often that transfixing image which I hesitate to mention lest the citation of reality cause offense to anyone, especially to the junior senator from the great state of Illinois.

SOME MAY WONDER WHY it is so important to the Senate now to undo the reunification sealed by the Senate 90-odd years ago. President McKinley pointedly paid homage to Confederate heroism, as a capstone to the victory in the Spanish-American War, and offered federal help in caring for Confederate graves on Northern soil. Two Confederate generals, Fitzhugh Lee and Joseph Wheeler, served in blue in that war—a point that was nationally noted. When Congress voted to return captured Confederate flags in 1905, it thereby acknowledged Southern honor. Other indicators of a gentlemanly reconciliation in that day included the celebration of Lee conducted by the younger Charles Francis Adams, brother of Henry and Brooks Adams, son of Lincoln's minister to England, grandson of John Quincy Adams, and great-grandson of John and Abigail Adams. In a related gesture, Charles E. Stowe, son of "the little lady who started the big war," repudiated abolitionism in a speech in 1911.

Confederate Memorial Day, complete with painful flags, was observed at Arlington *National* Cemetery beginning in 1903—appropriately so, when you consider in whose front yard that burial ground is located, and how it was acquired. In 1913, over 50,000 veterans—mostly Union, of course—gathered at Gettysburg for their 50th anniversary and a rather authentic if enfeebled reenactment of Pickett's Charge. They also heard a speech by a Southern-born president—one who, like many another citizen, was later to admire the film *Birth of a Nation*.

The powerful medium of the movies was used to promote the myth of American unity. Owen Wister in *The Virginian* (1902) instituted in the popular mind an acknowledgment of Southern virtue that had many echoes in popular culture, particularly in Hollywood films. John Ford had the most powerful and inclusive vision of the American past (in *She Wore a Yellow Ribbon* and *The Horse Soldiers* and elsewhere), but he was far from alone. The North-South conflict is played out in many a Western. In George Stevens' *Shane*, for example, the blowhard Southerner "Stonewall" Torrey is done in by the hired killer, Wilson. When the eponymous hero wants a settlement, he calls Wilson the worst thing he can think of: a lowdown lying Yankee. After such words, one of them must die. As far back as we can conceive of our country (and even for Yankees like Herman Melville, Henry James, and Henry Adams, as C. Vann Woodward reminded us), the Southerner has been a necessary part of the American imagination.

Now between you, me, and the newel post, I'd hate to bring up the point that the Confederate battle flag was just that: the banner of an army, and not the only one. (A vexillary excursus would assert that the cross of St. Andrew, the heraldic ordinarily known as a saltire, has been or is found on the flags of Ireland, Scotland, Great Britain, Spain, Jersey, Biscay, South Africa, Russia, Alabama, Florida, Georgia, and Mississippi.) The flag is *not* to be confused with "the Bonnie Blue Flag" or "the Stars and Bars"—flags of the nation. And if that's too demanding, then you didn't hear it from me. Yet for that reason and others, the recent flap about the Georgia state flag was quite absurd: The revisionists unknowingly wanted to change the part of the flag that repeated the motif of the battle flag with a pre-1956 version alluding to the Stars and Bars! The people of that state, ignoring the posturing of their governor, preferred to let things be. There have been, of course, similar controversies about Civil War memorials and flags, in attempts to rewrite or efface history in the name of some heightened consciousness or other.

But just as even in our country it is not absolutely necessary to choose our national leaders because of manifest lack of appropriate character, neither is it even in a postindustrial mass democracy necessarily impossible to make distinctions or maintain informed awareness—*Gettysburg* suggests that much. Similarly, the series *Civil War Journal* that runs on the Arts and Entertainment cable channel has in one recent episode devoted to "Banners of Glory" shown just how well a contemporary medium can serve the public interest and even present in context the Forbidden Image for which so many died. Even on television, 1861-65 is not to be confused with its own centennial, during which cheap copies of the Confederate battle flag were waved by unlettered and angry people resisting the civil-rights movement and the federal enforcement of unwelcome laws.

THE LATE WALKER PERCY, in *The Last Gentleman*, wrote definitively of the *déjà vu* caused by the degrading replication of the Civil War as a farce, not a tragedy. He also indicated elsewhere that when the flag was furled at Appomattox, no flag had ever been defended by better men—yet when the same flag was picked up by unworthy people or reproduced as a tourist's trinket, the icon had to be let go. He had much truth on his side—but his truth depended on his personal virtue and ironic intelligence, his extensive knowledge of the South, his aristocratic heritage, and his Christian conviction. How many Americans or senators are now fortified by such a combination? Even repudiation must rest on a proper foundation. In any case, Percy's irony today might well suggest that much harm as well as good has come from the civil-rights movement and that a final demonstration of the probity and wisdom of the federal enforcement of anything was recently shown to those sinister Branch Davidian women and children. Attorney General Reno's claim of "full responsibility" was—perhaps by some bureaucratic oversight?—unaccompanied by her resignation, but then again life without honor must today be our constant study. Janet Reno, as notable a "role model" as she is an attorney general, often came to mind during my viewing of *Gettysburg* (as did other members of the Clinton administration), because what life with honor was like *in our country* was demonstrated not so much in that movie as in that battle by the federal Colonel Chamberlain of the 20th Maine and by Buford and Reynolds and Hancock, not to mention their Confederate counterparts.

Yet those Confederates and their flags were more than a presence in *Gettysburg*—they dominated the movie as they failed to dominate that field. Somehow the story is theirs—a salient part of American history is theirs. The movie, like the battle, challenges and stimulates our imagination, showing our country to have been more wonderful and terrible, beautiful and mysterious, tender and cruel, idealistic and violent, selfish and sacrificing than anyone can ever fully know, yet which not to know is not to know ourselves. Because Lee lost the battle and Lincoln gave his address there, Gettysburg has been a synecdoche for the Civil War, and for the fate of the nation, since the smoke cleared—but it remains a deeply ambivalent symbol. The movie implies the tantalizing might-have-been that gives the battle its significance: if a mysterious dispensation had gone the other way . . . and why did it not? The film captures the freely determined fatedness (Longstreet a Starbuck, Lee an Ahab), the creation of a future that is now our past. "The stars in their courses fought against Sisera" (Judges 5:20).

Even the triumphalist view of that war, not to mention the tragic one, requires the Confederate presence. The South is a necessary part of the American story; a precipitating generator of our polity, our national mythology, our cuisine, our humor; a disproportionate share of our finest literature—even as "The Lost Cause." Massachusetts and Minnesota *need* South Carolina and Mississippi; the North *requires* the South (as it does the West); the Union literally *absorbed* unto itself the Secession by an epic violence as mental as it was physical. Who says "the U.S.A." says "the Revolution" and the Second Revolution, "the Civil War" (for our Revolution was a Civil War and our Civil War was a Revolution). Who says "the Civil War" necessarily conjures its imagery and notables. There can be no Grant without a Lee, no Sherman without a Johnston, no Lincoln without a Davis, no Custer or Sheridan without Stuart and Shelby, and no Gettysburg without Chancellorsville and Fredericksburg. There can be no monuments at the courthouse squares of towns in Ohio and Rhode Island without those other northern-facing monuments in Georgia and Alabama. There is no history without conflict, no honor without pain, no courage without fear, no victory without bloodshed, no contest without cruelty, no glory without sorrow, no irony without consciousness, and no memory without substance.

Gettysburg and *Civil War Journal* remind us that in spite of political grandstanding, commercialism, and public relations, though a Confederate soldier was not a federal one, he was still, after all, an American. He was sometimes quite memorably the best soldier in the history of our country, often the most pious, and usually the least destructive of private property. Though his battle flags were mostly surrendered, they were images of fidelity and independence and are not to be treated as images of opprobrium or as the moral equivalent of the swastika. That flag is no more to be shunned than is the old "Spirit of '76" flag, the flag of the Republic of Texas, or my own favorite, the rattlesnake with the motto "Don't Tread On Me." Anyway, I certainly hope that no senator of whatever race, gender, or orientation will suggest that nowadays something more like a red flag with perhaps a gold hammer and sickle or maybe even a lavender flag with a purple charge card and a pink condom would be a more appropriate national banner than the one whose history and resonance—because of pain and cognitive difficulty—we are presently arranging to forget. Or that the Daughters of the American

Revolution, the Colonial Dames, the Order of the Cincinnati, the Sons of Confederate Veterans, or the Association for the Preservation of Civil War Sites might be singled out for stoning.

AS THE DISNEY EMPIRE PROCEEDS with its 3,000-acre historical theme park six miles from Manassas, I'm sure that the nation's youth are, like other Americans, keenly aware that Gen. Joshua L. Chamberlain, who won a Congressional Medal of Honor at Gettysburg, was himself asked to receive on behalf of Grant the formal surrender of the Army of Northern Virginia on April 12, 1865. The Confederates stacked their arms and folded their flags in tears—some of their decimated regiments seemed composed of flags, not men. Chamberlain, later governor of Maine, president of Bowdoin College, and an accomplished rhetorician, composed a set piece called *The Passing of the Armies* in which he paid handsome tribute to the men whom he had fought for years and by whom he had been gravely wounded. The nation's youth used to read and recite the piece, written by a Yankee gentleman of the old school. He never scorned those men or their flags, but read the roll call of their units and their history as they passed by, assuming that everyone knew or should know the names of A.P. Hill and James Longstreet and John Bell Hood, as well as what they did. The more glory that was accorded to the gallant defeated, then how much more to the victors!

The North won Gettysburg and the war, but somehow the history as living memory was let go along with the values that made it worth remembering. If Farnsworth's Charge at Gettysburg had been a Southern disaster, it would not have been forgotten—it does not appear in the movie. Neither does the astounding mutual destruction of Pettigrew's 26th North Carolina and the 24th Michigan, at the climax of the first day on McPherson's Ridge. The Yankees lost over 80 percent of their men; the Secesh even more. One of Pettigrew's companies lost 100 percent; another had two unhit out of 83. Pettigrew's adjutant found the wounded howling in the woods and foaming at the mouth. Those were the kind of men who contested the battle of Gettysburg—on both sides. Today in Mogadishu, Colonel Aidid does not seem to be worried that he will have to tangle with such determination. Is he wrong?

In Atlanta's Oakland Cemetery, there is (or was, if any demagogues heard about it) an impressively painful memorial to the hard-luck Army of Tennessee in the form of a wounded lion, modeled on "the Lion of Lucerne," which commemorates the Swiss Guard that died for the Bourbons of France. Such an acknowledgment, if no more, is still appropriate in Atlanta and in Lucerne. When the French attempted to celebrate the bicentennial of their

Revolution, many in the Vendée and elsewhere begged to differ, and for good reason. William Faulkner, who entitled one of the stories that make up *The Unvanquished* "Vendée," also let us know that the past is not dead. It's not even past.

The startling images of *Gettysburg* reaffirm that assertion, even though the Library of Congress recently withheld *Birth of a Nation* from an exhibition of great American films for the usual pained reasons. Such national folly says perhaps less about our country than it does about our leadership, but we can hardly hope to come to terms with our history if we cannot bear to behold even the history of our movies.

The United Daughters of the Confederacy will doubtless continue their service toward sustaining the memory of courage and devotion, in spite of the insult directed at them. The South, or what's left of it, may continue to cultivate the rituals of memory. But one larger question is whether, in the national mythology, the South will be accorded the place it receives in history and in *Gettysburg*, or whether it will instead be confined to the role of scapegoat—and recyclable comic relief, as in the latest version of *The Beverly Hillbillies*. Jed and Jethro can sure help you forget a lot of things in a hurry, but somehow they just don't have the style of Lee and Longstreet and the potent yeomanry that the Yankees weren't so afraid of—then. It's reassuring to believe that all Southerners are as coarse and stupid as Senator Heflin appears to be, rather than to wonder why a man of Lee's stature and rectitude would . . . But good heavens, we hardly have time for such disturbing thoughts while we are busy insisting that the Constitution guarantees so many things it unaccountably doesn't state and that so many things it does say are unconstitutional.

The larger question is whether our nation can have an honest account of its past, and retain it. Henry Steele Commager entitled his indispensable two-volume anthology *The Blue and the Gray*, not *The Blue and the Unmentionable*. Refusing the chance to trivialize his own life, Booker T. Washington did not entitle his famous autobiography *Up From a Painful Condition*. Yet today there is pressure to change the names of schools and other institutions that have been called after those vile Southern slaveholders—George Washington, Thomas Jefferson, and James Madison—as though we were learning to will the destruction of the national memory rather than its maintenance and to exclude the Southern roots of our freedom from acknowledgment rather than to honor them. Ignorance of history and terror of truth do not preserve liberty or national coherence any more than they represent sound education or public policy. After all, if we need Sojourner Truth and Frederick Douglass and Susan B. Anthony in the national pantheon (and we do), there must also be room in the multicultural amplitude for Lee and Long-street—and their flag as well.

The kind of future we are liable to get without much sense of a past is rapidly coalescing. It will be determined by the college sophomores and juniors I have encountered who have never heard of John Brown, of his raid on Harpers Ferry, or of the song about his body moldering in the grave. Since neither the government nor the educational establishment seems interested in promoting awareness of American history without anachronism, private interests and contemporary technology of the kind that produced *Gettysburg* may restore to those quaint people who identify with this country and speak English what formerly was considered to be their heritage—a vision of their past heroic enough to be memorable, outrageous enough to be glorious, conflicted enough to be tragic, and particular enough to be theirs.

Reclaiming the American Story

Clyde Wilson

THE WAR OF 1861-65 is still the pivotal event of American history, despite all that has passed since. In the extent of mobilization, casualties, and material destruction on American soil, in the number of world-class events and personalities, and in revolutionary consequences, nothing else can equal it.

That is why Ronald F. Maxwell's epic portrayal of the first two years of the conflict, *Gods and Generals* [2003], a prequel to his 1993 *Gettysburg*, is more than just another film or a good recreation of history. It is an American cultural event of major significance.

The cataclysmic bloodletting of the war left a gaping hole in the American psyche. Late in the 19th century, we began to achieve a kind of healing by rendering the tragedy as a common ordeal of North and South. The Great Reconciliation went something like this: The victorious North agreed to stop demonizing Southerners as an inexplicably and irredeemably evil people, to recognize the courage and sincerity of their effort at independence, and to adopt the Confederacy's heroes, such as Robert E. Lee and Stonewall Jackson, as American heroes.

This had been anticipated by Joshua Chamberlain's respectful salute to the defeated at Appomattox. His sentiment was shared by most fighting Union soldiers, though not by their political superiors and ideological masters. (Ambrose Bierce and other combat veterans said they never met an abolitionist in the Union Army.) Because of deliberately whipped-up political hysteria, it was not until late in the century that much of the Northern public overcame their Southern-devil idea of the war.

In return for respect finally granted, Southerners agreed to be thankful that the country had not been broken up and to be the most loyal of Americans in the future. In other words, the war, instead of being a morality play of the triumph of virtue over evil, was accepted as having had good and bad on both sides and as a necessary trauma out of which had arisen a new, more united, and more powerful nation. This is why Southerner D.W. Griffith's *Birth of a Nation*, with its sympathetic recounting of Southern experience coupled with an admiring portrayal of Lincoln, was a great success.

THE GREAT RECONCILIATION prevailed for half a century. *Gone With the Wind* was immensely popular. The Confederate battle flag was carried by American fighting men to the corners of the earth in World War II (which today would subject them to security investigation and court-martial). Harry S. Truman chose a romantic portrait of Jackson and Lee for the lobby of his presidential library, and Dwight D. Eisenhower and Winston Churchill chose Southern expert Douglas Southall Freeman to show them around the field of Gettysburg. That *Gods and Generals* has Stonewall Jackson as its central character would have been considered, not too many years ago, as American as apple pie. Today, it is a feat of insight and courage. What Maxwell has done in this stunningly crafted and epically expansive recreation of the first two years of the war is nothing less than to restore American history to the Americans.

Although Southerners have kept and continue to keep their part of the bargain, the truce was broken around 30 years ago, and the Southern-devil theory reemerged—and has been gathering force ever since. The average historian's explanation is that Americans have achieved a new realization of their heinous history regarding African-Americans and can never go back to the callous views of previous generations. This rests on the unquestioned assumption that the African-American experience—or, rather, the current interpretation of it—is the central or even the only important experience of American history.

The real explanation for the revival of Southern demonization as a national pastime is actually more complicated and has nothing to do with the discoveries of "expert" academic historians. It reflects, first of all, the triumph of Cultural Marxism—of history at the service of a fanatical agenda. The mainstream academic interpretation of the Civil War—and of much else in the American past—that prevails today institutionalizes views that, 50 years ago, were current nowhere except in the communist neighborhoods of New York City. Our history has been rewritten under the rubrics of Race, Class, and "Gender."

The worst thing about this is not, as countless neoconservative publicists have wailed, that it makes for divisive politics. The worst thing about it is that it cuts us off from our history, rendering our forebears alien and dead abstractions.

With regard to the Civil War, there is another element of distortion that relates not to leftist politics so much as to the penchant of too many Americans to assume their own unique righteousness, which has been a problem ever since the first Puritans stepped ashore at Boston. If Sherman burning his way through Georgia and Carolina was a righteous exercise against evil, then obviously the bombing of Christian Serbs and the starving of Iraqi children reflects the same unsulliable mission of American triumph.

The classic illustration of this is Ken Burns' celebrated documentary on the Civil War. Surrounding his thesis with intrinsically attractive materials, Burns revived the portrayal of the war as a morality play in a way that was widely appealing. In Burns' interpretation, the war was about the benevolence of the Union and emancipation and the evils of treason and slavery. At bottom, this rests upon a convenient fantasy—the fantasy of Northern racial benevolence. It is child's play to demonstrate that such benevolence never existed before, during, or after the war. This historical fabrication—that a war of conquest was gloriously, unselfishly benevolent—remains a seemingly ineradicable foundation of the American *amour-propre*.

By contrast, Maxwell has largely given us a dramatization of Americans, including African-Americans, as the real people in the real context in which they loved, perspired, wept, struggled, suffered, and died. That context truly was epic and, like all great historical events, morally complex. I could go on at length about the many marvelous aspects of Maxwell's creation: the battles, the well-drawn characters from history, the recognition of the importance of Christianity in the lives of our forebears, and much else. Though based generally on Jeff Shaara's novel of the same name, *Gods and Generals* follows the book less closely than *Gettysburg* did *The Killer Angels*, which is all to the good.

THERE CAN BE no perfection on this earth, which brings me to the one small flaw in this dazzling gem. Southerners, generally—and, for all I know, Civil War students, too—found fault with Martin Sheen's portrayal of Lee in *Gettysburg*. I thought the condemnation excessive; Sheen did a good job, given the impossibility of recreating Lee in a world where not even a model remains. Many happily greeted the news that Robert Duvall would portray Lee in *Gods and Generals*.

Now, I am risking being ridden out of town on a rail for this, but I would rather have Sheen or, even better, an unknown performer as Lee. Duvall is a fine actor who has portrayed many Southerners with verisimilitude. As Lee, he is a failure. At the beginning of the war, Lee was a vigorous, late-middle-aged man with an audacious military genius lurking just below a placid surface. Duvall plays Lee from the start as a worn-out old man—as Lee must have been after Appomattox—and with an overdone Deep South, rather than a Virginian, accent.

I was privileged to view a prerelease screening of *Gods and Generals*. It was way past my bedtime and a hundred miles from home, but I kept hoping the screen would never go blank. The film, I understand, has been cut considerably for theatrical release. I deliciously anticipate both the complete six-hour version that is to be released on DVD and the final installment of Maxwell's trilogy, *The Last Full Measure*, which is already in production. *Gods and Generals* is an arresting example of how a people's history should be told—which ought to have a healthy effect on Americans' idea of themselves.

Gott Mit Uns

Egon Richard Tausch

A S MODERN IMPERIALISM GROWS, even the regions within those countries under its rule become homogenized. Within the subnational
regions, smaller ethnic enclaves, with their diverse cultures, tend to take one
of two paths. They become tourist traps where the natives are totally ignorant
of their own histories, differences, and contributions to the larger groups,
until, eventually, everyone wears the same garb (lederhosen, feathered hats,
kilts, identical regalia), employs the same false architecture, adopts the same
fake accent, sings the same pseudo folk songs, dances the only folk dance
he knows, and claims the same beliefs and ideologies. Or they just die out
altogether. I don't know whom this hurts worse—the larger "empire" or the
enclaves. It certainly makes the world a duller place. And contrary to the
philosophers, knowledge of history is its own virtue.

I first discovered this as a child. After living in Washington, D.C., for several years, my parents and I had returned to the Texas ranch that had been
in our family since 1845. The culture clash between the East and Southwest
was not as great as I had expected; too much time had passed. But I had been
taught by my family, as well as by mounds of books, that we were Texas Germans, as was the entire Hill Country of the state, including the towns and
cities of New Braunfels, Boerne, Fredericksburg, Dickinson, Seguin, Austin,
San Antonio, Castroville, Hondo, up to what we still thought of as the western frontier—indeed, all of South-Central Texas.

Most of the Germans had arrived in Texas when it was still a republic, under the guidance of the Adelsverein ("The Noblemen's Society for the
Protection of German Immigrants in Texas"), led by Prince Karl von Solms-
Braunfels (though he didn't stay). It was not long before over one third of all
Texans were German. Before the invention of barbed wire (1875), the Texas
economy was based on cotton, so the Texas Germans raised it and owned
slaves, though not as many as the East Texans did. As late as the eve of U.S.
entry into World War I, a rally for the kaiser was held in Boerne among the
(mostly) still German-speaking blacks, with the rallying cry: "Ve Chermans
haff got to schtick togedder!"

The Texas Germans went on to fight valiantly for the United States after we entered the war, despite the closing of our schools and violent harassment by groups of drunken Anglo teenagers from San Antonio. I lost two uncles to gas attacks on the Western Front.

As late as the 1950's, one could not buy groceries or feed in the small town nearest our ranch without knowing German. My grandfather founded New Braunfels High School, and almost all the textbooks were in German (though Greek and Latin—and English—were also taught). He was also the editor of the *Neu-Braunfelser Zeitung*, our first newspaper (since the 1850's), and cofounder of our first bank (the Guaranty State Bank). This whole section of Texas was closely knit. After all, the Germans arrived in the 1830's and 40's not knowing whether they were immigrating to Mexico, an independent Texas republic, or the United States.

Differences among groups of Texas Germans were common. The influential founders of New Braunfels were largely Prussian, atheist ("freethinkers"), and townspeople; Fredericksburg was founded by Bavarians and other southern Germans, Roman Catholics, and country folk; the German towns to the east were largely Lutheran (Evangelisch) and from all parts of Germany and all occupations. In addition, there were the Forty-Eighters.

The only question that had interested children back in Washington, D.C., was whether they were Southerners or Northerners. After all, Washington had been a Southern city for most of its history, was the center of the War Between the States, and the mid-to-late 1950's was the height of regional rivalry.

As soon as my family returned to Comal County, Texas, we ran into a similar conflict. I met the other descendants of the War Between the States. Every kid would announce that, although his own ancestors had fought for the Confederacy, everyone knew that the *other* Texas Germans had fought for the Union. About the time I concluded that the tooth fairy was a myth, I began to suspect that this Texas-Confederate history didn't make sense. If every German-American Texan I met had Confederate soldier ancestors, including three progenitors of mine, how could this ethnic group have been so pro-Union?

AT THE UNIVERSITY OF TEXAS-AUSTIN, I studied Texas history, and, for my master's thesis, I decided to unravel the myth of German Unionism. This proved to be a hopeless task. Every textbook of Texas history I could find simply stated, without footnotes, details, or any other support, that the Texas Germans were pro-Union and were either neutral or fought for the North during the War. The only evidence given was a mention of the Nueces Massacre. The books I found on the involvement of Texas in the Confederacy produced the same scant evidence and cited only earlier general histories, which used almost the same words (and often had the same typographical errors). Those books concerning only the Texas Germans simply skipped the crisis of the South in which the Texas Germans played so great a part.

Several years ago, the myth of German Unionism reached its climax in a series of newspaper columns by the late Maury Maverick, Jr., in the *San Antonio Express.* Maverick was a left-wing columnist and the lawyer son of an equally left-wing mayor of San Antonio in the 1930's; both devoted their lives to atoning for the sins of the patriarch of the clan, Sam Maverick, while keeping his money. Sam was not only a notorious cattleman (whence cometh the word *maverick,* which first meant "found" or stolen or rebranded cattle) but a Confederate officer and an anti-German, upon whose livestock he preyed. As a result, Maury Jr. defended Vietnam draft dodgers for a living and insisted that the Texas Germans shared his left-wing views. He began the series by stating that the Texas Germans fought for the North during the War Between the States and that "over a hundred German Unionists were lynched during the War and lived under a reign of terror." (This would have been a surprise to Adm. Chester Nimitz of World War II fame, about whom Maury Jr. always wrote admiringly, since the admiral's father, Capt. Charles Nimitz, had been the highest-ranking Confederate officer in the German area and was, indeed, the Confederate recruiting officer in charge of maintaining order.)

Several dozen Texas Germans challenged the series by Mr. Maverick on his allegations. After a lot of shilly-shallying, Maverick retreated to one mysterious nighttime murder, by unknown persons, for unknown reasons.

When presented with the facts and the statistics, most believers in the myth, including at one time even the *New Braunfels Zeitung-Herald* (successor to the *Zeitung*), merely declared that the Texas Germans must have been trying to "blend in" with the Anglo Confederates, an absurd proposition when one considers that there were among Anglos proportionately more Unionists than among the Germans. Germans overwhelmingly voted for secession, and pre-draft enlistment figures bear this out. It is far more likely that some modern Texas Germans are trying to "blend in" with political correctness. It strains credulity to argue that the same Texas Germans praised by Maury Maverick, Jr., for their courage, the same people who produced Admiral Nimitz and General Eisenhower, would be so cowardly as to vote against their principles in secret ballot, fail to speak out publicly or join the Union Army, and even join the Confederate Army (before the draft) to shoot and be shot by Yankees—all out of fear of offending Anglo citizens.

While researching my thesis, I had to perfect my German in order to read the dozen German-language newspapers circulating in Texas before and during the war. I discovered that no one had ever read any of these archives between that time and mine. I also read every German diary and private letter available, every letter to the Confederate and Reconstruction governors and legislatures in the State Archives, countless enlistment and unit rosters, and every published or unpublished primary source concerning the Texas Germans available at that time. My conclusions echoed those of John Arkas Hawgood in his 1940 book *The Tragedy of German America*:

> So many fallacious statements have been made concerning the Germans in Texas during the late 1840's, the 50's, and the early 60's, that perhaps it is wise here to express quite clearly ... that the Germans were not ... Abolitionists, ... that they believed in states['] rights, and that ... a majority of them were loyal to the Confederate cause, many fought for it, and quite a number died for it.

These Germans came over to Texas in response to emigration propaganda in Germany, all of which stressed that, if you were an abolitionist or of the political left, you should go to New York City; if you were neutral or undecided, go to Missouri; if you were a conservative, go to New Orleans or Texas. Ferdinand Roemer's *Texas*, which was widely read in Germany and distributed by the Adelsverein, warned those who were radical or opposed to slavery to avoid Texas.

In addition, Germany at that time was a loose confederation of autonomous states, similar to the United States under the Articles of Confederation. Those Germans were used to a system that respected states' rights, and most were very leery of strong central government.

After 1850, Texas began receiving a trickle of refugees from the German Revolution of 1848—*"die Gruene,"* who were sometimes both radical and nationalistic. These new arrivals were not well received by the Germans who had come under the Adelsverein or before. Some of these Forty-Eighters formed the communistic Bettina Colony under the leadership of Gustav Schleicher, a friend of Friedrich Engels. The collective failed within two years, and Schleicher soon became the leader of the conservative and pro-states'-rights element in the Texas legislature.

The Democratic Party (then conservative and pro-states' rights) won the enthusiastic allegiance of the Texas Germans thanks to the sudden growth of the anti-immigrant Nativist Party, the Know-Nothings. As the Know-

Nothing Party became identified with nationalism, Unionism, and abolition-ism, the Germans became more states'-rights and conservatively oriented.

There were occasional outbursts of radical sentiments (mostly on eco-nomic issues) among a few Forty-Eighters after that; a few singing societ-ies were founded for political purposes; and one German newspaper editor, Adolf Douai, was chased out of San Antonio by the other Germans because of his abolitionist views. Even he did not believe that the federal government had any business meddling with slavery in the states.

German social life centered on the Turnvereine (athletic clubs). When the National Turnvereine denounced the South in 1859, all Texas Turnver-eine immediately seceded, anticipating the Confederacy by two years.

The most influential German newspaper, the *Neu-Braunfelser Zeitung,* was edited by Dr. Ferdinand Lindheimer. According to R.L. Biesele—the first, and greatest, Texas German historian—Dr. Lindheimer was "the polit-ical barometer of the Germans in Texas." His newspaper's support for states' rights, secession, and (through four difficult years) the Confederate war effort mirrored that of the Texas German population.

THE FIRST TEST of Texas German loyalty to the South was in the presiden-tial election of 1860. It was a four-way race, with John C. Breckenridge rep-resenting the Southern Democrats and supported by secessionists; John Bell representing the Constitutional Union party, which hoped to hold North and South together by retaining states' rights; Stephen A. Douglas repre-senting the regular and Northern Democrats; and Abraham Lincoln for the Republicans.

No Texas German voted for Lincoln. Of the ten Texas counties that gave Bell and/or Douglas at least 40 percent of the vote, only one—Gillespie—had a substantial German population. Gillespie County voted against the seces-sion candidate by only 52 percent. The other 17 heavily German counties, including Comal (which was the most populous and most German one), voted almost entirely for Breckenridge. For that matter, the least secessionist area, western Gillespie County, gave a larger percentage of its votes to Breck-enridge than did any non-German western county. A fear, common in all the western counties, of frontier isolation in the face of savage Indians accounts for its hesitation toward secession.

Upon the election of Abraham Lincoln, Comal and Gillespie Counties called for a state convention to discuss secession, as did the *Neu-Braunfels-er Zeitung,* which reminded Germans that, just as they had renounced their allegiance to European despots, they should do the same to Yankee ones. All other German newspapers called for secession, except for one, the smallest, which called for caution and deliberation before such a step. Every German delegate at the Texas Convention voted for immediate secession.

On February 23, 1861, the question went to the citizens of Texas. Of the 17 German counties, only five voted against secession. Five of them favored it by 90 percent. Comal County—again, the most populous and most German—did so by 73 percent. In Fayette County, which had a large Anglo Unionist element and a Unionist newspaper, only 10 of the 400 German voters voted against secession. Of the 29 Texas counties that had a substantial unionist vote, only 5 had any German population to speak of.

Once the war broke out, Texas Germans joined the Confederate Army in droves. As early as December 1860, Lindheimer had urged the Germans to organize military companies of minutemen to "protect the rights of the South." By the middle of July, two volunteer infantry and two cavalry companies had been formed in New Braunfels—one led by the mayor, Gustav Hoffman, a former Prussian officer. Before the military draft was instituted, two thirds of the enfranchised population of Comal County were armed and in the field.

Gustav Schleicher organized units that would fight nobly in the Red River Campaign. Many of the first companies in Galveston were German to a man. The first Houston company to appear in the field was German. Most of their flags were embroidered *"Fuer die Constitution"* and *"Gott Mit Uns."*

Fayette County formed a company of Germans that joined and fought with the famed Terry's Texas Rangers in all of its battles, including Perryville, where Colonel Terry was killed. The last commander of Terry's Texas Rangers was one of these Germans.

German units formed important parts of the New Mexico Campaign, the Battle of Galveston, the Red River Campaign, and even served in Hood's Texas Brigade under General Lee in Virginia.

The ladies of German towns formed Southern Aid Societies, raising funds and making provisions for the troops. One such group in Fredericksburg alone raised over $5,000 for the cause and made countless uniforms and bandages.

There were, of course, some who were disloyal to the Confederate cause in German as well as Anglo counties. In Fredericksburg, the aforementioned Capt. Charles Nimitz was physically attacked and put in danger of his life by an Anglo-American bandit leader because some of his men had been drafted. In the later suppression of Unionists, Confederate German troops were often sent to arrest disaffected Anglo citizens.

Maury Maverick, Jr., cited Duff's Partisan Rangers as the greatest terror of Texas Unionists. August Siemering, a German of Fredericksburg who had formerly been a Unionist, was Duff's lieutenant. R.H. Williams' firsthand account of Duff's partisans, *With the Border Ruffians*, recounts that even Duff's fanatic scouring for Unionists in Gillespie County could only turn up "four or five men, and eight women with their little ones."

THIS BRINGS US BACK to the aforementioned Nueces Massacre. On August 1, 1862, 61 men met in Kerr County, with the intention of leaving Texas. Most of them were Germans and very recent arrivals in the state; some were Anglos, and a handful were Mexicans. Ted Fehrenbach, in *Lone Star*, his definitive history of Texas, and many other historians have pointed out that this group had no particular ideology and no intention of joining the federal forces; they just wanted to avoid a war of which they'd had no advance notice. Upon reaching the Nueces River, they were attacked by Duff's Partisan Rangers, who were guided by a German, Charles Bergmann of Fredericksburg. In the fight that followed, 19 of the refugees were killed, and 9 were wounded. Several witnesses later reported that the wounded were murdered. Thirty-three refugees escaped, of whom eight were killed later while attempting to cross the Rio Grande. None of the survivors ever chose to join the federals after entering Mexico, where they were met by Union forces.

It is not excusing such barbaric, behind-the-lines persecution to point out that this murderous slaughter of harmless, multiethnic draft evaders has no bearing on the question of whether Germans were, as a group, enthusiastic supporters of the Confederacy. But, somehow, an inscribed monument was recently built in Comfort, Texas, which honors these victims as being "Loyal to the Union." A novel, *Rebels in Blue*, was even written about them, ignoring the refugees' equal avoidance of both the Blue and the Gray.

It is often forgotten that Texas was under martial law throughout most of the war. This constitutional atrocity has turned out to be a windfall for historians, because my old mentor, Dr. H. Bailey Carroll of the University of Texas, managed to turn up the court-martial records of civilians, which accompany martial law.

The court-martial trials were convened in San Antonio, beginning on July 2, 1862, continuing through the greatest Unionist activity, and concluding after the Nueces Massacre. The court tried all those arrested in the Hill Country and Bexar County. Seventeen Anglo-Americans were tried, and over two thirds were found guilty of disloyalty. Only 12 Germans were prosecuted, and of these, only 5 were found guilty. Their punishment was imprisonment for the duration of the war. Prominent Germans testified for both the defense and the prosecution. In most of the cases, the evidence was all hearsay, and even that was nebulous. Julius Schlickum was accused of singing a Yankee song while drunk. In one case against a German, the charge of disloyalty rested on the accusation that the defendant appeared happy upon reading of a Confederate defeat. His accuser could not remember having heard the defendant actually say anything; instead, he judged by the latter's facial expression. One German was charged with having had a New York German newspaper at his store. He answered that his customers could read no English, and local German papers had no European news. Another German, accused of having spoken only of Confederate defeats, explained that, during the week the witness knew him, the South had had no victories.

Again, it is no defense of such police-state tactics to point out that these trials show less disloyalty to the Confederacy among Germans than among Anglos—insofar as they show anything, save that no government should really be trusted. It should, in fairness to Confederate authorities, be mentioned that such arrests and trials were much more common in the North. President Lincoln managed to arrest the legislature of Maryland, and Northern prisons were full of suspected Copperheads, who enjoyed no right of *habeas corpus* (it was suspended by Lincoln), let alone a hearing of any sort, military or otherwise.

Before, during, and after these trials in San Antonio, hundreds of Texas Anglos fled Texas to join the Union Army. They were not so unfortunate as the group caught on the Nueces River, however, so they have been largely forgotten. I would welcome any evidence that one Texas German ever wore the Blue.

Once, when a former member of the Know-Nothing Party made a slighting reference to Germans, the *Neu-Braunfelser Zeitung* replied that, proportionately, German-speaking soldiers were more numerous than any other language group among Confederate Texans and urged that a survey be made to determine German participation in and support for the Confederacy in order to prove their loyalty forever. Unfortunately, no such survey was ever conducted—a fact that might be the only one that matters for modern Americans, who are accustomed to weekly polls of the population on every question or opinion imaginable. However, at the time, there *was* a war going on.

The privation suffered during wartime had no relation to nationality, and the German families left behind while their men were off fighting had their share. In some areas, the women did all the farm work; in others, German families had to depend on the charity of their neighbors to survive. The well-known thrift of German families was ineffectual in the face of a rapidly depreciating currency. Indian depredations and bandit raids increased dramatically during the war, and many German soldiers who went to war to protect their homes against the Yankees returned to find their homes burned and livestock stolen by Indians or thieves.

As late as the close of May 1865, Ferdinand Lindheimer was still writing editorials in the *Neu-Braunfelser Zeitung* urging greater sacrifices for the survival of the Confederacy. Finally, on June 2, 1865, he printed a letter in German that he had received from a Lieutenant Bitter, CSA. In translation, it states:

> As you should know, our company F, 32 Texas Cavalry is coming back home today. It is true we are not coming back as everybody wished, as victors in the cause for which the county sent us, but our conscience is clear that we have done at every occasion our full duty, and that our behavior and good German honor gave us the respect of all our war companions, as of the citizens in that part of the country in which we have been. We have earned this honor and still hold it. Even in the last time of common demoralization of the Army, every citizen felt protected as long as Company "F" was near.

He closed the letter with the slogan inscribed on his battle flag: "*Gott mit uns.*" God be with us.

Clip Clop, Bang Bang

J.O. Tate

A review of
Quantrill's War:
The Life and Times of William Clarke Quantrill
by Duane Schultz

and

The Devil Knows How to Ride: The True Story of William
Clarke Quantrill and His Confederate Raiders
by Edward E. Leslie

THE MANIPULATIVE SENSATIONALISM regarding any display of the Confederate battle flag continues unabated. The *New York Times* gets hot and bothered, or sexually aroused—or whatever it is that the *New York Times* becomes—whenever that banner appears over the capitol of South Carolina or on a vanity tag in Maryland—indeed, anywhere. The shibboleths of liberalism are applied whenever it is possible to maintain power today by controlling the national memory of yesterday, and the day before. "Heritage Not Hate" is the motto of some who defend the right to display the disputed flag, but the problem may be that hate is precisely what our heritage is. Strangely enough, that hate was broadcast a century and a half ago by spokesmen for a gospel of love—and it still is. It has long since become the language of power in our society.

What a shame that our effort to remember our own history should itself be so contentious. But then again, the Civil War was a shame itself, and there is something perversely appropriate in having the national memory supervised by replicants of the most obnoxious personalities of that war. Sure, remembering the Civil War is one thing Americans ought to do, and for a host of reasons. The memory of heroic actions, of courage and sacrifice, have traditionally been thought to be the stuff of civic virtue, as Pericles memorably indicated. But while I do believe that there is something to be gained by cultivating the memory of great deeds, I also believe that there

143

can be a chastening profit in remembering cowardice, cruelty, and mendacity as well. The Civil War was a degrading as well as a glorious experience. Above all, it was a bloody one.

For every image of a brave soldier charging forward, we should also remember a skulking "bummer" burning down some old lady's house. Killing in combat is not murder, but there was plenty of murder in the Civil War and wanton destruction of property. "Mr. Lincoln's Invasion" was among other things a gigantic stick-up, and the pseudobiblical cadences to which we have resorted ever since in order to sugarcoat the bitterness are today parroted by those kindly humanoids who promote gross infanticide as a palliative for "women's health," all the while intoning their concern for our children. To whose advantage, some may wonder, is all the confusion and divisiveness? But not to worry. The editors of the *New York Times* are feeling fine.

Perhaps a little sober reflection and even humility are in order, for just as the Stars and Stripes do not exclusively represent everything we would wish them to, the Confederate flag does not either. I do not think that the Confederate flag was flown by the raiders who sacked Lawrence, Kansas, on August 21, 1863, burning over 100 houses and shooting dead some 200 unarmed boys and men. Quantrill was a captain in the Confederate Army, but his appropriate banner would have been the one nominated by Kit Dalton in his reminiscences, *Under the Black Flag*. Frank James and Cole Younger declared after the war that they never saw this black flag, but to me it is the black flag, not the Confederate one, that represents everything vile in violence. There can be no justification for the atrocities at Lawrence, but the story of the border strife between Missouri and Kansas—the real beginning of the Civil War—shows that there was a background of hatred and revenge. When the war began, the Yankee abolitionists were enfranchised, and the Southern fire-eaters were too. In this chaos, as Duane Schultz has suggested, a deadly trickster like Quantrill could not fail to see the opportunity of a lifetime.

THE STORY OF THE BORDER WARS is a story that every American should know, particularly because so few know it. The part of it that is familiar (though almost always misapprehended) deals with John Brown. Brown's massacre at Pottowatomie Creek, complete with night-stalking, corpse mutilations, and God's blessing, has never discredited him as a hero, though he is rather better interpreted as a madman. Since his bloody-minded insanity literally became national policy, he remains a model of rectitude, a prophet indeed. But we might ask why such a killer and schemer retains his aureole of righteousness, when Quantrill's name conjures revulsion. If Quantrill had thumped the Bible harder and taken money from the pious divines of New England, he would have made a better career move. And he could still have murdered to his heart's content.

But that was not his way. William Clarke Quantrill was an aimless youth from Canal Dover, Ohio, who inscribed abolitionist sentiments in letters to his mother. He wandered fecklessly, and he taught school rather successfully, which in those days indicated a certain order of intelligence. Unable to resist the temptations of the Border Wars, he sneakily participated in the anarchy he loved. He posed as an abolitionist, and then sold back the slaves he had stolen; he also pretended to be a "border ruffian" and lived with the Indians. He told either side he was a spy for the other, while stealing horses, burning houses, and probably murdering some individuals. Arson, thievery, and murder had a sanction in the Border Wars. Eventually, in the raid on the Walker farm, he turned on the "idealistic Abolitionists" (Schultz's phrase) he had conned. He arranged their betrayal and declared he was from Maryland—a Southern loyalist, indeed.

The struggles on the Kansas-Missouri border were magnified in the war. They show that our Civil War was both civil and a war in the worst senses of those words. The war justified unreason and attracted not only the flower of the nation's youth but also its lowest elements, including not just Quantrill but such saints as the vicious Charles Jennison (of "Jennison's Jayhawkers"), and the others of his ilk. Riding with Quantrill were men who became not soldiers but killers—men such as Bloody Bill Anderson, who draped the scalps of his victims around his horse's neck. To ask why Quantrill fought as he did is to face a mystery, but even Bloody Bill had his reasons. When he was killed and decapitated, a cord with 53 knots was found in his pocket. He was literally keeping score with the Yankees, who were responsible for kidnapping his sister and placing her in a decrepit building in Kansas City, the collapse of which killed her, crippled another sister, and killed a cousin of Cole Younger and three other women as well. The raw memories of the Border Wars were intensified during the war as the federal authorities not only raised the black flag in various proclamations but in one of the most remarkable episodes in American history created the "Burnt District" on the Missouri border, explicitly making war on the civilian population which fed and harbored Quantrill's men in some cases. The escalation of violence to such a dreadful scale is remembered if at all today by the names of Quantrill's massacres at Lawrence and at Baxter Springs. But what about the Palmyra massacre of captured Southerners, ten of whom were clumsily executed in 1862, or many another depredation?

Bill Anderson was bloody all right, but Cole Younger, author of *The Story of Cole Younger by Himself* (1903), must be the most interesting of the men who rode with Quantrill. If an American can be an aristocrat, he was one. His paternal great-grandfather had served at Valley Forge; his paternal great-grandmother was related to "Light Horse Harry" Lee. The son of a prosperous planter who was no secessionist, the young Cole was threatened by Capt. Irvin Walley of the 5th Missouri Federal Militia, who subsequently arranged his father's assassination. The Yankees persecuted Cole's mother from 1862 to 1870, enough so that at the cessation of hostilities he felt justified in continuing his lawlessness. But there are several stories which attest to Cole Younger's mercy in various incidents during the war. He had his opportunities to kill, and to refuse to do so. To read of all the bloodshed is a bone-chilling as well as a blood-boiling experience. Even Quantrill, who sometimes demonstrated qualities of intelligence and finer feeling, emerges as a man worth remembering, one who has something to tell us. Because the federal generals Halleck and Ewing and others raised the black flag, they forced Quantrill and his men to do likewise, for the raiders knew that death was the only thing they could expect if taken during the war. Quantrill himself was shot in Kentucky after Appomattox, where he had gone declaring he would kill Lincoln.

QUANTRILL IS REMEMBERED (or should be) as the man who exhorted at Lawrence, "Kill! Kill! And you will make no mistake. Lawrence is the hotbed and should be thoroughly cleansed, and the only way to cleanse is to kill!" Kill they did. But the first point to be noted about Quantrill's speech is that he sounds a lot like John Brown. The second is that it was the abolitionists years before who had cried, "War! War to the knife and the knife to the hilt!" The murderousness of Quantrill cannot completely cover up the violent gnosticism of the abolitionists.

But to engage even imaginatively with such tangled and bloody material is to engage also with a second order of mythology, for the story of Quantrill and his men has long since been treated, not always obliquely, in the movies. Because the Younger, James, and Dalton brothers rode with Quantrill's raiders, "Quantrill" is frequently cited in Hollywood Westerns still recycling on cable. There has been no remotely truthful treatment of Quantrill on celluloid, as far as I know, and that's a lack that may someday be supplied. Nevertheless, on screen Quantrill is always represented as a "heavy," though physically he was young and slender, unlike Walter Pidgeon, Brian Donleavy, Leo Cordon, or Emile Meyer, who portrayed him. His name on screen seems to mean what it should—"going too far," "crossing the line." Not many remember *Quantrell's* [*sic*] *Son* (1914), but some may recall through a haze of association with Raisinets and popcorn *Dark Command* (1940), *Renegade Girl* (1946), *Kansas Raiders* (1950), *Red Mountain* (1951), *The Woman They Almost Lynched* (1952), *Quantrill's Raiders* (1958), *Young Jesse James* (1960), *Arizona Raiders* (1965), and *Ride a Wild Stud* (1969).

Edward Leslie provides an ironic account of the premier of *Dark Command* in Lawrence in 1940, but then in modern America any attempt to remember the past is ironic even when naive. Yet Hollywood's invasion of Lawrence was a notable massacre of the historical imagination and of the truth. That embarrassment of a movie is a reversal of experience, but why blame Hollywood? Americans prefer lies.

> John Wayne, playing a fictional town marshal, learns of Quant-
> rill's planned raid at the last moment, sends the women and chil-
> dren to hide in the courthouse, rallies the menfolk, has barricades
> thrown up, and directs the slaughter of bushwhackers as they ride
> down the main street. The town is burned, but only one or two
> male residents are killed. Wayne chases down the fleeing Quant-
> rill and kills him.

In other words, the movie about the Lawrence massacre denies that the massacre ever happened, and the bad guy is killed by the good guy with an assist from the bad guy's mother. This happy ending suggests that America has been anxious to deny truth not for reasons of public relations, but because the truth is too terrible to contemplate, for if that truth were confronted squarely, the old conflicts and grievances might reassert themselves, and the old lies might be exposed.

But that movie was not enough. To add insult to injury, John Wayne, Roy Rogers, Gabby Hayes, Gene Autry, and others paraded in Lawrence at the premiere, and a reenactment of the "Burning of Lawrence" was mounted to the delight of thousands. Lawrence had in effect cooperated in effacing its own past while pretending to recreate it, in a miniature of our national obsession. Such repression and transference might have impressed even Sigmund Freud, if he had not died the year before.

Hollywood did not initiate the whitewashing—far from it. Frank James and Cole Younger, those veterans of violence, lived to become charming geezers whose byword was denial. In 1903, they got together to mount a Wild West show, beating Hollywood to the punch. And Quantrill's men continued to have genteel reunions until 1929, by which time the Western had been institutionalized as a displaced substitution for the national memory of fratricidal strife. The name "Quantrill" still sneaks in among all the chivalrous paladins wearing silk shirts, as though to remind us that violence is violence, after all. And perhaps the brutality and vanity and even fraud of Quantrill may remind us as well that our history is replete with shame and even horror which no amount of reverential rhetoric can quite gloss over. The populist mythology that made a folk hero of Jesse James in dime novels and bad movies had its base in something real, but the little boys in the backyards of 50 years ago did not quite understand what they played with or at: "Bang bang, you're dead." W.R. Burnett wrote the novel on which *Dark Command* was based—the same Burnett who wrote *Little Caesar* and *High Sierra*, glorifying urban violence and outlawry in a strong tradition that still packs them in at the multiplex.

SO QUANTRILL IS NOT FORGOTTEN, nor is he going to be, thanks in part to Schultz and Leslie, and thanks as well to Quantrill himself, who succeeded in securing notoriety if not fame by violating so many prohibitions and transgressing so flagrantly upon the bounds of human decency. Schultz sees Quantrill as a sociopath; Leslie has a more ironic, even absurdist view; and both are persuasive. Schultz, by the way, makes the error of mistaking Gen. Henry McCollough (the Confederate general who ordered Quantrill's arrest in 1864) for his brother Benjamin (who was killed at Elkhorn Tavern in 1862). His is a censorious account. Leslie's is expansive and pursues the story of Quantrill's remains perhaps further than it deserves. Even so, both show the context that allowed Quantrill to rise however falsely as a partisan in a conflict of reckless ferocity. Perhaps Quantrill's name survives simply to nominate a transgressor, and if that is so, then Quantrill succeeded in his aims. But behind his violence are the shadows of the abolitionists and the Jayhawkers, and the Union Army and the federal government as well. In what was truly civil war, he exposed the truth we do not want to acknowledge, the truth that no memorial can hide—the truth about the bloody-minded Jacobins who insisted on violence, on war, on a blasphemous crusade which is the basis of our law, mythology, and government today. No wonder Hollywood was nervous about Quantrill, for his story, telescoping red and black and white, North and South and West, is a reproach to our nation and to our complacency—to any easy assumptions of Southern honor or Northern virtue. Going beyond good and evil is not easy to routinize as digestible entertainment. Not many customers want to be reminded in the theater of what they ignore every day, nor do many Americans want to face the implications of the antinomian, millenialist, radically egalitarian rhetoric most recently displayed in Bill Clinton's

Second Inaugural Address. It is somehow easier to deprecate the Confederate flag and then watch somebody getting shot on television. Nevertheless, to the credit of Schultz and Leslie, individual readers will be powerfully shown some nasty truths about American history, and perhaps reminded as well of Nietzsche's insight: "He who fights with monsters should be careful lest he thereby become a monster. And if thou gaze long into an abyss, the abyss shall also gaze into thee."

The Character of Stonewall Jackson

Chilton Williamson, Jr.

A review of
Stonewall Jackson: The Man, the Soldier, the Legend
by James I. Robertson, Jr.

"Look, men, there is Jackson standing like a stone wall! Let us
determine to die here, and we will conquer! Follow me!"
—Gen. Bernard E. Bee, shortly before falling,
mortally wounded, in First Manassas

THE ERA OF THE WAR for Southern Independence illuminates the present time for what it is, and is not. As J.O. Tate has said, "Everything in American history went into the Civil War, and everything since has come out of it." Americans who agree with a well-known American magazine editor, now retired, that the crucial event in the national history is as irrelevant as the Wars of the Roses probably ought not to be permitted to vote. It is just possible, however, that of those Americans who know that a war was fought at all, or when it was fought, a majority considers it worth knowing about. The publishers' catalogues for the past several seasons [in 1997] list a substantial number of big books (Mr. Robertson's included) about the Civil War, and Shelby Foote's three-volume masterpiece, completed almost a quarter-century ago, is prominently displayed in most bookstores. Interest in the Late Unpleasantness shows no sign of diminishing; indeed it may well be increasing. It is tempting to speculate on the reasons for this. Surely the Second Reconstruction that leftists waged against the South in the 1950's and 60's has something to do with it. So does the current campaign, prosecuted by cynical politicians, black and white, to wipe every reminder of the Confederacy from the national consciousness, and also from the memory and awareness of Southern localities for whom it remains the defining element in their histories. With its legal and rhetorical onslaughts against the Citadel and the Virginia Military Institute (where Stonewall Jackson taught for ten years), the Bonnie Blue Flag, the Stars and Bars, state flags, state songs, and Confederate license plates, the left consistently generates the moral indignation it ordinarily expends on victims. Listening to it and watching it in action, one can almost believe that Grant *had* been drinking at Appomattox.

If a renewed preoccupation with Civil War history really is occurring, could it be a natural reaction to our contemporary civil barometer, which has been falling for decades and is now dropping like a rock? Do we hear new firebells in the night in response to judicial tyranny, intimidating acts by the FBI and terroristic ones by the BATF, and the rise of the militias? In the summer of 1860 Major Jackson and his wife spent some weeks at Norwood, Massachusetts, where the Virginia couple sensed "unhospitable elements" among the New Englanders who were their fellow guests at a popular water-cure establishment. This kind of social uncomfortableness is something with which contemporary Americans are increasingly familiar. Comparisons between the antebellum conflict over slavery and the late-20th-century impasse regarding abortion, though the parallel is scarcely an exact one, have become trite. Yet abortion is only part of the broader picture, as slavery was also. When the Rev. Richard John Neuhaus devoted a recent issue of *First Things* to a symposium on the moral legitimacy of the American government, many readers, including certain of the magazine's contributing editors, reacted as if the editor had touched off the first gun in Second Fort Sumter. The truth is, if the cultural and political divide in America today were drawn along regional or sectional lines rather than on social and economic ones, the Second American Civil War would have been declared long ago. This is a notion that certain people find terrifying—too terrifying, it seems, to contemplate. Others of us are made more sanguine, even sanguinary, by the thought.

At the time of the War for Southern Independence the American polity, having reached its apex with the Constitutional Convention of 1787 in Philadelphia, was already in decline: American civilization, however—North and South—was in many respects in its fullest flower, a product of the colonial past brought to full maturity and unblighted as yet by the vulgarity, coarseness, and abstraction of industrial empire. I refer skeptics or dissenters to the record, the primary literature, of the Civil War period. That a modern-day reader can find solace in the history of his country's hitherto greatest crisis as a people—not least for the nobility and heroism that our forebears were forcefully engaged in displaying a brief 130-something years ago—is testimony to the terrible condition of that country today. Southerners and Northerners, Union and Confederate, officers and enlisted soldiers, the men who fought the War Between the States were men indeed; offspring of a culture in which physical strength and stamina, resourcefulness, courage, and stoicism were balanced by cultivation, a little learning, fluency in self-expression (written and spoken), and the gentlemanly gentleness that used to be called gentility. These qualities were reciprocal, and reciprocated. Men who had been compatriots only months or a few years before remained brothers across the lines: The tragedy of this bungled unnecessary war is never more poignant than in the scores of instances, from First Manassas to Nashville, in which warriors paid homage to the bravery of their opponents—sometimes, as at Gettysburg, to the point of cheering them forward. It may be too much to say that the American Civil War, the first war in which troops (Jackson's) were transported by train to the front and the first that experienced trench warfare, was also the last major war to which the character of the combatants was intrinsic. But not by a lot.

A RIGID, DUTY-DRIVEN, almost painfully serious man, Thomas Jonathan Jackson appears at first look as one of the war's less chivalric commanders, more a model of the modern military man established, perhaps, by Cromwell. As a fighter, General Jackson was all business. Rather than praise the valor of opposing troops, he once remarked to a subordinate who had expressed regret at having to shoot gallant men in action that he would kill every man, as he did not wish the enemy to be brave. At least one review of Robertson's book I have seen speaks of a contradiction between Jackson's relentlessness in battle and his stern piety. In fact there was no contradiction on account of that very sternness, as I think Robertson himself would agree. Unlike Robert E. Lee, Stonewall Jackson was no Tidewater aristocrat but an orphan from the hill country of northwestern Virginia, where he led a lonely hardscrabble existence before winning admission to West Point. Taciturn and shabby beneath an old forage cap—he wore his blue VMI faculty uniform into the early months of the war, at the risk of drawing friendly fire—Jackson forewent Lee's quiet elegance in dress, even more Jeb Stuart's sartorial flamboyance. In many ways, he was more of a Roundhead than a Cavalier, whose strict Presbyterianism translated in the American setting as a Southern type of New England Puritanism. Jackson had hoped that war might be averted; when it came, he understood the crisis in theological terms. The infidel North intended the destruction of his sacred homeland, a country entrusted by God with His purpose. "Now," Robertson says, "he could begin the long but holy task of lifting the Almighty's scourge from the country and obtaining God's blessing on the most faithful side." However, as a professional military officer Jackson was acutely aware of the disadvantages the Confederacy was under in its defiance of the United States of America. "We cannot stand a long war," he told his wife. Yet the price of defeat was terrible. "I myself see in this war, if the North triumph," his brother-in-law recalled him saying, "a dissolution of the bonds of all society. It is not alone the destruction of our property, but the prelude to anarchy, infidelity, and the ultimate loss of free responsible government on this continent." Therefore, the South must not lose.

And so Jackson urged upon Lee that small bands of Confederate troops be organized to mount a series of invasions to the north, holding cities for ransom, paroling prisoners, attacking and retreating everywhere. "I would make it hot for our friends at *their* homes and firesides, all the way to Kansas." In laying his proposal before Lee, Jackson, as Robertson observes, "was advocating ruthless, uncompromising war with the enemy. His precedent was the Old Testament; his justification was the freedom of the God-loving people of the South," who after all were fighting a purely defensive war. At bottom, he was arguing that a weaker government could not defeat a far more powerful one using the means of conventional warfare. "That premise," Robertson remarks, "was current but unacceptable to Confederate authorities." Therefore, deprived of the chance to pursue what he considered the most effective and economical (in lives as in materiel) of possible strategies, Jackson was for hitting hard—killing every man—that the war might end as soon as possible, and the troops on both sides return to their homes and families. Jackson's own wife, Anna, gave birth to his only child to survive a few months before the events at Chancellorsville.

ONE ASPECT OF JACKSON'S FAITH is, undeniably, disturbing. On a night late in 1862, while the destruction of the railroad between Harpers Ferry and Winchester was in progress, Jackson had a long conversation with Surgeon Hunter McGuire about religion. "I have no fears whatever that I shall ever fall under the wrath of God," he stated. "I am as certain of my acceptance, and heavenly reward, as that I am sitting here." Jackson's assuredness on this point suggests the degree to which his admired, and admirable, righteousness pressed close upon self-righteousness, as it did on a number of occasions in his life and career. Most godly, even saintly, men and women, profoundly conscious of the inevitability of human sinfulness defiling those lives most humbly, conscientiously, and heroically dedicated to doing the will of God, have felt reason to fear falling under God's wrath. That Jackson believed divine punishment, in the case of himself, to be unimaginable is less suggestive of the unshakableness of his Presbyterian faith than of its imperfect formation.

That is, however, a personal consideration. The broader one has to do with Jackson's devotion to the Cause. For Stonewall Jackson the fact of his being a God-fearing man and his country a God-fearing nation produced the unquestioned, and unquestionable, conclusion that God was a Confederate. Now it may be that this sort of theological and moral certainty is necessary to men confronted by the intense suffering, privation, and sacrifice that war demands of them; also to their families at home. On the other hand, it is always bad theology—even if God *is* a Confederate. In our day of banished religion, relativistic morals, weak principles, and loss of nerve, the reality of a government supremely confident in the rightness of the society it represents, and a society equally well assured of itself, appears to us as a dream too good to be true. Yet such self-assurance may have contributed crucially to the South's weakest element, its quality of brittleness. No individual, and no country, should be too confident of having read God's will aright. It is doubtful that the more sophisticated Lee shared his subaltern's unblinkered faith in the Southern cause, since he himself opposed the war until the moment when Mr. Lincoln sent federal troops across the Potomac and, in its closing months, confided to his son the belief that his compatriots would live to regret secession—and soon. The Confederacy had legal, constitutional, and moral right on its side; also, as the more civilized of the two opposing cultures, it had the more humane vision, slavery or no slavery. But did God really wish the Confederacy to win the war? For that matter, did He hope to see the Union—the future bastion of abortion, napalm, and criminalized prayer—the victor? Who knows what God wants? What we do know is that the South lost its bloody bid for independence, and that with the death of Stonewall Jackson—shot *by his own men* in the Wilderness around Chancellorsville—shocked and grieving Southerners wondered, for the first time, whether God might really acquiesce in their defeat. Something else we know: that triumph, in this world, is only rarely a sign of the Lord's favor, but rather its opposite.

James Robertson's *Stonewall Jackson* is a long book with too-short paragraphs and a spare, plain style that exactly suits its reticent, laconic, supremely heroic subject. It is a splendid addition to the enormous literature on the Lost Cause that never was lost, the conclusive war that did not end but has continued to the present day when it continues to be fought, under different flags (some of them), and in a multiplicity of forms and guises.

THE PRESENT UNPLEASANTNESS

Southern Men, American Persons

Thomas Fleming

"SWEET HOME ALABAMA / Where the skies are so blue." It has been many years since anyone made money from patriotic songs dedicated to Illinois or New Jersey. Chicago and New York have their anthems of course, to say nothing of San Francisco, but no one is going to get into a fight over "the city that never sleeps" or "little cable cars climbing halfway to the stars." In the 19th century, we did celebrate the rivers of the midsection—the Ohio and the Wabash—but none of them was so famous as the inconsequential Suwannee celebrated by Stephen Foster and later taken up by New York songwriters as a code word for the sentimentalized South: "How I love ya, how I love ya, my dear old Swanee."

We are become a cynical and heartless people, more prone to deride than to celebrate our hometowns, and yet Charlie Daniels virtually drips with sentiment as he sings of "Carolina," and Merle Haggard was proud to be an Okie from Muskogee, which he was not. If Northern songwriters can occasionally write movingly of the troubles of Allentown, Pennsylvania, the tone of boosterism and defiance is almost exclusively confined to the South. "If the South woulda won, we'd a-had it made," Hank Williams, Jr., was singing a few years ago, just when the critics were praising him for giving up his Southern nationalism.

Lynyrd Skynyrd's "Sweet Home Alabama" remains the benchmark Southern song, because it is deliberately combative, throwing down the gauntlet to the Canadian leftist who had stuck his nose into what did not concern him. In "Southern Man," Neil Young had cried shame on Southerners for the usual reasons. One might have thought that an Anglo-Canadian could have better spent his time on the Ojibwa, victims of both toxic waste and toxic welfare, or the French, whose identity the English did their best to eliminate. "Mr. Young, does your conscience bother you?"

One does not need to turn to popular music to find signs of Southern chauvinism. Southern fiction has so dominated the United States in this century that some people have said there are only two kinds of American writers, Southerners and Jews. This is an exaggeration, but just barely, and despite the considerable differences that separate Southerners and Jews, the success of both groups depends on their atavisms: loyalty to kinfolk, preservation of tradition, and suspicion of aliens.

In America Faulkner could only have been a Southerner, because only a Southerner can spend his life wrestling with what it means to be a Southerner. A century and a half ago, when Nathaniel Hawthorne was crafting his nearly perfect stories of Puritan life, the Northeastern writer was already out of touch with his people, and as a thin stream of civilization flowed westward in the wake of the pioneers, region after region went through a brief period of literary exaltation—Ohio, Indiana, Illinois, the Plains States—before the stream lost itself in the deserts of the West. The closest approximation to a northern Faulkner may be Glenway Wescott, of an old Yankee family in Wisconsin. But Wescott left Wisconsin at an early age, and the narrator of *The Grandmothers*—an almost too beautiful novel tracing his own family's descent—is an expatriate, like Hemingway and Fitzgerald.

Not all Southern writers have been obsessed with the land and its history—Walker Percy and George Garrett are notable exceptions—but, as the essays in this number [May 1994] illustrate, the land and its people was the dominant theme of the Agrarians as well as of Faulkner, and it is still providing Fred Chappell and Wendell Berry with the matter of literature. There is nothing unusual in this; what is unusual is what has happened to the rest of the American Empire, where people of my generation can scarcely tell a single tale of their grandparents and where it is nothing for families to spread themselves across the continent like so many toys shaken on a child's blanket.

NO HUMAN CIVILIZATION has ever been created by nomads—although even true nomads have their sense of place—and whether one looks at Athens in the 5th century or Florence in the 14th or Edinburgh in the 18th, the great works that define our culture as "the West" were created by men who knew who their people were and knew the land they lived on. Here in the Middle West, only the Indians have a right to speak of their ancestors or call the land sacred, and when they complain of the desecration of funeral mounds, they are defended only by crackpot leftists who have forgotten to turn down the thermostat in their sweat lodge. Self-described conservatives—what a word that is becoming—make fun of people who do not like to see the bones of their ancestors put on display in Barnum's museum.

A people such as we have become in the United States is incapable of creating or even receiving the gifts of civilization. Because human beings are, as a species, almost infinitely creative, there are individuals sporadically writing books or composing music that is worth some attention, but there is nothing specifically American unless it be that self-abusive consumerism that has overstocked California with two-legged parasites and keeps the national economy grinding on to the doomsday we are preparing for ourselves. Eating and spending, we lay waste our powers. If in the next century there is a civilization in North America, it will have been the creation of Mexicans or French-Canadians or Indians or even, if they survive, Southerners.

One of the chief effects of the South's survival would be the challenge it would represent to other sections. An arrogant and overbearing Southern culture could antagonize Yankees or Midwesterners to rediscover their own identity. In the greatest political novel of the century, Chesterton's *The Napoleon of Notting Hill*, one of the dreariest of London's neighborhoods takes over the city, thereby inciting the other neighborhoods to assert their independence. The rest of the country seems to need the South, if only as a whipping boy. What will we do when it is gone?

Much of the South is no doubt gone, and I have never been persuaded by John Reed's Pollyannaisms about Southern distinctiveness surviving in the suburbs. So much talk about Southern identity and Southern culture cannot be a good thing: Members of authentic cultures do not have to wear shirts or attend conferences to prove who they are. All the various Southern culture projects are a Disneyland surrogate for the real thing, and the professional Southerner today is as authentic as a stage Irishman or a Stepford wife. They love the South, because, now that they have got over the race thing, Southerners are actually more tolerant, more humane, more—well—Northern than Northerners. I cannot print my response to this nonsense in a family magazine. It is better for blacks and whites to hate each other, if the fruits of toleration are lies and cowardice, just as I would welcome the return of the persecuting spirit to Christianity, if it meant the Faith was strong enough to justify torture and death.

The real South was and is a dangerous place, more like Mexico than Chapel Hill, and if you say the wrong thing or look the wrong way at the wrong time, there will be some cracker to make an issue out of it. And not just crackers. Southern men of good family may no longer fight duels, but they might just be willing to slap you silly or take revenge in less obvious ways. Ted Turner is reckoned to be one of the nastiest businessmen in America, and I sometimes wonder if he would be less ruthless, if he had been able to call out his rivals.

Everywhere I go, I meet real Southerners who are not about to apologize for either their family or their flag. The other night I received a telephone call from a perfect stranger who wanted some historical ammunition. At a local high school named for General Lee, some students had been displaying the Confederate flag until the superintendent issued a decree prohibiting it, and my caller—an articulate but not educated Southerner—wanted to defend the students. When all is said and done, there is only one argument that counts in these flag controversies, and that is loyalty. One can argue all day about the comparative sins of Southern slaveowners and Yankee capitalists, but for real men and women, all that matters is the love they bear their people and their land. If Southerners are going to be asked to repudiate their flag and their history, do not imagine it will make them good Americans. The most that can be hoped for is that they will turn into one more whining minority.

THE WAR AGAINST THE SOUTH did not end in 1865 or even 1876, when the last federal troops were pulled out of Southern states. After some years of peace, the war was renewed in the 50's and 60's, and under our rednecked Rhodes scholar president it has heated up again. Consider the Byron De La Beckwith trial. I had always assumed, without having any particular knowledge, that "Delay" was guilty, and if I had served on his first jury, I would have voted guilty. But the jurors felt differently, and I think I understand why. Mississippi was under invasion, by federal marshals, northern leftists, and a civil-rights movement that was every day proclaiming race war against Southern whites. If forced to choose between their people and its enemies, most decent, simple people will choose their own. We cannot ask ordinary people to get above their raising, and if we do, we are really demanding that they hate themselves.

In any event, Beckwith was tried twice, and one had thought that particular phase of the war was over. But no, this pathetic and cracked old man, who under other circumstances could have plead mental incompetence, was forced to go through it all again. I cannot blame the family of Medgar Evers for wanting vengeance. In their place, I might have done it myself. But a show trial of this kind implicates the entire nation in a sensitivity witch hunt that will be a source of embarrassment to our posterity, if there is a posterity that can read books and make up its own mind.

I am not in favor of any of these historic trials. There is something cold-hearted and nasty about the pursuit of supposed ex-Nazis, like John Demjanjuk, who after years of peaceful and harmless existence are dragged forth as scapegoats for the sins of our own insensitive society. I felt the same way about the middle-aged member of the Weather Underground—a successful businesswoman, a wife and mother—what purpose does it serve to put her in jail? Campuses in the 60's were the scene of civil war, and although I have no compunction about blaming the left for what it did in those days, the war is over, and it is time for amnesty—for the students and for the cops and for the National Guardsmen at Kent State and even for Richard Nixon and Mayor Daley.

For two decades after the War Between the States, the Kansas-Missouri border war was kept alive by a number of young men who had fought under the black flag with Quantrill and Anderson. The Youngers were caught in Northfield, Minnesota, and Jesse James was murdered by an assassin hired by the governor of Missouri. When Frank James finally turned himself in to be tried, no one thought Frank was exactly innocent of all charges, but his acquittal meant that after three decades of fighting, the war was over. Unfortunately, the war against the South is not over, and the South's enemies—the liberal-conservative Establishment that owns and operates the United States as a private monopoly—will not rest until they have erased every vestige of the Southern identity.

One typical complaint against the Confederate flag is that it is the symbol of treason and rebellion. I say "typical," because no one who knew anything of our history would be so obtuse. The withdrawal of a commonwealth from a federation does not constitute rebellion, much less treason, either in political theory or in international law. There are those who will say that the states of the Union did not have a right to secede. They are wrong, but let us concede the point. The Virginians and Carolinians of the 1860's certainly had better right to secede than their fathers and grandfathers who liberated their states from British rule, and yet we are not ashamed of Washington and Adams, and we do not curse the memory of these traitors to the only lawfully constituted authority that had been conceivable from the time John Smith set foot in Virginia. The government of Andrew Johnson had wanted to try Jefferson Davis for treason, but the President thought better of it when he realized that world opinion would be solidly against him.

So far from being traitors to the American Republic, Southerners have been, at least since the Spanish-American War, the greatest chauvinists, sensitive to any blot on the national honor, eager for war, and proud of the Stars and Stripes. It is a pernicious piece of nonsense to claim that a man cannot be loyal to his state or region without being disloyal to his nation. That is like saying a man cannot be a good father or a good Baptist, unless he is just a little bit of a traitor to the state that demands perfect and total loyalty.

I OFTEN THINK of our late friend M.E. Bradford. The only time I think we seriously disagreed was during the Gulf War. He understood and accepted all the criticisms I made against the injustice and imprudence of that crusade for democracy, and yet, at the end of a discussion, he would always come back to the same point: It would do Americans good to punish the strutting little despot who had insulted our country.

I do not think I ever met a more patriotic American: He had served his country in the Navy, had devoted much of his valuable time to political battles both in Texas and in Washington, and had spent much of his later years explaining the meaning of the Constitution to a nation that had turned its back on the rule of law. As a leader of the conservative coalition, he had been an excellent fighter on behalf of principle. His only weakness was that he was a very poor hater. He could get temporarily incensed against those who lied against him—Irving Kristol and George Will—but he could not bring himself to seek revenge and would not countenance it in his friends. As Paul Gottfried always used to say, Mel was too much of a Christian to make a good politician.

To his academic colleagues, even those who considered themselves his friends, Mel often seemed an anomaly. Here was a literary historian who could have carved out a very comfortable career, if only he had stuck to his trade and avoided controversy. When Clyde Wilson's volume of essays *Why the South Will Survive* was published in commemoration of the 50th anniversary of *I'll Take My Stand*, the reviewer in the *Virginia Quarterly* took all the contributors to task for politicizing the Agrarian inheritance. The shaft was aimed at Mel, of course, to make it appear that he had diverted a literary movement into politics.

But the contributors to *I'll Take My Stand* were nothing if not political, and several of them wanted to call the volume *Tracts Against Communism*. Indeed, it is hard to think of a man of letters more political than Donald Davidson. Even if he had tried, Mel Bradford could not have disentangled politics from literature, not in the trivial sense that he could not recognize literary merit in liberal writers, but because the career of the writer and scholar was bound up with the community that had given him life and cultural sustenance. His role was not to go off into the wilderness in order to discover some unheard of system of thought and expression to spark a revolution. On the contrary. Speaking of the resemblance of Southern writers to ancient Romans, he wrote: "[B]oth reflect the all-absorbing corporate spirit of the culture for which they speak. The Southern writer, like his ancient counterpart, has almost always felt the pressure to be a public man and to perform a service in relation to that powerful sense of cultural identity."

For me, Mel was a kind of touchstone of integrity. Whatever decency a man had was sure to be called forth and encouraged by the mere fact of knowing Mel, and if there were those who responded to his open nature with distrust and chicane, they revealed themselves for what they were. In offering this number of *Chronicles* to M.E. Bradford, we are paying tribute to a man who represented the last link in many chains: a man of letters who put his pen to his nation's use, a passionate Southerner and loyal American, a faithful friend, and a Christian husband and father who did his duty.

Tyranny by Sloth

George Garrett

WHEN I SAY that I thank you for asking me here to speak to you, that I thank you I am here, I have to confess that I am flying in the face of the latest status ritual practiced by many of my colleagues in the scribbling professions. The latest thing, as you may already have learned (I am a slow learner and also somewhat out of touch), is to prove your high place in the hierarchy of contemporary American writers by *not* showing up for scheduled and promised appearances and events. The greater luminaries simply don't arrive. At the next aspiring level, the basic idea is to cancel out, offering no good reason or proposing an obviously implausible one, about 24 hours before the event. And now that the word is out, there are many places, particularly in the status-conscious groves of Academe, where their disappointment and shame and contempt are clearly visible, as if etched, if and when you actually arrive at the right place at more or less the right time. It means they have been snookered one more time into wasting some of their limited resources on an obvious second-rater.

Of course, in the literary world other coincidental funny things have been happening lately—interesting mix-ups, for example. My Charlottesville neighbor Ann Beattie swears to me that she was recently flown out to a school in Ohio for a visit and a reading (and good money) and realized, after she got there, and no joke, that everybody thought she was Anne Tyler. The name on the posters and the programs was Anne Tyler. The name on the check proved to be Anne Tyler. She was introduced as Anne Tyler. Ann Beattie grinned and went through with it, although for some reason she chickened out and read from her own work and not Miss Tyler's.

In another recent incident—every chairman and toastmaster's recurring nightmare—novelist Nicholas Delbanco, professor at Michigan and one of the most elegant and eloquent of introducers, was asked, on about ten minutes' notice, to fill in for a colleague (who had been taken suddenly ill) by introducing Margaret Atwood to an expectant audience. Or so he understood his assignment. Quickly he prepared a few notes. Then he ran across campus to Rackham Hall, rushed on stage and up to the podium where he offered up a fulsome, deep-voiced, and impeccably suave introduction of the life and works of Miss Atwood. Turned then, smiling, to greet her as she came to the podium. Only to discover, to his almost unspeakable dismay, that he was looking directly into the familiar and glowering face of Margaret Drabble . . .

ANYWAY, FOR BETTER and for worse, here I am. I am not, however, completely alone. I have brought along with me my invisible and fictional companion, a character named John Towne, out of a novel of mine called *Poison Pen*. Not because I want to inflict him upon you. Not at all. But mainly because I can't trust him, left alone and behind in the pages of his home. Better I should keep an eye on him.

For those of you—the overwhelming majority, no doubt—who don't know him and have never heard of him, let me just quote a few (honest to God) journalistic descriptions of the fellow:

> *Publisher's Weekly*: "a vulgar scapegrace"
> *New York Times Book Review*: "a low life crank"
> *National Review*: "a coke-befuddled redneck"
> *The Washington Times*: "a man of *unsavory* character"
> *Charlottesville Daily Progress*: "a character of exquisite vulgarity"
> *Village Voice*: " . . . an academic charlatan of the lowest order"
> *Book World*: "a full-time con artist, misanthrope and lecher"
> *Chicago Tribune*: "a lecherous, misanthropic, failed academic"
> *Village Voice*: "an exceptionally sleazy picaro"

They didn't even like him much down home in my native Southland. Here's the *Greensboro News*: "a loathsome, racist, crude and gruesome creep."

Well, you get the idea. An interesting consensus of reactions.

One thing about Towne, he's got a lot of advice to offer.

For instance, true to character and form, he wanted me to build this little talk around something that interested *him*—namely, the truth and consequences of a headline and story in the *Charlottesville Daily Progress* (October 25, 1987): "Aging Sexpot Van Doren Tells All." Towne finds it especially exemplary of the inward and spiritual truth of our times. He is particularly fond of the following paragraph, which he takes to be a better than average example of the fine-tuned complexity and subtlety of contemporary morality: "Was the casting couch a Hollywood fixture in those days?"

"'Yes. I found myself on it—but I only did it because I wanted to,' she said. 'I never went to bed with anyone I didn't want to. I had opportunities, but I didn't do it. Had I done so, I might have had better parts.'"

Well. Towne has got a point. It is pertinent. I mean if Joe Biden had been an actress instead of a U.S. senator, he might have sounded exactly like that . . .

"Surely you don't plan to talk about *literature* and the (pardon the expression) literary life," Towne argued.

I agreed. Partly because in one aspect of one thing I find myself more or less in agreement with him. Towne's hydraulic law of uniform corruption—that is, that corruption everywhere seeks its own level and that, thus, all aspects of our life and world, at any given instant, are equally corrupt— seems to have some real truth to it. A corollary to the law, however, is that it doesn't apply to the literary world, which is unquestionably on a completely different level of corruption. Indeed, sad experience teaches me that it is hard to imagine any social unit as riddled with corruption as the American literary scene. My own personal opinion, on the basis of anecdotal evidence, is that next to the American Academy and Institute of Arts and Letters, the court of the Emperor Caligula would look like an early session of the Council of Trent.

More serious, however, is the fact that to the mundane practices of misinformation and disinformation, as widely practiced by our press, which at least has the general goal of national destabilization to justify its ways and means, the literary folk (whose mostly unspoken consensus is so ironbound as to ignore all political differences and cross the boundaries of social class) are dedicated to rhetorical games played at the expense of the full dimensions of the truth.

For example, although there have been some debates concerning matters of form, aesthetic arguments, in the world of poetry, serious questioning or discussion of any of the serious issues of our time have been almost completely absent in American poetry since the deaths of Pound and Eliot and Frost and most recently John Ciardi.

Saddest of all, nobody seems to miss this. Or them, very much.

I collect whole notebooks of splendid little examples, of which here is only one, only a typical and very recent one. Here is John Gregory Dunne in his piece "This Year in Jerusalem," in the December [1987] issue of *Esquire*:

> Surrounded by soldiers as I waited to pass through the metal
> detectors and security check, I was struck once again by the way
> the Israeli military was woven into the country's social fabric. In
> the United States, soldiers are those weird looking young men
> we usually see only in airports, this one with his hair too short,
> that one with the tattoo and the mottled complexion and the flat

hill accent, the black lance corporal here, the Hispanic Pfc. over there; in other words, no one we know. At the trial that morning the soldiers had the sentient mainstream faces so rarely seen in the contemporary American services.

Of course, all this is layered in appropriate and protective kinds of irony. A baklava of clever observation. He doesn't really mean all that. Forced to a final wall, he can always admit that he really doesn't mean anything. Meantime, however, in the form of an entirely typical piece of contemporary literary rhetoric, you have an aside, passing as an observation, a matter of opinion told as a fact as it were. And which is, in fact, a very lightly encoded cryptogram, a cheerful little message sent to other true believers, slightly disguised as a commonplace, unexceptional stereotypical comment about our volunteer armed services, offering a gesture of gratuitous, if relative, contempt for our country and its people, paid for by a little tip, a shrug, and a *pourboire* of self-contempt . . . *"in other words no one we know."*

I sometimes honestly think that a certain kind of liberal, equally the *literary* liberal, uses the overt profession of personal guilt as justification for an almost murderous contempt of fellow man.

All the assumptions behind Dunne's deft little aside are so familiar to us as to be more or less harmless if we notice them at all. They stand like crumbling statues in a weedy overgrown public park or garden. Not neutral, mind you, but more or less harmless . . . unless and until you allow yourself to consider the possibility that the relentless and largely unquestioned documentation and consumption of such distortions of reality can add up sooner or later to what constitutes a killing dose of poison. Meanwhile, though, it all has a certain sly charm. Even the little instances of pure and simple ignorance are socially if not rhetorically redeeming.

I said *largely* unquestioned. Not completely. We are here on this occasion [*Chronicles'* tenth anniversary banquet] to celebrate the existence and survival of *Chronicles*, which asks some questions and answers others which would otherwise be ignored.

And that is what I really should be talking about and what we should be thinking about: questions and answers in the unceasing search for the truth.

WHENEVER I GO TO WORK in the morning and go through the entrance of old Cabell Hall at the University of Virginia, I pass under some words of Thomas Jefferson: "Here we are not afraid to follow Truth wherever it may lead nor to tolerate any error so long as reason is left free to combat it."

170

Some words of Jefferson ought to be my theme.

Here Towne butted in and argued.

"Don't talk Jefferson at them," he said. "You give them Jefferson, they'll give you Sally Hemings."

"Hey," I said. "I am not speaking at a Norman Lear testimonial."

"Lucky you," says he. "But it's all pretty much the same old thing."

"We'll see."

"Well," he said. "If you have to talk about Mr. Jefferson, go for it. Don't give them the sweet violins."

I tried my best to explain to him that in my own Episcopal Church even the *hard sayings* of Jesus Christ have now been put on the back burner, if not actually banned. How can I give them the iron fist of Thomas Jefferson?

"Here's how," he said. "As an example of exactly the kind of thought or idea which ought to be part of any full and free discussion or debate about ourselves, but which is not, because we are these days so concerned about monitoring our thoughts, even as we permit ourselves the crudest possible luxury and license by using the worst words our language allows."

"Look," I said. "Here we are living at a time when everything you can think of has been weighted with political symbolism and significance. Even baseball teams (it was racist to wish for the Minnesota Twins' win in the [1987] Series); *musical instruments*—if you listen at all to what might accurately be called Radio Daniel Schorr, I mean National Public Radio, you know that the flute and the acoustic guitar are the instruments of compassion and that compassion is a virtue exclusively reserved for the left and especially for those who most publicly assert that they have compassion; even the care and cure of dread diseases are politically weighted. Fabrics, clothing, and hairstyles, bottles of beer and soda pop—it's a political minefield out there. How can I possibly say anything that will catch attention and mean anything?"

"You want me to attract their attention?" Towne asked.

In the end we compromised. From radically different points of view we both agreed that if our way of self-governing were to survive much longer—and by the way, we even in our absolute privacy allowed ourselves to consider whether survival of our ways and means of self-government is a hopeful or a baleful prospect; for *ourselves*, I mean; never mind the multitudes outside of our particular traditions and history, for whom all democratic forms are at the least exotic; anyway—we compromised on the choice of a single passage, one example among many, from the words of Thomas Jefferson, one which carries the imperative necessity of the full and free debate of issues and assumptions to a logical, if honorable, extreme.

HERE, THEN, ARE HIS WORDS, taken from a letter written in Paris and dated November 13, 1787 (a wink or two beyond two centuries ago). You probably remember them well enough: "God forbid we should ever be 20 years without a rebellion. The people cannot be all, and always, well-informed. The part which is wrong will be discontented in proportion to the importance of the facts they misconceive. If they remain quiet under such misconceptions, it is a lethargy, the forerunner of death to public liberty. . . . " (I skip a little.)

> What country before ever existed a century and a half without rebellion? And what country can preserve its liberties if the rulers are not warned from time to time that their people preserve the spirit of resistance? Let them take arms. The remedy is to set them right as to the facts, pardon and pacify them. What signify a few lives lost in a century or two? The tree of liberty must be refreshed from time to time with the blood of patriots and tyrants. It is its natural manure.

No question but that is a *hard* saying. No question, either, but that it is complex, thorny with prescience and pertinence, and I think eminently relevant to our very times and this very occasion tonight.

But before we go into some of those things, try to imagine, for a moment, the uproar and outrage which would follow if any contemporary public figure, at any point in life, early or late, and in any form, from letter to the editor to a diary note, had ever said such a thing.

The only one I can think of who could get away with it is Joe Biden. Because everybody would correctly assume it was just plagiarism, anyway.

Thomas Jefferson said it and seems to have meant it, too, though some of the terms he used meant different things then than now. Take tyrant, the concept of tyranny, for example. For somewhat more than 2,000 years, on up through and including the times of Thomas Jefferson, tyranny was defined and equally applied to the overzealous exercise of rigorous justice without mercy and to the squandered blessing of reflexive and thoughtless mercy without the context or foundation of rigorous justice. Thus any leader or statesman, from the citizens of the Greek city-states, through every kind of emperor and monarch, absolute or benevolent, on through the rebellious generation of Jefferson, would surely and easily define our contemporary American social situation, with its elaborately formulated, indeed *codified*, absence of any system protecting the rights of the law-abiding citizens and their civilization from predatory assaults, as clearly, unequivocally tyrannical.

172

And, as such, it was always deemed worthy of the strongest possible kind of resistance.

The most usual and immediate response to this passage that I have received from reasonably thoughtful and thoughtfully reasonable people is that we must consider the relativity of historical context. That in the period (brief or long, depending on your own historical scheme) since Jefferson we have come to value the sanctity of human life, have come to view life, in and of itself, as precious. Certainly more precious than our ancestors viewed at least the lives of others.

This is an answer, a position which might be regarded as simply and brutally laughable, coming as it does out of this bloody, bloody century, this century whose appropriate image is of rivers, Amazons, Mississippis, Congos of human blood. Century in which even the holocaust, defined by both intent and execution, can only be claimed to be one enormous genocidal example among many, first among many parts . . .

It is certainly not becoming, it ill behooves anyone from this 20th century to regard Jefferson's statement as evidence of a more bloody-minded disposition or blithe disregard for the lives of others than our words and acts.

Indeed, once the idea of hypocrisy has been introduced, a good strong case can be made that Jefferson's approach, even taken by a literal mind, is closest to that of a good general—Patton, for example, whose own casualties (*and the casualties he inflicted*) were always minimal precisely because his tactics were sudden, ruthless, and anything but tentative.

Thus I can see that it can be decently and honorably maintained that certain complex and confusing issues troubling us in these times probably should have been settled in the streets, sealed in the blood of patriots and tyrants, rather than vaguely resolved in legislatures, courts, or in the press.

As to the sanctity of human life in our own country, we must never allow ourselves to forget that in fact a good many years ago we settled for the deaths of roughly 65,000 people—men, women, and children—on our highways as a statistically acceptable year. Sixty-five thousand is a number our society has somehow agreed to live with. I don't need to remind you that that is, of course, more than the total number of American dead in all the years of the Vietnam War.

Do you suppose they would consider putting up a series of black walls in honor and memory of all the dead drivers, drunk and sober alike, of America?

A possibly more plausible argument, one that is frequently heard from intellectual sources, is that (with perhaps the exception of Israeli preemptive and retaliatory strikes on terrorist targets) warfare as an instrument or extension of national policy, even the policy of self-defense, is no longer really feasible.

Unthinkable is, I believe, the correct adjective. That there are wars going on, here and now, within and between most of the nations of the earth is a fact beyond the interest of most of these advanced thinkers.

I am reminded of the celebrated 60's, when rape seemed statistically likely to become a new national pastime and women were advised not under any circumstances ever to resist a rapist. Exactly the opposite advice is freely given in courses and seminars nowadays. I am reminded of the Navy Shark Repellent in World War II, a colorful dye which, while it evidently had no effect on sharks one way or the other, at least allowed a brief feeling of safety and security *before* the jaws clamped down.

Never mind.

Let us return to text. To Jefferson.

Clearly, despite all his good wishes and even high hopes for some measure of domestic tranquility, he envisioned the quality which he conceived of and called liberty as enduring only in a state of constant, unrelenting testing. Interrogation by means of full debate and argument where facts are assembled and known and where reason, itself, is allowed to be and run free. Absent those conditions, he likewise clearly believed (at least on this occasion) that it was meet and right that genuinely significant issues should be sealed and settled in blood.

That, if need be—no, more accurately, *when need be*, for he simply assumed that, come what may, ignorance and misconception were inevitable companions—that when need be we should be ready, willing, and able to die for and kill for our principles.

But let us be pragmatic and try to get at the heart of what he was saying as it may possibly apply to us.

One cannot (to use that lovely *media* word) *rule out* the possibility, now or ever, of bloody acts of resistance and rebellion (in whatever form) in the United States. What, after all, was the seizure of federal prisons and hostages in Atlanta and Louisiana but a clumsy act of rebellion? One cannot ever rule out the possibility. But since the race riots of the late 1940's and the late 1960's, although we have had plenty of violent events and incidents, large and small, we have witnessed no full-scale, real and honest rebellion. And for the present such a thing seems highly unlikely.

Which may well mean that, in Jefferson's own terms, we live at a time when the love of lethargy has at last replaced even the hope of preserving liberty. Maybe . . .

Or it may mean that, for the time being, resistance and rebellion must take place on the other fields where our great life-and-death issues are being settled.

Settled, for better and worse. Not well or deeply discussed. Many things are discussed, if only lightly debated, but next to none of the great and deep questions are being asked.

THIS WHOLE PROBLEM, which ought to have attracted our attention and, at the very least, aroused the passion of intellectual anger, has been most passionately discussed *not* by any American thinker of any persuasion, but by the great Russian writer Aleksandr Solzhenitsyn, and only on one occasion— his baccalaureate address at Harvard in 1978.

You will remember it. And I hope you will refresh your memory of his words by seeking them out again.

His observations are remarkable, subtle, profound, and, I think, as accurate and prescient as they are controversial. May I quote from a couple of paragraphs?

> There is yet another surprise for someone coming from the East, where the press is rigorously unified; one gradually discovers a common trend of preferences within the Western press as a whole. It is a fashion; there are generally accepted patterns of judgment and there may be common corporate interests, the sum effect being not competition but unification. Enormous freedom exists for the press, but not for the readership, because newspapers mostly give emphasis to those opinions that do not too openly contradict their own and the general trend.
>
> Without any censorship, in the West, fashionable trends of thought are carefully separated from those that are not fashionable.
>
> Nothing is forbidden, but what is not fashionable will hardly ever find its way into periodicals or books or be heard in colleges.

It continues . . .

It earned Solzhenitsyn immediate and rabid denunciation by the press he criticized. Gentle and wimpish liberals suddenly discovered the "America-Love-It-or-Leave-It" standard and applied it directly to him.

Time has only allowed the uniform derogation of Solzhenitsyn by the press to slack off a little bit. One week ago the *Washington Post* ran a lengthy feature: "Solzhenitsyn and His Message of Silence." If you were to read the article, you would have discovered that his *silence*, in this case, means that he turned down an opportunity to be interviewed by the *Washington Post*. They don't suggest that he is crazy up there in Vermont. But they do at least imply that he is keeping a low profile for a self-serving reason: "It has even been suggested that, if Gorbachev means what he says, the work of Aleksandr Solzhenitsyn might be published in the Soviet Union for the first time in more than two decades. Some of his fellow émigrés believe Solzhenitsyn is silent for that purpose too: that he not jeopardize the best chance for his return to the motherland, in word if not in deed."

A bullet wound would, of course, be considerably more painful. But I doubt if firing a bullet at him could be a more *hateful* act than writing those words.

As long as they can kill their opposition with *words*, why waste bullets on any of us?

World of words, that's where the battle—the ceaseless war of rebellion and resistance against intellectual and spiritual lethargy, and for the sake of liberty—is going on.

THINGS HAVE NOT IMPROVED much, if at all, since Solzhenitsyn spoke. Indeed the stereotypes he noted—the sculptural museum of modern group-thinks—have acquired the patina of dignity since then. Whole topics have been declared to be off-limits, beyond all legitimate discussion or even historical reconsideration. In history and the so-called social sciences, and even (alas) in the stricter sciences, especially medicine and biology, it is now widely accepted and understood that evidence which weighs against fashionable contemporary political and social positions is to be suppressed, or at least modified and limited so as not to offer any ammunition to the skeptical opposition. I can recall that once upon a time we laughed at science under Stalin, never dreaming that most of its practices, if not all of its excesses, would come to pass here.

In literature there are such inhibitions as the prevalent critical notion that even for the sake of verisimilitude, fictional characters must not be allowed to maintain views, prejudices, or, indeed, use words which offend stereotypical contemporary standards. Or if they do so, they must be known to be irredeemably wicked and must be *punished* for their sins.

Even the exalted arena of Shakespearean criticism is not safe from this kind of agitprop scrutiny.

If I may be so bold as to second Solzhenitsyn's proposition, I would have to tell you that I have only recently returned to the 20th century from a couple of decades spent living as an expatriate, an alien, in the 16th century. And it is my best and considered judgment that then and there, in Tudor England, when the consequences—and *legal* consequences—of asking certain questions, voiced opinions, even (at times) thoughts and intentions, were deadly serious, there was probably more honest, deep-digging, and far-reaching debate and dissent than we have experienced in this free society for more than a quarter of a century.

Even under the rigors of almost absolute monarchy they were not afraid to debate not only current issues but also, maybe more important, first principles.

Of course, they had at least *some* of the same problems and concerns. Here, for example, is Sir Walter Raleigh writing in his *History of the World*: "How shall the upright and impartial judgment of man give a sentence, where opposition and examination are not admitted to give in evidence?" He then quotes from Lactantius: "They neglect their own wisdom who, without any judgment, approve the invention of those that forewent them; and suffer themselves, after the manner of beasts, to be led by them."

To which Raleigh adds his own observation, coming amazingly close to the words and views of Jefferson: "By the advantage of which sloth, dullness and ignorance is now become so powerful a tyrant, that it hath set true philosophy, psychic, and divinity in a pillory."

We are gathered to honor not the voice, but the various and sundry voices of *Chronicles*. Which, as it happens, is one of the very few and very precious forces actively engaged in the war against lethargy.

It is with words, with ideas, with facts, with questions, and, God willing, with passion that the good fight is being fought.

We are much beleaguered, more so than we would like to admit, if only for the sake of sanity. We need each other. And I am proud to be here and to be a part of all this and all that.

John Towne's cynical laughter echoes in my inner ear like a car horn in a tunnel.

"You'll be sorry. You and your big mouth!" he says. "One thing about the American Establishment, regardless of race, creed, color, country of origin, gender, or sexual preference, they will never forget and forgive."

"So what?" I say. "I never wanted to be on the Supreme Court, anyway."

Witchfinder:
The Strange Career of Morris Dees

Samuel Francis

THE TRIAL, CONVICTION, and death sentence of Timothy McVeigh for the Oklahoma City bombing of April 19, 1995, passed quietly this year [1997], far more quietly than most reporters and some political leaders wanted. The main reason for the calmness of the McVeigh proceedings was probably the utterly uninteresting mind, character, and personality of the defendant. Unlike Charles Manson, who carved swastikas in his forehead and stared satanically at the public throughout his trial, McVeigh simply stared, and no swastikas were in sight. Ever since his arrest 90 minutes after the bombing, McVeigh has said virtually nothing, and certainly nothing of any interest. Even his brief quotation, before he was sentenced to death, from a fairly obscure Supreme Court dissenting opinion by Louis Brandeis, was too cryptic to excite much curiosity, and despite the heinousness of the crime for which he was convicted, it was almost impossible to sustain any public interest in the man who perpetrated the crime.

Nevertheless, some people did find the McVeigh trial interesting, though not because of the defendant, his deed, or the legal, moral, and political issues involved in it. Almost at the beginning of McVeigh's trial last March, an organization known as the Southern Poverty Law Center (SPLC), headquartered in Montgomery, Alabama, issued a publication that made McVeigh and his crime its centerpiece.

Entitled "Two Years After: The Patriot Movement Since Oklahoma City," the publication is the latest contribution to scholarship of the SPLC, which specializes in keeping track of what it calls "hate groups." Founded by lawyer Morris Dees in 1971, the SPLC has kept up a running account of the minutiae of the far right, and its most recent delvings into the world that supposedly bred the bombing of the Murrah Building and the deaths of 168 people within it are fairly typical of its products.

The thesis of "Two Years After" is that the extreme right—including white racialist groups, tax protesters, Christian Identity churches, anti-gun-control activists, Confederate flag defenders, conspiracy theorists, and the "antigovernment insurgency"—is deeply involved in further plotting to carry out acts of terrorism similar to the Oklahoma City operation. The publication, like most of what is produced by the SPLC, makes no distinctions among the various groups, individuals, and causes that it "exposes," and in at least some cases it has managed to loop in some perfectly ordinary and law-abiding conservative organizations.

"TWO YEARS AFTER" enumerates no fewer than 858 distinct organizations in the United States that are said to be part of the "Patriot Movement," a term that is never precisely defined or distinguished from Klan groups, white separatist groups like the Aryan Nations, neo-Nazi groups like the National Alliance, or groups like the various "citizens' militias" that have sprouted in recent years. It offers a listing of the 858 "Patriot" groups, though without describing the size, nature, beliefs, or activities of any of them. In some cases, even the listing is meaningless, as with the entries under Ohio: "Unknown Group Name, Grove City" and "A Concerned Citizen, unspecified location." Groups like the "Aryan Republican Army" (also "unspecified location") are lumped in with the "Keystone Second Amendment Foundation" (yet another "unspecified location"). Whether as a research guide to the far right or as a directory of which groups not to invite to cosponsor your local community barbecue, "Two Years After" is worthless.

Some of the groups, locations specified or not, that the publication lists may actually exist; some might even have more than two or three members; and a few might actually be dangerous. But according to the publication, which reproduces photographs of the bombed Murrah Building throughout the text, all of them are part of the vast and sinister "Patriot Movement," whose goals were succinctly characterized by the SPLC in a media briefing for "Two Years After" on March 4, 1997: "The Patriot Movement poses a continued danger to the country, including the threat of biochemical weapons." Though repeated again in the text, this claim is never substantiated, although a few pages later we learn that "The United States faces an increasing threat of biochemical terrorism—possibly from elements in the Patriot Movement— that would result in massive death and destruction. Patriot publications are filled with stories about an impending biological or chemical attack on U.S. citizens by the federal government." This fear of the *federal* use of biochemical terrorism against Americans is interpreted by the SPLC to mean that the "Patriots" are planning to use such techniques themselves.

Not only are many of the extravagant and sensational claims of the publication never substantiated, but a false unity is attributed to the "Patriot" movement. Ideological as well as behavioral distinctions among different groups are ignored, the actions of individuals are ascribed to the "movement" as a whole, and organizations that are entirely law-abiding and essentially mainstream are lumped in with fragments of the Klan and neo-Nazis. This is what has happened to conservative activist groups such as the U.S. Taxpayers Party and the Council of Conservative Citizens, which have been portrayed as part of the bomb-throwing "Patriot Movement." In the list of the 858 Patriot organizations throughout the country, local and state chapters of the USTP and the CCC, as well as of the John Birch Society, are included, with no differentiation among them, or between them and the more extreme fringe groups. The USTP, founded by movement conservative Howard Phillips, is a political party that seeks repeal of the income tax, abolition of abortion, control of immigration, withdrawal from the United Nations, and a restoration of constitutional government. The CCC, mainly a Southern-based organization of grassroots conservative activists but with chapters throughout the nation, is a hard-line conservative but hardly extreme group. Both the USTP and the CCC tend to be Buchananite in their orientation, both are entirely law-abiding, and neither has ever been accused by any responsible source of harboring any sympathy for political violence or engaging in it. The same is true of the John Birch Society. One may agree or disagree with their versions of conservatism and their political views, but to place them in the same category as Timothy McVeigh or the National Alliance is clearly irresponsible.

YET THIS STYLE OF SCHOLARSHIP is not untypical of the SPLC's products; and the man behind the center, Morris Dees, enjoys a long track record of similar distortions, as well as some amazingly high financial returns from it. In 1988, the *Progressive*, hardly a magazine of the far right, reported that Dees was raking in some $5 million per year, "about twice as much as [the SPLC] manages to spend," and *USA Today* reported in 1996 that the SPLC is "the nation's richest civil rights organization" with assets of $68 million. In 1993, the American Institute of Philanthropy ranked the SPLC as the fourth least-needy charity in the country. "We're interested in much more than poverty," Dees told the *Progressive*, and his center has the bank account to prove it.

Originally a direct-mail fundraiser by profession, Dees sold his marketing firm in 1967 for a tidy six to seven million dollars and then headed for the big time in civil rights. With partner Joe Levin, he set up the SPLC in 1971, won the support of black Georgia civil-rights activist Julian Bond, and embarked on the lucrative crusade in which he has been enlisted ever since. He raised funds for George McGovern in 1972 and made use of the McGovern mailing list afterward. In 1975, he raised money for the defense of black convict Joan Little, accused of stabbing a jail guard in North Carolina, and an anti-death penalty project in Georgia with lawyer Millard Farmer. The two men quarreled over money, and Dees wound up settling with Farmer for about $500,000. "I was naive at first," Farmer told the *Progressive*. "I thought he was sincere. I thought the Southern Poverty Law Center raised money to do good for poor people, not simply to accumulate wealth."

Farmer's characterization of the SPLC is not unique among Dees' former associates (Dees says of Farmer, "He's a fool"), but the former marketing wizard was now launched on a new career. He was soon raising funds for Jimmy Carter, though Carter wasn't far out enough for Dees, who says, "You can't fire them up with a middle-of-the-road cause or candidate. You've got to have someone who can arouse people." If Carter wasn't useful for harvesting the cabbage, however, Ted Kennedy and Gary Hart were better, and Dees raised funds for both of them in the 1980's.

But it was still bush league. It wasn't until Dees discovered the Ku Klux Klan and the far right that he really started munching in the high-dollar pastures. In 1980, Dees founded a research institute and newsletter called *Klanwatch*, which kept an eye on the Klan and related (and not a few unrelated) political groups. Even some of his own associates argued that the Klan, at that time with a national membership of less than 10,000, wasn't worth the trouble, but Dees understood where the money was buried. "The money poured in," reported Randall Williams, the original director of *Klanwatch*, who, like so many of Dees' other associates, departed in disgruntlement. "We developed a whole new donor base, anchored by wealthy Jewish contributors on the East and West Coasts, and they gave big bucks." But Dees soon found that if you start watching the Klan, the Klan might start watching back. In 1983, Klansmen firebombed the center's offices in Montgomery, an attack that helped bring in even bigger bucks.

By 1994, Dees was reported to be hauling in a personal salary of $136,000 a year, but even liberals who supported his causes were starting to wonder. In the same year they began to notice that, for all his fulminations against "white racism," Dees' center employed no black attorneys and that only one of its eight department managers was black. The *Montgomery Advertiser* reported that since the center's opening in 1971 it had hired 14 lawyers, only two of whom were black, and both left the organization unhappy. One of the former black lawyers, Christine Lee, a Harvard Law School alumna who interned at the center in 1989, told the *Birmingham News* in 1994, "I would definitely say that there was not a single black employee with whom I spoke who was happy to be working there." Dennis Sweet, also a former black staff attorney for the center, said, "overall blacks were treated in a patronizing manner" at the offices. Others reported hearing racial slurs and epithets used there.

Richard Cohen, the SPLC's legal director, responded to such claims by saying that the center did indeed have two black directors on its board and that 14 percent of its legal staff has been black. Dees himself was perhaps less eager to placate those who were suggesting that the czar of antiracism was himself less than egalitarian. "We don't have black slots and white slots," Dees told the *Birmingham News*. "Probably the most discriminated people in America today are white men when it comes to jobs because there are more of those who had more education opportunities and who the test scores show are scoring better and on paper look more qualified. That's why you have so many reverse discrimination cases around."

But even aside from his own views of blacks, Dees remains a controversial figure even on the left. Not only has Millard Farmer challenged his good faith, along with former employees who insinuate racial bias, but so have civil-rights workers in other organizations. "He's a fraud who has milked a lot of very wonderful, well-intentioned people," Stephen Bright told *USA Today* in 1996. "If it's got headlines, Morris is there." In 1994, Dees was instrumental in establishing a $700,000 Civil Rights Memorial outside his offices in Montgomery, but when civil-rights veteran Ralph Abernathy showed up at the dedication ceremonies, Dees seized him by the arm, told him he wasn't welcome, and ordered him to get off his property. Abernathy's autobiography, which recounted the irregular sexual life of Martin Luther King, Jr., had excited controversy among civil-rights supporters, and Dees released a statement afterward saying that Abernathy's attempt to put himself on the stage at the dedication ceremonies was "a ploy . . . a cheap effort to bring himself back into the fold of the civil rights community after selling out its most honored hero."

WHATEVER THE TRUTH about the authenticity of his commitment to racial equality, there is no doubt that Morris Dees has made himself more than a nuisance to white racialists of the extreme right. In 1987, he sued the United Klans of America on behalf of a black lynching victim and won seven million dollars in damages. The *Montgomery Advertiser* series on Dees reported that only $52,000 of the money won actually went to the mother of the Klan's victim; the rest wound up in the center's bank accounts. His legal actions against white racialist Tom Metzger in 1990 virtually ruined Metzger and put his White Aryan Resistance out of business by winning $12.5 million in damages, and Dees has launched similar lawsuits against other activists. The late Robert Matthews, the neo-Nazi who founded the secret terrorist group called "The Order" in the 1980's and who carried out the murder of Colorado radio host Alan Berg and the armed robberies of several armored cars, reportedly placed Dees' name next on the hit list after Berg's; Matthews, who was killed in a gunfight with federal agents in 1984, wanted to kidnap Dees and skin him alive—a sentiment that may be shared, for different reasons, by some of Dees' former employees and business associates.

But there's no doubt also that Dees' "research" is of questionable value. Not only does he seem to specialize in scare sagas like the ones told in "Two Years After," but he is often just plain wrong. Last year during the black church burning hysteria, Dees' *Klanwatch* listed five acts of arson against black churches in Kentucky in 1990, but it never mentioned that the supposedly "white racist" fires were in fact set by a black man.

DEES WAS ONE OF THE FIRST to make capital out of the supposed rash of church burnings. At a news conference in Washington in April 1996, Dees announced that "Those [black] churches that have been burned in the South were certainly burned by racists." In fact, as subsequent investigations by the Associated Press, *USA Today*, and other mainstream newspapers showed, there was no wave of church arsons at black churches by white racists. The AP reported that "A review of six years of federal, state and local data by the Associated Press found that arsons are up—at both black and white churches—but with only random links to racism. Insurance industry officials say this year's toll is within the range of what they would normally expect."

Fewer than 20 of the 73 fires at black churches that the AP counted since 1995 can be blamed on "racism." Five states have suffered more fires at white churches than at black churches, and in only 12 to 18 fires is there any evidence of racial motivations. In nine fires at black churches, black suspects have been named, while in six other church burnings, white churches were also targets of the arsonists. *USA Today* found that 64 black churches in Southern states had been burned since January 1, 1995. Of these, eight were torched by black suspects and one by a racially harmonious trio of two whites and one black. Only three cases involved whites who might have had racial motives. In Morris Dees' own state of Alabama, the state fire marshal investigated all 15 fires at black churches in his state since 1990 and found no evidence of racial motives in any of them. Earlier this year a federal task force appointed by President Clinton to investigate the church burnings concluded that white racists were responsible for such acts of arson in "only a handful of cases."

Yet whatever the value of Morris Dees' scholarship and whatever motivates him to sponsor it, he continues to bamboozle much of the media. Reporters eager for a sensational story can always rely on the friendly experts at the SPLC to feed them uncorroborated details about the numberless white legions lurking in the cow pastures and munching sandwiches down at their klavern meetings, all the while plotting more "biochemical terrorism," more church burnings, and more bombings of federal buildings. One who fell for the "Two Years After" tale was Abe Rosenthal of the *New York Times*, who, in a column of June 20, 1997, titled "The Traitor Movement," swallowed the whole whale. Rosenthal regurgitated the "Two Years After" account almost verbatim, including the "858 groups" operating in "every state." Rosenthal used the SPLC propaganda to call for federal legal measures against the "hate groups," "militias," and the "Patriot Movement" as a whole.

Even the federal government pays a lot of attention to Morris Dees, though not perhaps in the way it should. The Special Operations School Catalog of the U.S. Air Force for 1997 lists a course entitled "Dynamics of International Terrorism," taught at the classified level of "Secret." One of the guest lecturers in the course was Joe Roy, the current editor of *Klanwatch*. What exactly Mr. Roy instructed the flyboys on is not clear, but the course did include a section on the terrorist "Threat in the United States," and since *Klanwatch* and the SPLC confine their researches on terrorism and extremism to these shores, it is likely that is what Mr. Roy lectured about.

And that, for all his apparent flaws, both personal and professional, is Morris Dees' real use. As Randall Williams, the original director of *Klanwatch*, told the *Progressive* in 1988, "We were sharing information with the FBI, the police, undercover agents. Instead of defending clients and victims, we were more of a super snoop outfit, an arm of law enforcement." Outfits like that run by Dees can carry out intelligence-gathering operations on law-abiding targets that government intelligence and law-enforcement agencies do not have the funds, the time, the brains, or the *authority* to investigate; they can keep and disseminate the information they gather and develop it (or embroider it) in any way they please, and they can then convey that information (or disinformation) to government investigators and to students in government-sponsored seminars, leading them to believe in the existence of a far-reaching and dangerously violent underground of right-wingers that must be stopped before it kills again.

Dees' own conception of the threat, which he unbosomed on National Public Radio's *Diane Rehm Show* this spring, makes clear what the real target of his crusade is: "Fear of immigrants; fear that the government has grown too large, overregulation, over-taxes, is insensitive to people; fear of the English language not being the mother language of the country—in other words, multiculturalism, fear of giving gay people more rights; fear of the laws that allow abortions." In Dees' mind, and in the minds of those on the left and in the federal leviathan who listen to him and share his authoritarian and paranoid phobia of anyone who dissents from their agenda, those who share and act on these "fears" to try to stop immigration, halt abortions, end multiculturalism, promote economic liberty, and reduce taxes, even if they do so peacefully and democratically, are no less a danger than Timothy McVeigh and the fictional terrorists of *The Turner Diaries*. As the new federal police state continues to evolve, men like Morris Dees and his associates can expect to serve as its demonologists-in-chief and head witchfinders, and to enjoy a bright and prosperous future advising, informing, and shaping the reign of terror that they want to unleash against the dissidents of the right.

The South and the New Reconstruction

Michael Hill

ATLANTA, THE SELF-STYLED "capital of the New South" and the host of the annual debauchery known as "Freaknik," was a natural to host the 1996 Olympics. The quadrennial event has become a giant block party to celebrate the smiley-face aspects of the New World Order: universal brotherhood, multiculturalism, diversity, and tolerance. But amidst the revelry and self-congratulation, the "City Too Busy To Hate" has discovered a target for its pent-up indignation: the Old South.

The 1996 Centennial Olympics revealed the dichotomy between the two Souths. On the one hand, the New South greeted the gathering of the world's tribes with its usual boasting and civic boosterism. On the other, the Old South viewed the garish pagan spectacle in much the same way it views the annual descent of the sandals-and-black-socks crowd from Ohio—as an aggravation to be borne until it goes away.

In order to spare the feelings of international visitors, the Atlanta city fathers and ACOG (the Atlanta Committee for the Olympic Games) went all out to banish every vestige of the Old Confederacy, including the Georgia state flag, which contains in its design the Confederate battle flag. A resident of Crawfordville, the home of CSA Vice President Alexander H. Stephens, told me that when a vanload of federal bureaucrats came to scout out Liberty Hall as a potential Olympic tourist site, several of them refused to go inside, and one spat on a monument to "Little Aleck," calling him a "honky racist." Needless to say, politically incorrect Liberty Hall was not put on the official Olympic pilgrimage.

But traditional Southerners fought the international octopus in their own small ways. A lawsuit was filed against the Atlanta suburb of Roswell, which forced the city to allow Confederate reenactors to march in a parade escorting the Olympic flame. In the rural north Alabama hamlet of Battleground, named in honor of Gen. Nathan Bedford Forrest's victory at Day's Gap in 1863, city officials were asked to remove the battle flag that waves over the volunteer fire station on Highway 159 so as not to offend the bearer of the sacred flame. The local Bubbas reacted by hoisting two additional flags over the roadside plaque commemorating Forrest's triumph. "Them 'lympic folks ain't gonna tell us what to do," one retorted.

Why have loyal Southerners come under such heavy fire from the New World Order's artillery? In part, I think, because the traditional South is seen as the world's largest (and maybe the last) bastion of historic Christianity, the last "infamy" to be wiped out. Southern Christians (the Southern Baptist leadership perhaps excepted) see in biblical scripture the mandate for a hierarchical society in which modern egalitarian notions have no place, and they view the scattering of the nations at the Tower of Babel as an indictment against the United Nations. The Bible is also one of the sources of the Southern view of the nation as an organic expression of loyalty to kith and kin. The impersonal modern state, like the universal rights of man it is supposed to protect, derives from the delusion of human perfectibility. The Southern identity—largely Anglo-Celtic—is not dedicated to any proposition; it is bound up in that vast memory of the blood captured so well in Stark Young's *So Red the Rose*. Young's protagonist, Hugh McGehee, tells his son as he sends him off to join the Confederate Army: "It's not to our credit to think we began today and it's not to our glory to think we end today. All through time we keep coming into the shore like waves—like waves. You stick to your blood, son; there's a fierceness in blood that can bind you up with a long community of life."

The social and political ideals of the traditional South contrast markedly with those of the North, and especially New England. While the Southerner held fast to biblical inerrancy, allegiance to place and kin, patriotism, local self-government, and social hierarchy, the Yankee embraced individual conscience, universalism, nationalism, centralism, and egalitarianism. Lincoln's and the black Republicans' victory in 1865 assured that the North's worldview would prevail, at least for a while. The first chapter in the story of the destruction of the Old American Republic indeed was written at Appomattox Courthouse. Nonetheless, for the better part of the last [in 1997] 130 years, Southerners have tried hard to "get over it" and be good Americans, despite the destruction of the social and political arrangements left them by their forefathers.

ONE AREA OF NATIONAL LIFE in which Southerners have been willing to participate for the last century has been the Armed Services. They have shed their blood far out of proportion to their numbers in the general population. The most highly decorated American soldiers in World War I and II, respectively, were Alvin York of Tennessee and Audie Murphy of Texas, and our most feared World War II general, George S. Patton, was descended from a Confederate soldier.

But in more recent days, the military's attitude toward Southerners has changed. For example, many Southerners in the Armed Services, as exemplified by Michael New of Texas, are apprehensive of America's loss of national sovereignty to transnational agencies. New's tribulations have been well documented, and I shall not go into them here. What I would like to show, however, is a disturbing anti-Southern trend within America's mercenary Armed Services.

When it is not bombing the people of Iraq into submission or aiding Muslims against Christians in the Balkans, the New American Military is busy preparing to be the global peacekeeper of the 21st century. In an article entitled "Ambushing the Future," published in the April 1995 issue of *Special Warfare*, an official publication of the John F. Kennedy Special Warfare Center at Ft. Bragg, Dr. James J. Schneider reveals some of the darker purpose of this seemingly noble effort. The tone is set in the preface written by Maj. Gen. William F. Garrison. "We may forget," chides Garrison, "that our own Civil War [*sic*] was a nationalist-separatist conflict; that during Reconstruction our Army performed peacekeeping, nation-building, and humanitarian-assistance missions; and that our Indian wars were a long-running ethnic conflict."

Schneider takes the same lesson from the past, hopping from one cliché to another. Schneider is not sallying forth into never-never land. "The future," he says, "is already before us, hidden in a fog. It is like a living thing that we must seek out, discover, and ambush," and to set his ambush, he turns to the South's past: Reconstruction. Citing the Army's role as a domestic counterterrorist force arrayed against the Ku Klux Klan, the Redeemers, and other manifestations of white Southern resistance, Schneider and others of his stripe foresee a time in the coming century when U.S. Armed Forces could be profitably employed against "Good Ole Boys with guns" foolish enough to believe that the Bill of Rights still means what it says.

Should Schneider's view of the future role of the military prevail (as it seems to be doing), then not only the present-day South but much of the rest of the world is likely to get a taste of what "peacekeeping" really means. He contends that "for the Army and for Special Forces, the future will be a period of global reconstruction" under the auspices of the United Nations. This "global reconstruction," he reveals, will be sold to a gullible public through the international media. "Today the media knows no national boundaries," he writes, "it is international. The media is a powerful lever of public opinion. Through its global extension, universal presence, and speed-of-light technology, today's media can change world opinion in a matter of hours. As a consequence, local issues become laden almost immediately with global implications and therefore *become U.N. problems*" (italics added). In light of the well-publicized black church burnings and the pipe-bombing of Atlanta's Olympic Centennial Park, one wonders how long it will be before the U.N. blue helmets descend upon the South in their rainbow-colored paddy wagons to haul away scores of redneck terrorists to stand trial before The Hague Tribunal.

It is clear that the South and its long-standing patriotism are the main obstacle to the implementation of policies that subordinate the United States Armed Services to the interests of globalists. Southerners have in large part provided the backbone of the American military since the founding of the Republic. One might claim that the American Empire has been built on the bones of Southerners, just as the British Empire was built on the bones of Scotsmen. But today the Armed Forces are conducting a campaign to demonize the South, as evidenced by the Navy's attempt to ban the use of the state flags of Mississippi and Georgia in a 50-state display at a change of command ceremony in Pennsylvania in 1995. More disturbing are reports from Southern soldiers on the anti-South propaganda coming from some of their officers during basic training. One young man tells of entering basic at Fort Jackson, South Carolina, shortly after the Oklahoma City bombing and learning that the real enemy was not a hostile foreign power but domestic "terrorists" and the ubiquitous militia. A bit further on in his instruction, this Southern soldier was shocked to hear that the U.S. Army's standard example of a large-scale domestic disturbance was not the recent Los Angeles riots but the American "Civil War." The instructors pointed out that several Southern states still fly the battle flag in certain public venues, and that the flag stands for "disorder" and "treason." Moreover, Southerners are depicted as being more likely to stockpile weapons and ammo and to be distrustful of the federal government than are other Americans. This young man, along with his comrades, apparently is being brainwashed to take his place in the new Union Army that will finish the job Grant and Sherman started.

THE SOUTH IS DECADES "BEHIND" the rest of the country in accepting feminism, children's rights, and a privileged position for homosexuals. Before the South will fit neatly into the puzzleboard of the New World Order, it will have to be reshaped to rid it of these old-fashioned virtues. And perhaps this is what the New Reconstruction is all about.

With this in mind, what can traditional Southerners (and our friends in other regions) do to ward off the global demons who threaten to carry the country straight to Hell along with the rest of Western civilization? The first task is to develop a Southern consciousness based on our predominantly Anglo-Celtic roots: The Anglo-Celt (by definition someone who is mainly of Celtic descent but who speaks English) is perhaps the most despised creature on the face of the earth because he holds to an Old World Order—a sort of Filmerian patriarchy—that makes him unsuitable raw material for productive citizenship in the coming global utopia. He holds fast to the creed of the Mississippian: "A man ought to fear God, and mind his own business. He should be respectful and courteous to all women; he should love his friends and hate his enemies. He should eat when he is hungry, drink when he is thirsty, dance when he is merry . . . and knock down any man who questions his right to these privileges."

Self-protection is the hallmark of traditional Southerners of Anglo-Celtic descent, and if we are to survive, or better yet prevail, as a distinct people, then we are going to have to rekindle the spirit of defiance that burned within the hearts of our ancestors, from Wallace and Bruce to Lee and Forrest. Unless we are willing to be unswerving in our devotion to furthering the interests of our own kith and kin, we shall be absorbed into a multicultural nightmare in which our identity will be destroyed. No other ethnic or racial group in America (or the world) hesitates to defend its own. It is a vain hope that European-Americans in general will call forth the courage to develop an ethnic and cultural consciousness as a means of advancing their own interest and well-being. For one thing, there are too many outstanding historical grievances from both the Old and New Worlds that still exacerbate tensions among the various European ethnic groups. For another, Americans of European ancestry have been subjected to an effective campaign of antiwhite, anti-Western brainwashing that has rendered them incapable of defending their birthright.

At present, it appears that the best chance we have of saving at least part of our Western patrimony from the clutches of the New World Order is to raise the most recent banner of the Southern Anglo-Celts—the starry St. Andrews Cross—and hope that we can rally that particular group to serve as a nucleus for the revitalization of a general European cultural hegemony. Barring parts of the Western United States, the rest of the country lacks both the will and the ethnic and cultural cohesiveness to act decisively. Only in the South, and particularly the rural South, is there a sufficiently large population rooted in the old ways to allow for a successful movement against the forces of global reconstruction.

In reflecting on our current plight, I am reminded of the words of Donald Davidson in his 1984 essay "The Center That Holds":

We have come to the moment of self-consciousness . . . when
a writer awakes to realize what he and his people truly are, in
comparison with what they are being urged to become. . . . The

Southerner does not have to labor to learn some things. We already know, from the start, who we are, where we are, where we belong, what we live by, what we live for. That priceless inheritance is something given to us. But in the thoroughly modernized, anti-traditional society, it is not given; it can be achieved, if at all, only after long struggle. It is exactly what the apostles of the new Reconstruction, in the pseudoscientific language of the modern power-state, are saying we must not have, must give up if we do have it.

Should we fail to rally our people in the South to a defense of an historic blood-and-soil nation, we shall have had a hand in fulfilling Thomas Babington Macaulay's dire prophecy. In writing to an American friend in 1857, Macaulay predicted: "your republic will be as fearfully plundered and laid to waste by the barbarians in the twentieth century as the Roman Empire was in the fifth, with the difference. . . that your Huns and Vandals will have been engendered within your own country by your own institutions."

The defense of civilization has never been easy or cheap. If we are to succeed against the new barbarian hordes, Southerners must call forth the moral fortitude to reassert our own dominance in our own land. When the armed globalists come calling at some future time to usher us into the New World Order, then we will have to consider whether to take the good and practical advice of that fierce Southern man of action, Nathan Bedford Forrest. I shall alter his words but slightly to fit the looming situation: "Shoot everything in [U.N.] blue and keep the skeer on."

GOP Country: A Troubled Marriage

Jack Trotter

B ACK IN FEBRUARY [2007], music historian J. Lester Feder published an article in the *American Prospect* entitled "When Country Went Right." As Feder would have it, country music wasn't always as "conservative" as it is today. Once upon a time, it seems, country music was a left-leaning, "populist" American art form. Then Richard Nixon, taking his cue from George Wallace, invited country-music stars to join him on the 1968 campaign trail and was fêted, in turn, by the Country Music Association at the opening of the new Grand Ole Opry House in 1974. "Once fiercely allied with working people," claims Feder, country music "married" into the conservative movement and never looked back. It is certainly true that, in recent decades, mainstream country music has become increasingly identified with Republican politics, and that the music's fealty to its hillbilly and blue-collar origins has all too often been compromised by Nashville's craven appetite for popular acceptance (and the sales figures it generates). It is also a fact that, before the 1960's, to the extent that it was political at all, country music and its fans were firmly Democratic. But the true story of country music's migration from the Democratic Dust Bowl to the Republican Tar Pit is a tad more complicated than what Feder chose to reveal.

First of all, if I may follow Feder's lead and speak of country music as populist art, we will do well to remember that populism has always been Janus-faced. Since the golden days of William Jennings Bryan, populist movements have generally championed the downtrodden factory worker, farmer, or middling small-business owner against the interests of "elites"— usually Eastern bankers, railroad magnates, establishment politicians, or, more recently, pointy-headed intellectuals. Frequently, this defense of the "real producers" of wealth against the bloodsuckers who exploit them has taken the form of egalitarian political and economic positions. On the other hand, the "populist persuasion" (as Michael Kazin has called it) has generally been culturally and morally conservative, and especially so in the South. The most enduring motifs in country music have always been those of kinship and homestead, heartbreak and the hope of a better world in the hereafter. If country music has sometimes raised its blue-collar hackles in class-conscious anger or celebrated those it believed to be the political champions of ordinary folk, it has far more often been deeply apolitical, or, when political, atavistically so. This is perhaps because of the powerful strain of Calvinist religiosity so prevalent in the Appalachian Scots-Irish, whose balladry and fiddle playing have been the wellspring of country music since its commercial inception in the 1920's.

Nevertheless, during the Great Depression, when country music was still in its infancy (and when the distinction between "country" and "folk" music had not yet been firmly drawn), the populist impulse often found expression in lyrical laments for the poor farmer's plight in hillbilly songs with a political bent, such as Vernon Dalhart's "Farm Relief Song," first recorded in 1929, or Bob Miller's "Those Campaign Lyin', Sugar Coated Ballot-Coaxin' Low Down Farm Relief Blues." Some of Woody Guthrie's Dust Bowl ballads also possess an enduring populist pathos, though his best-known composition, "This Land is Your Land," vies with "We Are the World" for sheer, unadulterated banality. Yet Guthrie, who first achieved commercial success on country radio, borrowed the melody for that folk anthem from a gospel song, the Carter Family's "When the World's On Fire" (1930), and I would argue that the finest country songs of the Depression era are those derived from the apolitical gospel tradition. Consider, for example, Alfred Brumley's haunting "I'll Fly Away" (1929), whose vision of liberation from a life of earthly toil has been taken up again and again by country and bluegrass singers: "When the shadows of this life have gone, I'll fly away; / Like a bird from prison bars has flown, I'll fly away."

If country-music fans in the 1930's voted overwhelmingly Democratic, that is hardly surprising. After all, most of them were Southerners, and Southerners had always voted Democratic. It is equally true, however, that FDR was enormously popular in the South. In such songs as W. Lee O'Daniel's "On to Victory, Mr. Roosevelt" or Billy Cox's "The Democratic Donkey Is in His Stall Again," country singers celebrated FDR, scion of the Eastern elite, as a populist hero. But the real story here is not about populist aspirations fulfilled in the warm embrace of an invalid who understood the heartbreak and misery of the landless and the unemployed. To be sure, FDR was a master of smooth and all-embracing populist rhetoric. In his First Inaugural Address, he proclaimed his salvific mission to cleanse the temple of American civilization of the predatory capitalists who had profaned it: "The money changers have fled from their high seats in the temple of our civilization. We may now restore that temple to its ancient truths ... social values more noble than mere monetary profit." Of course, as numerous critics of the New Deal have shown, FDR's true mission was not to drive out the moneychangers but to invite them to sit down and break bread with the Pharisees of Labor, and to offer a desperate American people sanctuary in exchange for their self-reliance. This bargain with the devil culminated in the proclamation of the Social Security Act, a secular vision of the Promised Land that seduced millions who should have known better.

During and after World War II, the popularity of country music began to reach well beyond the Sunbelt, spread by fiercely patriotic GIs and the millions of Southerners who migrated off the land and crossed the Mason-Dixon line in search of work. As this slow-motion diaspora unfolded, a subtle process of what has been called "Southernization" occurred among the nation's working classes. As labor sociologist James N. Gregory has documented, by the early 1960's, native-born Southerners accounted for as much as 20 percent of the blue-collar labor force in key industrial sectors outside the South: auto and aircraft manufacturing, trucking, the steel and rubber industries, and the construction trades. To Northern cities such as Detroit, Akron, Chicago, and Columbus, and to Los Angeles, San Diego, and Bakersfield, Southern laborers brought with them not only conservative cultural and moral values, but their religion, their love of stock-car racing, and their music. Bobby Bare's plaintive 1964 ballad "Detroit City" articulates the powerful nostalgia for the South that these laborers left behind:

> 'Cause you know I rode a freight train north to Detroit city,
> And after all these years I find I've just been wasting my time.
> So I think I'll take my foolish pride
> Put it on a southbound freight and ride
> Back to the loved ones
> The ones I left behind.

But most of them never did return; they remained and spread their influence beyond the "Little Dixies" where they first congregated. Over time, country music became the musical voice, not just of the South, but of the American working classes, which, in turn, became increasingly conservative during this same period, years before the "right" turn that Feder describes.

THIS SOCIOLOGICAL and demographic development, though it is only one of several factors, strongly contributed to the eventual embrace of Republican politics by country music and its growing congregation of listeners. Equally important were changes in the agenda of the Democratic Party and the dawning perception among significant numbers of its traditional blue-collar constituency that the interests of the working man were no longer the party's first priority. Big Labor was increasingly seen as bloated and corrupt, its politics virtually indistinguishable from those of a federal bureaucracy committed to a radical civil-rights agenda that seemed to threaten blue-collar job security as well as the integrity of working-class neighborhoods. Opposition to federally mandated busing and massive welfare taxation were rampant among Northern blue-collar Catholics, who needed no instruction from Southerners to recognize that their traditional way of life was in danger. By 1968, with George McGovern's embrace of campus flag-burners—not to mention feminist bra-burners—the Democratic abandonment of its traditional base was a *fait accompli*. Into this electoral breach stepped Governor Wallace, achieving significant Northern victories in his 1964, 1968, and 1972 bids for the presidency, flanked by country-music stars such as Tammy Wynette and Webb Pierce.

Country music was a barometer of the changes transforming the American political and social landscape in the 1960's and early 70's. When Merle Haggard recorded "Okie From Muskogee" and "The Fightin' Side of Me" (both in 1969), the response was overwhelming. What Nixon was calling the "Silent Majority" found its anthem in "Okie," for, by then, country music was no longer just hillbilly music; it had been discovered by millions of middle-class Americans as well, hard-working suburbanites for whom the drug-induced excesses of rock music had no appeal. Appalled at the televised spectacle of the "free love" generation running amok on college campuses spewing anti-American hatred, they felt vindicated by Haggard's reactionary anger, just as their resentment of those who refused to work found an outlet in Guy Drake's 1970 hit, "Welfare Cadillac." The swelling ranks of country-music fans also supported the war in Vietnam, if only as a matter of national pride. Arguably, though, they were duped by the so-called domino theory, just as their predecessors had been by the Social Security scam of the 1930's, and duped yet again by Nixon's adoption of the populist rhetoric of Wallace, shorn of its blue-collar bellicosity.

Certainly, after 1968, country-music fans and evangelical Christians have been the core constituency of a Republican populism, which, though it draws upon millions of blue-collar voters, is largely a middle-class phenomenon. This is a cultural and moral, rather than economic, populism combined with a traditional Republican emphasis on deregulation, the "free market," and reductions in Big Government. As readers of *Chronicles* are well aware, however, under the Reagan and Bush administrations, the federal government has continued on an expansionist course, while the evangelical moral agenda has amounted to little more than pious window dressing. Nonetheless, Nashville has been only too happy to supply the soundtrack to this supersized cozening of the American people. The list of Nashville luminaries who have performed at Republican election rallies, or provided endorsements and/or contributions to Republican candidates, is a long one, but includes (just to name a few) Darryl Worley, Tanya Tucker, Sara Evans, Brooks & Dunn, Lee Ann Womack, Travis Tritt, Alabama, Loretta Lynn, Ricky Skaggs, Lee Greenwood, Reba McEntire, George Jones, George Strait, Hank Williams, Jr., and Wynonna Judd. (For the reader who does not follow country music, every singer on this list is a top-drawer country act.)

Endorsements are just the tip of the iceberg. Most of these stars are promoted by a miniscule band of Nashville producers who are themselves, with a few notable exceptions, Republican stalwarts. Moreover, most of the more than 2,000 country-music radio stations nationwide are owned by a few media conglomerates, including Cox Radio, Cumulus, and—the most powerful—Clear Channel, which also controls a huge share of the "conservative" talk-radio format (Limbaugh, Beck, and Hannity, among others) and is a well-known contributor of "soft money" to Republican campaign coffers. Clear Channel is widely believed to have conspired with Republican operatives to orchestrate the boycott of the Dixie Chicks after the March 2003 debacle in London, when radio stations from coast to coast refused to provide the Chicks airtime. Little conclusive evidence has emerged either to confirm or deny these persistent claims of behind-the-scenes shenanigans. Clear Channel executives, of course, claim that the stations' DJs acted independently in response to hordes of angry country-music fans who had "spontaneously" risen from their Barcaloungers by the tens of thousands to demand the silencing of Natalie Maines. Well, if you believe that, I've got a piece of oceanfront property in Arizona that might interest you. It is doubtful that Clear Channel DJs have ever acted independently.

Over the course of many decades, then, populist sentiment has been shamelessly exploited by both wings of the American political duopoly, which, like the vampires they are, require periodic infusions of populist blood to maintain their factitious vitality. What has changed in country music since the 1960's, however, is that Nashville's insatiable appetite for profit and respectability has driven a marketing agenda focused on capturing an ever-larger share of the middle-class consumer demographic. Thus, it has been willing to sacrifice its rural and blue-collar fan base in quest of a more lucrative suburban audience, one far more likely to drive SUVs than pickup trucks. That this has coincided with GOP electoral strategy since 1968 is, you might say, a happy coincidence for both. Country music's transformation is perhaps best symbolized by the 1974 relocation of the Grand Ole Opry from the hallowed Ryman Auditorium in downtown Nashville to a site adjacent to a theme park, Opryland, just down the road from Andrew Jackson's Hermitage. Before the theme park was shut down in 1997 and rebuilt as a shopping mall, country-music fans and their families could take a cruise on the *General Jackson Showboat* or a wild ride on the Rock and Roller Coaster, stuff themselves silly on corn dogs, then enjoy a show at the new Opry House. There, they could (and still do) listen to performances by traditionalist entertainers, chuckle over folksy Martha White radio commercials, and find themselves reassured by the illusion that country music is still, well, country. Meanwhile, by the mid 90's, the real action was unfolding in huge concert venues and stadiums across the country, where the likes of Garth Brooks and Shania Twain were strutting their stuff before adoring new metropolitan fans who hadn't the faintest idea that what they were listening to was about as country as MTV. And those same neophytes were buying up CDs in numbers that made Nashville record-company executives wet their well-pressed trousers with sheer delight.

Today, the country-music airwaves are dominated by youngsters who grew up listening to the Eagles and Southern rock, and, though they profess their admiration for Hank and George and Loretta, their music is often little more than pop music with a twang—the perfect soundscape for Republican campaign rallies. For the traditionalist who dares to tune in in the hope of hearing an oldie such as Lefty Frizzell's "I Can't Get Over You to Save My Life," there ain't no satisfaction to be had. Instead, he will find that the wailing steel guitars of the past have all been buried beneath a sonic wall of synthesized, guitar-driven, neo-honky-tonk dreck. Of course, there are still some authentic country singers who somehow make the charts. George Strait has, astonishingly since the late 1970's, continued to produce a splendid New Traditionalist country sound. More recently, Lee Ann Womack has proved that honky-tonk angels still cheat. (Listen to her 1998 "I'd Rather Have What We Had," and get your hanky out.) And then there's the young Gretchen Wilson, who sometimes sounds like a girl truck driver jacked up on little white pills, but whose recent duet with Merle Haggard, "Politically Uncorrect," is about as country as it gets. These are exceptions to the Republican rule in Nashville, however, where anything that might upset the soccer moms is generally verboten.

It is likely that, for the foreseeable future, Nashville's low-rent rendezvous with the Republican Party will continue. After all, the party and the producers are stalking the same demographic. But there are some signs of revolt. Back in 2004, a group of Nashville producers and performers formed an organization called the Music Row Democrats and supported the failed

Kerry bid for the presidency. Somehow, they were under the impression that Kerry would, if elected, prove to be a more reliable advocate of the concerns of "ordinary Americans" than George W. Bush has proved to be. (Such delusions suggest either rank ignorance or desperation.) Still, there are Democrats in country music—a sizable number, in fact. Emmylou Harris, the queen of traditionalist singers, regularly campaigns for Democratic causes, as does Rodney Crowell, one of Nashville's best songwriters. Willie Nelson, a longtime associate of Jimmy Carter, does his thing for the farmer, while the Bush-obsessed Steve Earle badmouths the Republican "fascists" at every opportunity. (According to Republican speechwriter Mike Long, Earle "was a great musician until he decided to become the pet monkey of the New York cocktail scene.") Toby Keith himself, whose "Courtesy of the Red, White, and Blue" (2002) promised to "put a boot" in the posterior of terrorist coddlers, claims to be a lifelong Democrat. But even if Nashville were to sue for D-I-V-O-R-C-E and get herself a blow-dried Democratic bedmate, it's hard to tell whether much would change.

It's Hard Times, Cotton Mill Girls: Manufacturing, Gone With the Wind

Tom Landess

HISTORIANS TEND to make the same argument: The South lost the Civil War because its economy was agrarian rather than industrial, with too few munitions factories to supply Confederate troops with weapons and too few textile mills to clothe them. According to these same historians, the postbellum sharecropper system proved to be an economic disaster, in part because it was grounded in agriculture. Only when the South turned to industry in the late 19th century did she begin to live for the first time. Color flooded into her cheeks. She was able to get her hair done and buy a couple of new dresses. Looking at herself in the mirror, she asked, "Why didn't I do this before?" The textile industry in the Carolinas is routinely cited as the best example.

Such historical accounts illustrate the degree to which the ideology of industrialism has wormed its way into the soul of the nation, as if Southern farms were never prosperous or even self-sufficient and all antebellum women went around wearing ragged dresses made from flour sacks, their hair perpetually in tangles.

At the beginning, the rise of the textile industry in the South primarily enriched Northerners. Eventually, Southerners scraped up enough capital to get into the game—or else, like Confederate Capt. John Montgomery of Spartanburg, secured the backing of New England investors.

The Northerners did not come South to save the conquered region from hoeing and plowing in the hot Southern sun. They came for the same reason 21st-century manufacturers have begun moving their operations to Mexico and other Third World countries: cheap land, cheap labor, and few legal restrictions. The South had no child-labor laws in the 19th century, and New England mill owners preferred to hire children because they were more submissive, cheaper, and less likely to strike.

Sarah Norcliffe Cleghorne, a New England Quaker, wrote a memorable quatrain on this subject.

The golf links lie so near the mill
That almost every day

The laboring children can look out
And see the men at play.

By the 1830's, the trade-union movement had begun to take hold in the Northeast; and, from the beginning, unions criticized child-labor practices (though not necessarily out of humanitarian concern). In 1836, Massachusetts outraged local mill owners by passing the first child-labor law, which required children under 15 working in factories to attend school at least three months out of the year. In 1842, the state crossed the line between responsible government and zealotry by restricting the workday of children to ten hours.

Small wonder that, after the War Between the States, New Englanders saw in such states as South Carolina an oasis of half-starved children and few restrictive laws. With these optimum conditions, the textile industry blossomed in the Piedmont. In 1880, there were 14 mills in South Carolina. By 1920, there were 184, employing over 55,000 workers. And by 1925, the state boasted more mills than Massachusetts or any other state.

In order to lure folks down from the mountains, mill owners built entire villages for workers, the rent for each unit determined by the number of rooms. Lined up in rows on both sides of the street, the wood-frame houses were identical: Each was identically tiny, painted an identical off-white, its clapboard siding the color of unginned cotton. Each had an identical front porch almost too narrow to accommodate a metal glider comfortably, and the identical front lawns were so small they could easily be mowed in five minutes. Though mill houses were not in the backyards of owners, they were hauntingly reminiscent of the slave quarters. If these workers were not postbellum slaves, they were the Mexicans of the late 19th century.

IN THE SOUTH, the mills once again favored the hiring of children. In the late 1930's, Fannie Miles told a WPA interviewer about her first day at work in a textile mill:

> I was just nine years old when we moved to a cotton mill in Darlington, South Carolina, and I started to work in the mill. I was in a world of strangers. I didn't know a soul. The first morning I was to start work, I remember coming downstairs feelin' strange and lonesome-like. My grandfather, who had a long, white beard, grabbed me in his arms and put two one-dollar bills in my hand. He said, "Take these to your mother and tell her to buy you some pretty dresses and make 'em nice for you to wear in this mill." I was mighty proud of that.

Her story was by no means unique. An old folk song (or perhaps qua-si-folk song) has as its chorus:

It's hard times, Cotton Mill Girls.
Hard times, Cotton Mill Girls.
It's hard times, Cotton Mill Girls, hard times everywhere.

A couple of stanzas reinforce the message:

Us kids worked 14 hours a day
For 13 cents of measly pay.
It's hard times, Cotton Mill Girls. It's hard times everywhere.

When I die don't bury me at all.
Just hang me up on the spinning wheel wall.
Pickle my bones in alcohol. It's hard times everywhere.

This, then, was the industrial revolution historians have come to admire, the one that brought prosperity to the South and its emancipation from the torturous drudgery of farm life. Of course, children worked on subsistence farms. But that was seasonal, and they were still able to attend school for much of the year. In fact—as advocates of a longer school year now point out—a lengthy summer vacation is a relic of the nation's agrarian past, originally built into the school calendar so children could work in the fields.

Eventually, child-labor laws came South, after much finger wagging and lecturing from New England, which—by the early 20th century—had forgotten its own history, just as, in an earlier time, it had forgotten who first brought slaves to America. Strikes came South as well. In 1929, violence erupted in Gastonia, North Carolina, in one of the bloodiest labor-management confrontations of that era.

INDEED, THE WORLD the textile industry made was quite different from the agrarian world the South was leaving behind. Among other things, industry produced a substantial blue-collar class that had not existed before. The millworkers—also known as "mill operatives"—became a political bloc and were mobilized by such historically significant South Carolina Democrats as Cole Blease and Olin D. Johnston, each of whom served as governor and as U.S. senator, largely because of their appeal to textile workers.

Yet after more than 50 years of the redemptive textile industry and other industrial ventures, the region was still poor. In fact, in 1938, in the midst of the Great Depression, President Franklin D. Roosevelt called the South "the nation's number-one economic problem."

World War II took care of the Depression and the economic backwardness of the region. Today, the South is thriving—not only because of increased manufacturing but because of its expanding service economy, its financial institutions, and its tourism. Northern companies have migrated to Florida, North Carolina, and Texas to escape Northern cities, which have become dangerous and unlivable. Caught up in the euphoria of greed, Southern city councilmen, mayors, governors, and congressmen are knocking one another down, pulling hair and gouging eyes in their attempt to attract new companies to their respective jurisdictions. Members of Southern chambers of commerce have become, like ancient Jews, the watchers at the gate, scanning the northern horizon, looking for the Messiah to come roaring down I-95, driving a Lamborghini.

IN THE MIDST of all this prosperity, the textile industry has all but disappeared from South Carolina and neighboring states. In 2005, Spartanburg textile magnate Roger Milliken warned:

> Since January 2001, nearly 300,000 textile and apparel jobs have been lost—and that number does not even include the job losses from the tragic Pillowtex bankruptcy. Moreover, the United States ran a $61 billion trade deficit in textile and apparel goods in 2002. If the federal government refuses to change the flawed trade policies that generated those numbers, the U.S. textile and apparel industry is in grave danger. The government needs to act now to save South Carolina and Georgia textile jobs.

Indeed, in 2001 alone, 62 Carolina mills closed. Many now blight the South Carolina landscape, windows broken, skirted by head-high weeds— red-brick eyesores waiting to become rubble heaps. As if to mock its own fate, a textile mill in Anderson has been transformed into a dinosaur museum.

No one knows for sure why dinosaurs disappeared from the face of the earth. But everyone agrees that the textile industry has died out because of international competition, principally from China. Spokesmen demand the return of quotas, arguing that China has been able to undersell American manufacturers by using slave labor and by subsidizing their industry.

Free-market economists reject this argument. Thus, Robert Barfield of the American Enterprise Institute has said: "The textile people have seen this coming for 10 years. The government should do something about trade adjustment assistance for workers whose jobs are put in jeopardy, but I don't think we ought to re-institute quotas."

The history of textile mills in South Carolina—and in several other Southern states—gives new meaning to Robert Frost's line "Nothing gold can stay." A once-lucrative industry is moribund. Mill villages—monuments to the idea that human beings are as alike as Ford carburetors—have become ghost towns, covered by green blankets of kudzu, or else salvaged by wrecking crews.

A century ago, the New South crowd would have bet their sacred fortunes that the textile industry would last until men and women stopped wearing clothes. Today, the same bunch is hailing the advent of high-tech companies and the automobile industry. After all, for New South adherents, paradise is always just around the corner, just over the next hill.

When presidential candidate John McCain was confronted by a textile worker who complained that his children would not be able to follow in his footsteps, Senator McCain replied:

> Sir, I did not know that your ambitions were for your children to work in a textile mill, to be honest with you. I would rather have them work in a high-tech industry. I would rather have them work in the computer industry. I would rather give them the kind of education and training that's necessary in order for them to really [sic] have prosperous and full lives.

Putting aside the effrontery of publicly lecturing a father on what's best for his children, Senator McCain was up to his chin in shallow water. Like earlier boosters of textile mills, he clearly believed in the immortality of present economic conditions, the inviolability of the fragile industrial dream. He drew the wrong lesson from the father's complaint. The global marketplace is just as dicey as Las Vegas, whether the industry be textiles or high-tech or computers.

Economist Paul Craig Roberts recently [in 2006] wrote:

> The declines in some manufacturing sectors have more in common with a country undergoing saturation bombing during war than with a super-economy that is "the envy of the world." Communications equipment lost 43% of its workforce. Semiconductors and electronic components lost 37% of its workforce. The workforce in computers and electronic products declined 30%. Electrical equipment and appliances lost 25% of its employees. The workforce in motor vehicles and parts declined 12%.

The father who addressed Senator McCain saw a world disappear before his eyes, one he had taken for granted his entire life. He may have lived in a mill village; been a textile machine setter and operator since graduation from high school; fed yarn, thread, and fabric through guides, needles, or rollers; and eaten a peanut-butter sandwich for lunch. But for him, those things constituted a precious reality, his own piece of God's created order—even more so, perhaps, than the check at the end of the week. He could not believe that such fine particularities could be gone forever, stolen by people chattering in a strange language on the bottom side of the earth. He just asked Senator McCain to explain why this had happened and what could be done to bring back that lost world. He is still waiting for an answer.

The irony of this history—shorn of ideology and boosterism—should be apparent: Whatever light the textile industry brought to South Carolina and its neighbors, most of the same conditions existed that led William Blake to wonder if Jerusalem could be built "among these dark Satanic mills." From nine-year-old Fannie Miles to that bereft father, the victims are scattered across a hard century like so many stars. None of us has the wisdom to measure accurately the worth of the light against the darkness. If you took a survey, most people would vote for the light. But then, they probably never heard the children singing in high, frail voices: "It's hard times, Cotton Mill Girls, hard times everywhere."

American Historians and Their History:
Scratching the Fleas

Clyde Wilson

FOR THIS OCCASION [the acceptance of The Rockford Institute's first John Randolph Award at the Menger Hotel, across from the Alamo in San Antonio, in November 2004], I have been asked to reflect on "the historian's task" and "the American republican tradition." To do so could be a gloomy undertaking—examining two things apparently suffering through terminal illness. I shall try not to make it too gloomy.

First, let us consider that shrine of heroism nearby known as the Alamo. How should we think about it—or, rather, what is wrong with the way most Americans do think about it? We are taught to see the Alamo as one of the great exhibits of American valor. I beg to differ: It depends on what you mean by "American." The Alamo is an exhibit of Texan valor and Southern valor. If we call it "American," we might be tempted to think of the U.S. Army and then of the U.S. government, neither of which deserves any credit for the Alamo. Soon, we will have conflated the heroes of the Alamo with the U.S. government soldiers so eloquently eulogized by Lincoln, who destroyed the "Union" and founded the "nation" at Gettysburg. When we have slipped into this way of thinking, we have falsified the central story of American history by erecting a fake nationalist continuity of struggles for liberty. We have perverted the meaning of the Alamo, whose heroes sacrificed for the liberty of their land and their posterity.

The forces that triumphed at Gettysburg were still in the making at the time of the Alamo. But already, a significant segment of Northern Americans were denouncing the heroes of the Alamo, their fellow countrymen, as enemies—as violent frontier barbarians and pirates engaged in spreading the sin of slavery and stealing from the harmless Mexicans. These people kept Texas out of the Union for ten years. Texas finally was allowed to join, wisely reserving in her accession the right of secession. Fifteen years later, these same Northern forces mobilized two million men, a fourth of them foreigners, to destroy the liberty of Texas and keep her captive, as they openly boasted at the time, for the North's economic benefit. At the same time, triumphant New England pundits and German 48ers used the victory to convert

American history from what had been a story of constitutional republican liberty into the story of a Redeemer Nation leading the march of humanity into an ideal future of Massachusetts-writ-large.

So, let us be careful to know what we mean when we say "American history," lest we misrepresent both history and the republican tradition. Otherwise, we might even end up, God forbid, equating the heroes of the Alamo with imperial wars against remote foreign peoples. While I am at it, let me point out the nationalist trick of adopting from the South as "American" anything that is favorably regarded, while only disfavored things are described as "Southern." Thus, we have books on "Celtic" valor to avoid discussing the disproportionate contribution of Southerners to American heroism. We have "country" music rather than Southern music. We have Texas, when she is in good favor, denominated as "Western" and "not Southern." In fact, historic Texas has been what she has been only because she is the offspring of Dixie. The Texans of song and story are Southerners on a new and bigger landscape. Otherwise, Texas would be just another Kansas or South Dakota of sodbusters, land speculators, and Yankee schoolmarms.

AFTER ALMOST A LIFETIME of considering what historianship is, I am satisfied that what it should be is storytelling. History is about human beings, and human beings do not live as a scientific experiment, nor as a logical proposition, nor as an ideological exhibit. Our existence is a drama, a story taking place in the mind of God. Through history, we have our only knowledge of the mysterious drama of our existence, beyond what has been granted us as Revelation.

I like the delightful saying of English historian Veronica Wedgwood: "History is not a science—it is an art, like all the other sciences." Even better, one by the great English poet and classicist A.E. Housman: "A historian is not like a scientist examining a specimen under a microscope. He is more like a dog searching for fleas." Or, more seriously, we can make the same point by calling on John Lukacs's perfect definition: "History is a certain kind of memory, organized and supported by evidence." In asserting that historians do not achieve certainty, I am not denying that they may be judged according to their degree of honesty and competence in handling evidence.

If history is best understood as a story, at least two things follow. First, a story—like that of the Alamo—is somebody's story; it is not everybody's story, as those with an agenda, whether they be nationalist ideologues or multiculturalists, claim. Everybody can learn from a story, but, if it is to be real and valid, it has to be some people's story. It follows that America in our time cannot have a real history, because America today does not have a real people. There was a time, peaking in the World War II era, when the inhabitants of this vast and diverse nation-state almost mingled into one people. That opportunity is now past. The inhabitants of the United States are corralled under the same territorial monopoly of force and exploitation; they share the same bread and circuses. They are not a people, only the motley subjects of an empire. Aggregations of Oprah watchers, sports fans, and mall shoppers do not a people make. After Augustus, the story of Rome ceases to be the story of an heroic and patriotic people. The Roman people pass from sight, and the history of Rome becomes only an account of more or less evil emperors and a chaos of peoples without stories. Such is America in the Era of Bush. The future history of the last national election can be written only as a meaningless contest in which the Jocks barely beat out the Nerds for possession of the imperial palace.

What is a poor historian to do if there is no core people whose story is to be told? For certain, we cannot turn to the academy. Most of the work of academic historians today can portray the American story in no other terms except those of an abstract fantasy of oppressors and oppressed. No society has ever had more professional historians and devoted more resources to historical work of all kinds—or produced more useless, irrelevant, and downright pernicious products—than modern America. I know an historian who teaches that the great Virginians of the American Revolution were like the Taliban—presumably because they carried weapons and were not feminists. This is to reduce human experience to a paltry and partial perspective, to remove from it everything that is worthwhile and ennobling, usable and true. But this is what academic historians mostly do these days.

SECOND, IF WE ACCEPT that the historian's task is to tell somebody's story, it follows also that all stories may be told from more than one perspective—historians should not be engaged in categorical political and moral judgments. An historian should be trying to say something true and useful about human beings, and doing so modestly and cautiously. No historian can discover an indisputable truth, at least not about anything important. But that is what historians are claiming to do these days by reducing the drama of human experience to abstract, supposedly universal theory.

Now, because I am arguing the immutable variability of human perspectives on human experience, please do not accuse me of being a relativist or a deconstructionist. My text here is not Foucault. It is Scripture: "Judge not, that ye be not judged."

THE AMERICAN HISTORICAL ASSOCIATION recently gave its grandest prize to a politically correct work that was later shown to be based on fabricated evidence. Then, there is Eric Foner. Professor Foner, at the time of the fall of the Soviet Union, was organizing public statements urging Russian leaders to save the noble communist experiment by crushing the Baltic peoples with the same ruthlessness, as he put it, with which Lincoln crushed the South. Foner has been elected president of both of the two most important academic historians' organizations in the United States and is retained by the Disney Corporation as a consultant.

The sins of omission are even greater. The most important work of history published in this country in the second half of the 20th century was John Lukacs's *Historical Consciousness*. It has been through three or four editions. To the best of my knowledge, it has never been reviewed or even noticed by any of the leading academic historical journals in this country. Why? Because it lies outside of the blind alley where academic historians follow their road to perdition. By the same token, if Jesus were to return tomorrow, the news media would not report the story. As in the case of the historians, it would not fit into their prefabricated pseudoreality. If the story became widespread enough, reporters would go to work to discredit the motives and sanity of those who were testifying to it. That would be the only reaction to truth of which they are capable.

History can take many forms, but I am speaking chiefly here about its most familiar form—history as the story of the nation-state—and in its American version. This history is supposed to be objective and factual, but it is also implicitly charged with a social purpose—to sustain a community with the stories of common ancestors and their legacy. As Ernest Renan remarked: "Getting history wrong is part of being a nation." The conflating of the Alamo and the U.S. Army is a product of the nationalist history that long dominated American thinking but has now been virtually supplanted by multiculturalism. The nationalist history was fake. It was really the history of New England Yankees, and it ignored, slandered, or coopted the stories of other Americans. Early on, the "intellectuals" of Massachusetts set out very deliberately—and you can document this with great specificity—to make the American story their exclusive property. After the War to Prevent Southern Independence, their mission was complete. The proud fox-hunting Virginia planter George Washington was turned into a prim New England saint, and the heroes of the Alamo were coopted for Lincoln's war on the South. To explore how Bostonian "American" history became multicultural/"gender" history would take many pages. I will only say that the two things are more closely related than many are willing to admit, just as debauchery and Puritanism are two sides of the same coin. But at least the old nationalist history had a limited fungibility. The new history has no redeemable value whatsoever.

It used to be that academic historians were trained by immersion in primary sources. An historian might have a bias or a theory to prove, but his first duty was to absorb the primary materials and bring back an honest summary of what they had to tell. This was a pretty good rule, and I will not deny that there is still such good craftsmanship going on here and there. But academics as a group have abandoned the search for accuracy and proportion and weighed judgment. The primary sources are there to comb for illustrations of preestablished dogma, no matter how ripped from context. What is this dogma, and where does it come from? It is an abstraction about the conflict of classes. The prevailing "mainstream" interpretations of American history today are interpretations that 50 years ago were current only in the communist neighborhoods of the New York City boroughs—except that now few practitioners are naive enough to deal only in economic class conflict. Today, they wield the much more destructive weapons of race and "gender."

Back to my all-too-commonplace example of the historian who equates George Washington with the Taliban: It is a sadly true consequence, I think, of the dissolution of American peoplehood that the great Virginians of the War of Independence really are not a part of this historian's story. They are really not a part of the story of most of the inhabitants of the American Homeland Insecurity today—for whom George Washington can signify little more than a cartoon character with wooden teeth. What this historian has done is superimpose on the Virginia story something familiar from his own story—the oppressors of the Old World, the Cossacks who harassed his ancestors. But that is not all: This historian has further confused things by a false theory that human life is forever and only a story of oppressors and oppressed. As a result, the czar's Cossacks, the Taliban, and the great Virginians are best understood as equivalent oppressors. Such historianship constitutes neither a contribution to knowledge nor a useful teaching for society's young. Such, however, is the educational regime that is being dispersed today with immense resources and the prestige of the supposedly learned. Such malicious word games destroy the chance that we, or the rest of humanity, might gain wisdom from the stories of our forefathers.

Even when it is not badly distorted, academic history has become not the remembered story of human life but only a commentary on dogma. This falsifies the vast contingency and complexity of our existence and action in time and converts it into a tawdry, diminishing determinism. It poisons the community by denying its existence apart from conflicting elements. It converts great segments of humanity into oppressors who deserve only annihilation. The result is today's academic history—a weird combination of supposedly objective "social science" and romantic exaltation of favored minorities designated as "the oppressed." This history fails both as accurate record and as material for social comity. As Christopher Lasch pointed out years ago, scholars have abandoned the search for reality in favor of the classification of trivia. But it is worse than that. It is in the nature of dogma that dissenters are quickly suppressed. Conformity of opinion about what is significant and true about the past has never been as rigorous among academic historians as it is today.

WHAT, THEN, ARE WE TO DO about our stories, and about the historian's duty to tell stories that are true and useful? Our only hope is where it has always been found: in art—that is, imagination disciplined by honest evidence. It was observed long ago that the novel and history have a common ancestor: narrative. It has been more recently observed by John Lukacs that the two, where they are of the pure descent, may be moving together back to their origins. We already see much evidence that I could cite. It is not coincidence that the greatest history of the American war of 1861-65 was written by a novelist, the late Shelby Foote. Foote observed at the end of his 20 years' labor that the novelist and historian are both engaged in the same work—a search for understanding—though operating by partially differing methods. The academics do not treat the works of Solzhenitsyn as history. But how could the history of the Russian people in the last century ever be told more truthfully than by this great artist and thinker?

Henceforth, American history is likely to be only the story of the rise and fall of the imperial machinery and its masters. There is no people who can cherish an American story. However, there are some remnants of peoples with stories to tell who remain in this imperial heartland: traditional Catholics and Southerners, the real Californians described by Roger McGrath and the authentic Westerners about whom Chilton Williamson writes. Let us hope that the future brings forth scholars of art and integrity to craft and preserve for these remnants their stories. For it has been truly said that we are what we remember.

Losing Federalism:
When Did It Begin?

Donald W. Livingston

HUMAN LIBERTY has two distinguishable but inseparable dimensions: the liberty of the individual to act according to his own reason and the corporate liberty of a moral community to pursue a vision of the good lived out in institutions and traditions that bind generations. These two dimensions are necessarily in tension. The individual's autonomy can always transcend the current dictates of the community. Yet autonomy is not meaningful without the authority of an inherited culture through which it can be exercised.

Liberalisms of various kinds are inclined to see only the individual, abstracted from his moral community, as real. The task of politics, however, is to provide a system of legal protection for the liberty of the individual *and* for the corporate liberty of a valuable way of life uniting generations.

American federalism seemed the perfect solution to this timeless problem of politics. The states, as sovereign political societies, created a central government, endowing it with only enumerated powers, the most substantial of which were providing defense, making foreign treaties, and regulating commerce among the states. What was not delegated to the central government or necessarily implied in the delegated powers was reserved to the states. Individual liberty was protected both by the state constitutions and by federal authority, which created a vast free-trade zone among the states in which individuals were free to move. The states themselves, however, were the sole legal instruments for protecting a valuable way of life. What did they need protection from? The very central government they had created! The Bill of Rights was insisted upon not to protect individuals but to protect the corporate liberty of the states as distinct political societies. The First Amendment, which prohibits Congress from establishing a religion, was intended, among other things, to provide legal protection for the tax-supported churches still retained by some of the states.

American federalism was to be—and, in fact, long was—a rich mosaic of distinct political societies. If an individual found one of these societies and its laws oppressive, he could move to another. Local and regional economies flourished, and crossing into another state was often an adventure. Today, the states have been reduced to little more than administrative units of the central government. Cultural and moral distinctiveness has been flattened along with local and regional economic independence. The sterile, oversized, stainless-steel-and-glass office buildings that have become symbols of American cities and of the centralized managerial American state are faithful reflections of the abstract public soul of Americans. Only in private imagination and in private associations is an alternative vision of the moral life preserved.

The darkest warnings of the Antifederalists concerning what would happen to the political societies of the states if they joined the Union have been realized—and much more. How are we to understand this revolution? Many point to the Supreme Court as the main culprit. Through its expansive reading of the Commerce Clause, the Court has privileged economic centralization over local and regional economies and, in so doing, has rigged the rules to favor political centralization. And through perverse readings of the 14th Amendment, it has usurped powers reserved to the states and local communities under the Ninth and Tenth Amendments. Federal judges regulate law enforcement, voting criteria, and redraw voting districts without regard to the communities within them. They regulate morals, speech, welfare, and the public place of religion. To achieve abstract egalitarian goals, federal judges have coerced private contracts of all kinds; have forced children to attend schools out of their neighborhoods; and have ordered communities to raise taxes—something only the legislature can do—to meet social policies favored by the courts. Federal judges strike down state referenda and amendments to state constitutions that do not reflect their public-policy goals. They have even bothered themselves with the architecture and interior decorating of the school buildings they have ordered built and have regulated public-school dress codes and the length of students' hair.

Notwithstanding these absurdities, however, it would be a mistake to see the Supreme Court as the cause of federalism's demise. It is merely a symptom. The Court can do nothing without the support of Congress and the president. Blaming the Court encourages the illusion that, if only the Court could be reformed, federalism would be restored. But federalism is not a *legal* gift of the Court; it is a *political* gift of the states themselves. What the Court can give by a vote of five to four, it can take away by the same vote. The central government was created by political actions of the states and can only be restored by corporate state action.

THERE WAS A TIME when states were jealous of their corporate liberty and took action to protect their citizens from usurpations of the central government. James Madison, in the Virginia Resolutions (1798), argued that a state—being a sovereign party to the constitutional compact—had the authority and *duty* to "interpose" in order to block an unconstitutional act of the central government. Thomas Jefferson, in the Kentucky Resolutions (1799), went further and declared that a state had the authority to "nullify" an unconstitutional act of the central government. The case of *Chisholm* v. *Georgia* (1793) affords an example of how state-centered federalism was supposed to work. The Supreme Court ruled in favor of the plaintiff, who had sued Georgia over a bond issued before the Revolution. Georgia nullified the decision, arguing that, as a sovereign state, it could not be sued without its permission. The Georgia House of Representatives went so far as to pass a bill declaring that any federal agent attempting to enforce the Court's order would be "guilty of felony and shall suffer death, without benefit of clergy by being hanged." Jefferson also held that an unconstitutional act of Congress should be thought of as the act of a "foreign legislature" and "an act of treason against the State," punishable by death. Other states did not deny Georgia's nullification of this absurd act of the Supreme Court. Indeed, they agreed with Georgia and immediately put forth the 11th Amendment, which declared that an individual cannot sue a state without its permission.

From shortly after the first Congress met in 1789 down to 1860, states in every section of the Union frequently interposed and nullified what they judged to be unconstitutional acts of the central government.

A striking example of how state-centered federalism worked is found in the reaction to the deeply contested Article 25 of the Judiciary Act of 1789, which gives the Supreme Court appellate jurisdiction over cases in which state laws are declared unconstitutional. From the beginning, a number of states held the law to be unconstitutional. The Virginia Supreme Court heard arguments for six days and concluded, in December 1814, that Article 25 was unconstitutional. In 1830, the governor and legislature of Georgia also nullified it. President Jackson supported the state and worked to repeal the act. In 1854, the California Supreme Court nullified the act, as did the Ohio Supreme Court in 1856. The Wisconsin Supreme Court nullified it in 1854 and continued to do so up to the War Between the States. Thus, from 1789 to 1860, the constitutionality of Article 25 of the Judiciary Act was disputed, with the sovereign states themselves forming authoritative judgments on the matter in an effort to reach a true constitutional consensus. That this process was taking a long time is exactly what we would expect of a federal system based on the consent of the peoples of distinct political societies on a continental scale.

During the first 70 years of its existence, the central government was kept within the bounds of its enumerated powers largely by state interposition and nullification. After Jefferson was elected in 1800—save during the War of 1812—the central government was restrained from imposing inland taxes and had to content itself with living off tariffs and land sales, which were more than sufficient for its enumerated powers. The freedom the states enjoyed under federalism was not lost by the secession of the Southern states, for that would have enhanced the liberty of states and individuals by creating a competing jurisdiction in the form of a second union. In just this way, liberty was enhanced by the peaceful secession of 15 states from the Soviet Union, which was 70 years old when it was dissolved—exactly the same age as the American Union in 1860.

FEDERALISM'S DECLINE BEGAN with Lincoln's doctrine that the states were not and had never been sovereign political societies. They were creatures of the central authority of the Union and, thus, could not secede. Though historically absurd, this doctrine was seared into the national consciousness by war and conquest. Interposition and nullification lost their authority as instruments of civil resistance to centralization. From then on, the only question would be *which* agency of the central government would take *what* role in the protracted project (a disposition of all modern states) of centralizing power.

Lincoln took the lead, expanding the powers of the presidency through force by raising money and troops illegally. He rounded up thousands of political prisoners by suspending the writ of *habeas corpus*, and he ordered the arrest of the Chief Justice of the Supreme Court when the latter declared this action unconstitutional. After Lincoln's death, however, it was Congress's turn to usurp power by using the military to impose the 14th Amendment by force.

On Lincoln's theory that the Union is indivisible, no state had, or could have, seceded. The war was about putting down *insurrectionists* who had seized state governments. Once the pirates were removed—so Lincoln's theory went—and loyal unionists put in control, representatives of the Southern states would be seated in Congress. It is essential to the legitimacy of a unitary American state to insist on this historically and legally absurd theory because, as Chief Justice Salmon Chase would rule in *Texas* v. *White* (1869), if it were acknowledged that a state *had* seceded, the invasion would have been an unjust war of conquest. Accordingly, governments conditioned by loyalty oaths were established—a few shaped by Lincoln himself—and Southern states were included in the votes necessary to ratify the 13th Amendment, abolishing slavery.

The 14th Amendment, however, was a different matter. It reserved to the central government the power to determine who would be a citizen of a state and further declared that "No State shall make or enforce any law which shall abridge the privileges or immunities of citizens of the United States; nor shall any State deprive any person of life, liberty, or property, without due process of law; nor deny to any person within its jurisdiction the equal protection of the laws." It seemed to many that this latitudinous language could be broadly construed to consolidate all important powers in the center and, thus, destroy the states as genuine political societies, though the framers of the amendment insisted this was not their intention.

The bill proposing the amendment was introduced in a rump Congress that refused to accept representatives from the Southern states—in violation of the Constitution, which guarantees representation to each state. The bill passed the House, but a straw vote showed it would fail in the Senate. Congress voted to unseat an outspoken critic of the amendment, Sen. John P. Stockton of New Jersey, even though he had been duly elected and legally seated by the Senate. The Constitution requires a two-thirds majority to unseat a senator. The vote, however, passed by a simple majority of one. He was, nevertheless, unseated. In this dark way, the bill was sent to the states for ratification.

There were 36 states, so it would take ten states to block ratification. Ten Southern states voted against the amendment, as did Maryland, Kentucky, Delaware, and California. Congress was undaunted and passed the Reconstruction Act on March 2, 1867, which declared that "no legal state governments" existed in the Southern states that had refused to ratify, despite the fact that no change had occurred in these state governments, which had been included by Congress in the number of states necessary to ratify the 13th Amendment!

The South was placed under military commanders who were to disfranchise most Southerners who had supported the Confederacy; these were to vote on a constitutional convention, ratify a new constitution enfranchising blacks, and ratify the 14th Amendment. The bill passed, despite President Johnson's veto.

When Southerners appealed to the Supreme Court for relief, the Court claimed that it had jurisdiction only over rights of persons and property, not over the political rights of the states. On another occasion, when confiscation of property was made the basis of a suit, Congress passed a bill removing the Court's jurisdiction over the Reconstruction Acts. Weary of military rule, and fearing the draconian threats of members of Congress to confiscate property—beyond the massive confiscations already under way—the Southern states "ratified" the 14th Amendment. Without the Southern states, the ratification would have failed. However, the "ratification" was not valid, because the votes taken were not acts of legal governments—by the express declaration of the Reconstruction Acts!

There were many other legal irregularities surrounding the 14th Amendment. Ohio and New Jersey rescinded their ratifications while other states were still considering the amendment. Oregon later rescinded its ratification. Congress, however, refused to accept rescissions. West Virginia was illegally carved out of Virginia, and Nebraska did not have the required number of people for representation in Congress.

THROUGH BRUTE FORCE, the Lincoln administration and the radical Republican Congress opened the floodgates that held back the waters of centralization. During the early 20th century, it was the Supreme Court's turn to lend its hand to the protracted work of centralization. Through the Incorporation Doctrine, the Court so broadly construed the 14th Amendment as to turn the Bill of Rights on its head. Instead of protecting the corporate liberty of the states from the central government, the Bill of Rights would now protect the *sovereign individual* from the political societies of the states.

This had two baneful consequences. First, when the shape of the public sphere began to be determined by federal judges, politics and civic virtue started to dry up. Americans have become so accustomed to this regime of legalism that they wait breathlessly to see what new shape the Supreme Court will give to their public sphere. Much of the entertainment on television consists of court dramas, real and fictional. The heroes of the managerial state are lawyers, and the clergy of liberalism are federal judges.

Second, taking social policy out of the realm of politics and transmuting it into constitutional rights has led to civil discord. If I am outvoted on a question of social policy, my position remains in the public realm as a legitimate minority opinion to be pursued on another day. If the question has been transmuted into a matter of constitutional right, however, my position suddenly becomes *illegitimate*. To insist on it is to invade your constitutional rights, thereby provoking a constitutional crisis. The Supreme Court's adventure in social engineering has played a major role in wrecking the social fabric of America and perpetuating a condition of chronic civil discord.

Legal scholars, such as Raoul Berger in *Government by Judiciary*, have shown conclusively that the framers of the 14th Amendment meant only to extend basic civil rights to freed blacks, not to overturn federalism. But so what? No agency of the central government has an interest in enforcing a reversal of usurped power to states and local communities. The people themselves must *recall* those powers. What Americans must now acknowledge openly—and what some law professors are already saying—is that the

Constitution, as a federal instrument preserving the corporate liberty of states and local communities, no longer exists. If the people wish to restore constitutional government, they will need to frame a new constitution, one that will limit the central government to jurisdiction only over delegated federal powers and provide—as Madison and Jefferson urged—some sort of veto by the states to protect against inevitable usurpations by the central government.

At present, the only veto the states have is the right to vote on calling a constitutional convention of the states. The convention must be called by Congress, however, which could refuse to do so on the ground of some legal sophistry or manipulate the agenda to render it ineffective. There is no reason to think that a contemporary Congress would not be as arbitrary and violent as the rump Reconstruction Congress was. That is why, in the pages of *Chronicles*, William Quirk once proposed a constitutional provision that would allow any state to initiate a constitutional amendment that, when ratified by three fourths of the states, would automatically become part of the Constitution.

The Confederate Constitution, which was designed explicitly to limit the centralization of power, allowed any *three* states to initiate and compel a vote on a constitutional amendment. This provision was intimated in Madison's doctrine of state interposition and in Jefferson's doctrine of state nullification. Had it been in effect, at least three states would surely have challenged the Supreme Court's fantastic readings of the 14th Amendment regarding school prayer, abortion, and a host of other powers reserved to the states and local communities. Indeed, the mere threat of such a state constitutional initiative would have put a brake on the Court's arrogance— itself a reflection of the arbitrariness and violence of the 14th Amendment's origin. The fires being kindled today for Confederate symbols are consuming one of the most important historic ties to the federative republicanism of the Founding Fathers.

HIGH TIMES AND HARD TIMES

A (Pardon the Expression) Baccalaureate Address

George Garrett

I WANT YOU TO KNOW I share your disappointment that nobody you really care about and wanted could be here to make this speech. Sorry that Gary Hart is indisposed. Alan Alda was too busy and so was Gloria Steinem. As for all the others, I am almost as sorry as you are that you couldn't get Claus von Bülow or Jean Harris, Jodie Foster or Brooke Shields, Mother Teresa or Maya Angelou, the Refrigerator or James Baldwin, Gordon Liddy or Gordon Lish, Fawn Hall or Donna Rice. I am especially sad you couldn't get yourselves a Norman—Norman Mailer or Norman Podhoretz or Norman Lear, singly or as a kazoo trio. Believe it or not, there just aren't enough famous people out there to be everywhere these days. Same old faces in *People* and *W* . . .

Whoever came up with the idea of inviting a *fictional* character is either an inspired genius or a Woody Allen copycat. Anyway, here I am and I'm glad to be here, free for a while from the printed pages of a minor novel. I am not Joe Bob Briggs. Joe Bob is out on assignment. And some of you may already have guessed, on account of my preppy, slightly down-at-the-heels WASP appearance (actually, appearance-wise, if you'll pardon the expression, I am a dead ringer for the brilliant young novelist Madison Smartt Bell), that I am not Nathan Zuckerman. Sorry about that. The odd thing about Nathan is, all things considered and not excluding the success of the books *he* gets to live in, that he and his author get along pretty well. You can't even invite one without the other, and you can't afford either of them, anyway.

My name is Towne, John Towne, and I don't get along at all with my author. We aren't speaking to each other, not since he exposed me to outrage and ridicule in a novel called *Poison Pen*. Boy-oh-boy, the critics! Here's how they described me to potential readers (if any): *Publishers Weekly*—"a vulgar scapegrace"; *New York Times Book Review*—"a low-life crank"; *National Review*—"a coke-befuddled redneck"; *Book World*—"a full-time con artist, misanthrope, and lecher"; *Chicago Tribune*—"a lecherous, misanthropic, failed academic"; *Village Voice*—"an exceptionally sleazy picaro"; and, best of all, Fred Chappell's description of me in the *Greensboro News*—"a loathsome, racist, crude and gruesome creep." Enough stuff like that could eventually hurt a guy's feelings, you know? Anyway, I'm pleased to be here with you instead of back in that book hiding from critics. Thanks for thinking of me.

FIRST THING, I want to congratulate all of you who have managed to win prizes and awards. I hope you enjoy them to the fullest, if only because irrefutable statistics prove most of you will never win another blessed thing as long as you live. For most of you, this is it. The rest of you, the huge majority who didn't win anything, aren't going to change your luck out there. And no amount of weeping and wailing, praying and fasting, goals, guidelines, and affirmative action is going to change the odds against you very much. Relax. We are all mostly destined to be losers together. *I lose; you lose; he, she, it loses.* Call it a conjugation for clowns, syntax for suckers. Then try to think positively about it. Chances are you will always have next to nothing to lose. No Book of Job for you. When Death comes knock, knock, knockin', early or late, you'll be about half glad to unlock, unbolt, and open the door. And if the Idiots start trading off missiles and nukes, well, you don't have to worry about all your trophies and medals melting down. There are advantages to being a nonentity, a nobody, as Emily Dickinson pointed out a couple of times.

Of course, the great anxiety is that you can never be perfectly sure that you won't be recognized, sooner or later, and spoil your record. My (pardon the expression) author looked like a sure thing, a shoo-in to avoid and escape every known prize and award. He never figured They would go out and *invent* one just for him. Who would have guessed that the silly little parody magazine, *Poultry: A Magazine of Voice*, Second Series, No. 2 (Fall 1986), p. 6, the selfsame page whereon poet Dave Smith received his richly deserved Pullet Surprise and Charles Simic was named winner of the National Duck Award, would present *Poultry's* First Annual Forgot to Duck Award to my author?

One other thing. A lot of people criticize my bad language. I don't know where they get off bad-mouthing me. Mostly they complain about my constant use of the F–Word. Well, here I am almost halfway through this address, and I haven't used the F–Word one time yet. And I don't plan to, either. Except in that precise form. If I have to, I will use some variation in the euphemism, itself. As in: "F–Word you!" Or "Who invited this F–Word-ing guy to speak at my graduation?"

Fair enough?

Where are we? Well, you probably know where you are, anyway. Sitting out there in your rented cap and gown getting ready to graduate. Real life is waiting. Like a cop behind a tree or a billboard. About 15 minutes, on average, after you turn in your cap and gown, it's going to start to dawn on you. How you have spent a whole lot of money, yours and other people's, and, minimum, four years of precious time, to acquire a rolled up piece of paper that won't buy you a beer or a cup of coffee. F–Worded again! And bear in mind that this isn't the last time you will hear from the folks here. This institution has already targeted you as a source of funds for the future. Your name is already in the computer.

How are you ever going to earn enough money to be able to afford to give them some of it? If you are rich already, then just don't worry about it. Statistics prove conclusively that, barring the Nuclear War, which will change everybody's luck and numbers significantly and looks like a more attractive prospect every day, you will most likely stay rich or end up even richer. Numbers also prove that most of you will stay pretty much the same as you are. You will never quite realize it because you will be earning more dollars. But those bucks will always be worth less and will buy less. In the end you will be very lucky if you make as much as your old man whether he went to some college or not. Unlike him, you stand a good chance of never being able to own your own house. You will, however, make out a little better, in the long run, than if you had *not* attended college. Let that truth cheer you up every spring at Tax Season. And you can take some consolation in the fact that you will be supporting at least one other guy (more if the F–Wording Liberals come back in fashion) who may or may not have been to high school or college, but who never cared if school kept or not. Who is perfectly happy to take your money and use it to F–Word a whole lot more than you have time or energy for, to drink, to smoke Mexican Mary Jane and snort Colombian snow, to sing and dance, play the banjo, and then, for serious fun and games, to go out and yoke and mug your old, crippled grandmother. Try to be positive about this. It helps to think of the fellow (or fellows) you are supporting as being, in a real sense, your own more ethnically interesting other half or shadow self. When things get really dull, when hard labor and drudgery are all, you can pause to think of him and what he is up to, relishing the vicarious experience of it all.

I don't want to get into a taboo subject like politics, but I feel I should point out that much which you learned here is, well . . . *inapplicable.* Don't take my word for it. Read *America in Perspective* by (no kidding) Oxford Analytica. They claim that political parties, Democrats and Republicans, Dixiecrats and Progressives, Commies or Nazis, don't mean much anymore. What we have really comes down to is Right-Wing Rednecks and Liberal Pussies. Nothing in between. The RRs are invincibly ignorant and darn proud of it. They can't (or won't) find places like Liberia and Nigeria on a printed map. They can't pronounce the capital of Honduras. They are adamantly unpersuasive, and they don't care. That's a very large part of their charm. The LPs, on the other hand, are usually very persuasive (partly because they own all the means of persuasion), and their charm is just charm. Their chief domestic goal is to take *all* of your hard-earned money and give it to that shadowy fellow you have been supporting all along. Whether he will then share it back with you or blow it all on a Mercedes remains to be seen. Judging by the example of his (excuse me) Third World kinfolk, he will go for the car. LPs believe in national defense without resort to deadly force, and they are prepared to negotiate about anything. They like to give things, especially other people's things, away. High on the LP giveaway list are Florida and Alaska. The only thing RRs and LPs have in common is the desire to F–Word you and me and anybody else they can catch in the missionary position.

Speaking of which, I guess I better at least mention Feminism and The Sexual Revolution. Feminism has been a huge success. It put the women to work so guys can goof off more and don't have to pay as much alimony and child support when we move on to greener grass and younger stuff. It has also worked out that most of *them* can't ever make enough money ever to feel free and secure. If and when we want them back, they have a very powerful incentive. As for sex, the basic stuff, well, let's face it, the great advantage of the feminoid, on-top position is that they have to do most of the work.

Of course, the collapse of The Sexual Revolution is changing everything. The leaders, those who haven't had strokes or been shot or something, are praying night and day that somebody will come up with a quick and easy miracle cure for Herpes II and AIDS. Good luck to them! But, cure or no, it looks like serious masturbation is here to stay. Never mind, it's one thing that most of you kids are really good at. Cultivate a full rich fantasy life and try to behave yourself. Being an integral part of someone else's fantasy life, maybe that's the modern definition of true love . . .

WHERE DOES ALL THIS LEAVE US, except almost out of time? Since this is a (pardon) commencement, we need to end on an uplifting note. In a few minutes I am going to have to climb back between the pages of my book. At the same time you are going out into the Real World. I don't envy you. I believe there is some kind of a natural law (probably a matter of hydraulics) which keeps the *level of corruption* just about the same in every given area of human endeavor. No matter what you do or don't do, the natural depravity quotient will remain roughly the same. The Arts are an exception, attracting more than an average share of scumbags. But please remember we are an open, free society. And one good working definition of freedom is they can't make you be an artist and you don't even have to pretend to appreciate Art. Be careful, though. Best to keep your aesthetic contempt to yourself.

Let me conclude with a few words about Freedom. Since the *economic* aspect of the American Dream is long gone, except to people coming here from Latin America or other places like (pardon) Bulgaria, Freedom is the main thing we have got left. Enjoy it. We have fairly free speech. You can say pretty much what you want to, including the F–Word, provided you do not openly or seriously question any of the assumptions which grease the cogs and wheels of our society. I wish I had time to discuss some of those assumptions with you. But you know them all already or you wouldn't have come this far. You have learned a thing or two. You know how to watch what you think. That's where all serious trouble begins, with unmonitored thinking. At this late stage of your development, while you are as good-looking and healthy (even though plenty of you are as plain as pig tracks and probably feel lousy a whole lot of the time) as you ever will be, it will not occur to you to question anything important. And even if it does occur to you, not to worry and never mind, you won't know how.

Maybe you are wondering where a fictional character, a truly bookish guy, gets off making big fat generalizations like that. I mean, here I am, about as alien as E.T., trying to tell you things about yourselves that you don't even know. You want to know what some other aliens, smart and legal ones and not a bit fictional, have said? Here's Solzhenitsyn and his notorious 1978 commencement address at (pardon) Harvard: "Enormous freedom exists for the press, but not for the readership, because newspapers mostly give emphasis to those opinions that do not too openly contradict their own and the general trend. . . . Nothing is forbidden, but what is not fashionable will hardly ever find its way into periodicals or books or be heard in colleges. Legally, your researchers are free, but they are conditioned by the fashion of the day." Well, you can shrug that off. He's a Russki who never went to college and spent more years in the Gulag than I have in my book. They didn't even have TV in Siberia. No wonder he can't tell Kiwi from Shinola . . . Well, then, here's another who, even though he's a foreigner, too, had a better (British) education than any of you did. Here's V.S. Naipaul, in 1979: "The young people at the university, the ones you try to talk to, are really like old men. Their minds are closed, by television discussions, by newspapers, by their own successes." Get it? Good, but don't worry about it. Always remember that being happy is the best F–Wording revenge. Always remember the handy-dandy, accurate definition of happiness—the state of being well deceived. And I hope you will all live happily ever after.

Thanks for your kind attention. May the good Lord bless and keep you all.

Bubba-cue Judgment Day

John Shelton Reed

DID YOU NOTICE last spring [of 1992] how the national media—the *New York Times, Newsweek, NPR,* all of them—almost simultaneously began talking about "the Bubba vote"? I seriously doubt that many of these folks have actually met Bubba, much less discussed politics with him, but at the Memphis in May World Championship Barbecue Contest they sure could have.

Just before I went to Memphis, I'd spent a couple of days in Washington, reading college professors' grant applications at the National Endowment for the Humanities. Imagine, if you can, leaving earnest consideration of such subjects as how-texts-reflect-and-resist-the-emergence-of-information-as-the-form-capital-takes-in-the-signifying-environment to go hang out with the Porkaholic Beefbusters, ZZ Chop, and Pap-Paw's Pig Pokers as they cooked pig, drank beer, and raised hell. I don't like to brag, but a lesser man would have suffered cultural whiplash.

Yeah, Bubba was there in force. And Tyrone was, too. (I don't think that piece of shorthand's going to catch on with NPR, do you?) Southern barbecue has always been a fine, biracial, working-class enterprise, and it still is. In Memphis, private teams were mostly all-black or all-white, but there were plenty of each, and the spectators and some corporate and government teams were unself-consciously salt-and-pepper. We all sweltered together cheerfully in the 90-degree heat.

But I wasn't there as a mere tourist. No, sir. I had been invited to judge the barbecue. So that evening, while the competitors were applying mysterious dry-rubs to their meat and getting the coals just right for a long night of cooking, I walked up Beale Street to the Orpheum, a splendidly restored old downtown movie theater, for an orientation meeting and reception.

It struck me once again that there's something synthetic now, and a little sad, about Memphis's most famous street. Urban renewal has turned it into a sort of Potemkin village, three or four blocks of downtown storefronts surrounded by acres of parking lots. Several clubs, including a new one owned by the great B.B. King, offer genuinely good blues, but the neighborhood's tradition has been demolished almost as thoroughly as its architecture.

But that may be just as well, from the Convention Bureau's point of view. The old Beale Street would have been hard to market to most out-of-towners, because its whole point was that it was a *black* street, the heart of black Memphis under Jim Crow. When Elvis came to Schwab's department store to buy his first sharp threads, he was making more than a fashion statement. That time has passed, though, and if urban renewal hadn't killed the old Beale, the end of segregation probably would have, just the way it killed black business districts in other Southern towns. Schwab's is still in business, which is something, but its window is full of tourist souvenirs.

In the absence of a living tradition, Beale Street's entrepreneurs now try to emulate New Orleans. Since my last visit the blues clubs and obscene T-shirt vendors had been joined by oyster bars, beignet stands, and converted Slurpee machines spewing frozen daiquiris into paper "go-cups." There aren't enough drag queens yet, but my sister says they're working on it. Memphis probably needs to import some Louisiana Catholics, too: Beale Street's borderline-desperate "are-we-having-fun-yet?" atmosphere feels mighty Protestant to me.

Anyway, I'd been feeling pretty smug about getting picked as a judge, but when I got to the theater I found that the honor was spread pretty thin: A couple of hundred other judges were already there. As the seats filled up, I checked out my colleagues. Some of the black folks were dressed to the nines, but shorts, T-shirts, and gimme caps seemed to be the uniform of the day for white boys. I was almost the only one in a coat and tie, the over-dressed Eastern dude again.

As I waited, I listened to some of my judicial brethren—guys from Kentucky and Alabama and a North Carolinian from the great barbecue town of Lexington—discuss other contests they had judged. One told me that he had completed a judge-training course offered by something called the Sanctioned Barbecue Contest Network, which sponsors some 30 major contests per year. Lord knows how many bootleg, minor-league contests there are, but the schedules in a fat newspaper called *National Barbecue News* suggest that there are enough to keep you busy most weekends if you're inclined that way. (Later, talking to some of the contestants, I discovered that some folks are. We Americans can make a way of life out of some of the damnedest things, can't we?)

Listening to these guys, I began to wonder if I was out of my depth, but I was reassured when the orientation began. Obviously I wasn't the only novice. Our instructor began with the basics ("If you don't eat pork, please let us know") and moved on to matters of deportment ("Stay sober until *after* the judging") and ethics ("If your ex-wife's boyfriend is on a team, you should disqualify yourself"). He told us that prizes had already been given for the best "area," for hog-calling, for showmanship, and for something called the "Miss Piggy in Italy" contest. (One team's Miss Piggy, I read in the paper, was provided with an honor guard of Bacchae from the International Barbecue Bikini Team.)

There were also prizes in a category for "other meats," which includes everything from exotica like gator, snake, rabbit, and ostrich to chicken and beef (sorry about that, Texans). We were given to understand, however, that we were the elite: judges of barbecue, which starts with B, and that rhymes with P, and that stands for *pork*.

We were introduced to the rating scheme, told what to look for in the meat and sauce, and warned not to be impressed by how much money teams spent on their areas, cookers, or uniforms. Our instructor explained why there were so many of us. There were nearly two hundred teams, he said, some with entries in more than one of the three divisions (ribs, shoulder, or whole-hog). Each entry was to be judged by six of us, and each judge was to judge only three to six entries, because you don't want your barbecue judged by someone whose taste buds have already been seared by the competition.

Fair enough. I was as ready as I was going to be.

THE NEXT MORNING I found the headquarters tent, checked in, and put on my special apron and judge's badge. I was to be a rib judge, and "on-site," as opposed to "blind." Each on-site judge was assigned a keeper: Mine was a pleasant lady from Memphis who had done this several times before. Her job was to get me to the right places at the right times, and incidentally to rate my performance as a judge (sobriety counts, I gathered).

Waiting nervously for the tasting to begin, I talked with another judge, a man from Boston down for his seventh Memphis contest. He had taken up barbecuing to impress a girlfriend whose previous beau had been a Southerner, he said, and he assured me that he now produces the best barbecue in Massachusetts and upstate New York, which (he added modestly) ain't saying much.

At last the signal came to begin the judging. As the blind judges went into their tent, where the platters were arriving, the rest of us were led off to begin our tasting. All the fun and games, Miss Piggy and all the rest, were irrelevant now. We were down where the pork meets the palate.

Well, I'll cut this short: The worst I had was good, but the best—cooked by a team called the Rowdy Southern Swine, from Kossuth, Mississippi—was out of this world. The smell of the smoked pork made my mouth water. When I picked up a rib and examined it, as instructed, I saw a crisp brown crust over moist tender meat, pink from smoking, the color even from end to end. The meat came easily off the bone, but kept its integrity (none of the mushiness that comes from parboiling). This meat had been cooked with dry, cool smoke, and lots of patience. A dry rub sealed in the juices, but most of the fat had long since melted and dripped away. The rib tasted as good as it smelled: sweet and smoky; crunchy, chewy, and melt-in-your-mouth, all at the same time.

And the sauces . . . Well, after 23 years in Chapel Hill I've become fond of simple vinegar and red pepper. East Carolina Minimalism. It respects the meat. But, oh my goodness, there's a lot to be said for Overmountain Baroque, too—except you can't say it without sounding like an ad in *Southern Living*: "A symphony of Southern flavors: tart Sea Island tomatoes, mellow onions from Vidalia, sweet-and-sour molasses from Louisiana cane fields, and the Latin kick of peppers from South Texas. A sauce the color of Tennessee clay, with the fiery heat of an Alabama afternoon and the long slow sweetness of a Kentucky evening."

Or, worse, like a wine critic: "A sauce of great character and finesse. Bright claret color, with a complex peppery nose. Lusty full-bodied taste: tomato catsup and chili the principal notes, with a definite garlic background and hints of—could it be grape jelly? Balance sustained throughout. An assertive finish and a pronounced afterburn." (I just made all that up, actually, except for the grape jelly, which I'll bet anything was the secret ingredient in one sauce I tasted. And why not? Applesauce isn't the only fruit that goes well with pork.)

Anyway, I was pleased to find that I could discriminate intelligently among several first-rate plates of ribs. After I'd filled out my rating forms, I went back to two of the teams for second helpings and for the beer that I'd turned down earlier, with an eye on my keeper. I also had a pleasant chat with the Kossuth D.A.: Small-town Southern lawyers generally know their barbecue.

I had a date for supper with my sister that evening (just a salad, thank you), so I missed the announcement of the winners, but the next morning's *Commercial Appeal* reported that the championship in the ribs division and overall Grand Championship had gone to a team from—well, from Illinois, of all places. It was no accident, either: The same guys had won two years earlier. They graciously pointed out that they come from Murphysboro, only 35 miles north of the Mason-Dixon line, and you have to admire them for going back to basics (no high-tech cooker, just concrete blocks with a grate and a piece of sheet metal to hold the smoke in). But, still, from *Illinois*!

It just goes to show what Yankees can do when they put their minds to it. But I'll bet the Rowdy Southern Swine had more fun.

The Flamingo Kid

Jack Trotter

IT IS A TRUISM to note that H.L. Mencken, like his great vitriolic predecessor Jonathan Swift, was a thoroughgoing misanthrope. So perverse was Mencken's vision of human existence that he preferred to read *King Lear* as farce rather than as tragedy—since nothing, he was fond of saying, could be more farcical than death. But if Mencken's loathing for his fellow man prevented him from discovering some remnant of dignity in the antics of the intelligent ape, it made him one of our most acute observers of the American political scene. "Mirth," Mencken wrote in his "On Being an American," "is necessary to wisdom. . . . Well, here is the land of mirth, as Germany is the land of metaphysics and France is the land of fornication. Here the buffoonery never stops."

The "buffoonery" that so regaled Mencken was of the unconscious sort, the buffoonery of those, especially in political life, whose grotesquely inflated sense of their own self-importance provides the rest of us with endless mirth. (The honorable senator from Massachusetts is perhaps our most unadulterated contemporary [in 2005] American specimen of such buffoonery.) Yet Mencken's own satiric art was itself a kind of buffoonery, albeit of the wickedly honed and self-conscious variety, and one intended to remind us that, the moment we begin to take American politics *too* seriously, we join the parade of unconscious buffoons. Thus Mencken would approve, I suspect, of Rep. John Graham Altman III (R-Charleston District 119), a politician who, for several decades of public life in South Carolina, has supped with the scribes and Pharisees with tongue planted firmly in cheek.

Everyone in these parts remembers the "dress code" incident at the State House in Columbia, when, during the 2001 legislative session, an overzealous clerk's office in the House forbade female pages to wear blouses exposing cleavage or skirts more than four inches above the knees. Shortly thereafter, a memo was released by a group calling itself the "Men's Caucus," instructing the pages to ignore the dress code. Instead, "they should save valuable materials used in blouse construction" and consider undergarments strictly "optional." They were further encouraged to regard "the terms 'babe,' 'honey,' 'sugar,' and 'little missy' as compliments and terms of endearment."

Although authorship of the Men's Caucus memo remains a well-guarded secret, it is widely rumored that Representative Altman was one of the "handful of Republicans" responsible. Of course, virtually all the Democrats in the House waxed apoplectic over the incident, obliging state Attorney General Charlie Condon to call for a State Law Enforcement Division investigation of the matter. Well, that was a bit like using a pile driver to kill a fire ant. The not-so-surprising upshot was that, six months later, the General Assembly was compelled to hold a sexual-harassment seminar for its members. When asked whether he would be attending the seminar, Representative Altman was widely reported as saying, "I won't be able to come. I forgot to pack a dress."

ALTMAN GOT HIS START in local politics back in 1976 when he was elected to the Charleston County School Board, subsequently serving in that capacity for 20 years. Then, as now, the progressive worthies on the board regarded him as their *bête noir*, and no doubt with good reason. Altman obstructed or attempted to obstruct every politically correct piece of nonsense proposed by the board during those years. After 20 frustrating years of bickering with the education bureaucrats, Altman stepped down. Later, he expressed some of that frustration: "There are more people in Charleston County that believe in the tooth fairy," he lamented, "than people who believe in the school board."

To his credit, however, Representative Altman has continued to work tirelessly for local control of schools, for real parental involvement in decisionmaking, and, most recently, for returning authority to teachers in the classroom. Ironically, these very efforts have drawn Altman into a running battle with the organization that, traditionally, might have been most supportive. When, earlier this year, Altman signed on as a backer of Gov. Mark Sanford's initiative "Put Parents In Charge," he was opposed by the hired muscle of the national PTA. In an editorial published in a number of papers across the state, Altman accurately depicted today's PTA as little more than a PAC: "What happened to the old PTA?" he wondered. "One year [when] I was on the school board, I joined 32 PTAs and went to a meeting every week. Now the PTA is just the political arm of whatever educrat blob there is out there." Needless to say, that didn't go over well with the PTA's local defenders. *Charleston City Paper* pundit Bill Davis responded in his usual patronizing fashion: "Poor John Graham Altman just can't seem to get his mind around the concept that the PTA has shrugged off its apron and put down its sheet of cookies to knot its neck scarf and pick up a briefcase." A briefcase, indeed. Those of us who live in Altman's district are just grateful that there are some ideas that poor John Graham just can't get his mind around.

Even his most persistent detractors admit that Representative Altman's traditionalist advocacy for state and local sovereignty is genuine. In April 2005, after the state supreme court struck down a Charleston County ordinance that would have placed caps on property-assessment increases for tax purposes, Altman introduced a constitutional amendment intended to allow counties to secede from the state—at least for the purpose of tax valuation. "Property tax is a monster that is devouring our Charleston community," Altman told the Charleston *Post and Courier*. "We pass bill after bill to try and get property tax relief. . . . I was thinking of how to get us around the constitution. So I decided to take us out of the constitution." While local progressives argue that the property-tax cap was intended to protect the rich, Altman, in fact, spoke for the overwhelmingly middle-class majority in his district, whose mortgages in one of the hottest real-estate markets in the country are backbreaking and whose tax payments are eating away at their children's college funds.

While the South Carolina chapter of the League of the South has consistently awarded Representative Altman its "Patriot" designation for his legislative performance, others—blacks, liberal women, and homosexuals—would be only too happy to see him hog-tied and castrated (that is, if their cuddly views of human nature allowed them to admit to such vengeful fantasies). Indeed, sometimes Representative Altman seems to relish baiting such victim groups with an almost Mephistophelian glee. In March 2000, he joined a number of State House Republicans in opposing a proposed Martin Luther King, Jr., holiday, a measure that would make South Carolina the last state in the nation to honor the civil-rights leader in this manner. Altman, at a crucial moment in the debate, took the floor and began to quote from a biography of Dr. King that, according to the *South Carolina News*, "alleged that the civil rights leader had extramarital affairs and plagiarized parts of his college papers." Altman's point was that, while it would be appropriate to celebrate a "Civil Rights Day," King himself was unworthy of such an honor. "You can run from the real Martin Luther King," he said, "but you can't hide from him!" Enter the chorus of breast-beating accusers, maligning Altman as one of those white-supremacist bigots of yesteryear who slandered the spotless civil-rights leader out of sheer hatred for his cause. No one, not even the "conservative" *Post and Courier*, bothered to name the "biography" in question or to report honestly that the "alleged" charges against King have long since been established beyond any reasonable doubt.

A few months later, during the Confederate flag debate, Altman wrote a letter to Education Secretary Barbara Nielsen after she came out in support of removing the flag from the State House dome. "The kindest help I can offer you," he wrote to Nielsen, " . . . is to get you quickly qualified for the Federal Witness Protection Program." In response to claims that his letter could be considered a threat, Altman countered, "I'm not a threat to her. She's a threat to our children." When he learned that, to appease the NAACP, the Citadel had resolved to remove the battle flag from public view, Representative Altman managed to kill two lovebirds with one stone: "I never thought," he told the press, "that we'd find the Citadel Board of Visitors and the NAACP holding hands and whispering sweet nothings."

THE *POST AND COURIER* once characterized Altman as a "quote machine," but it is not just the lash of his tongue that enrages the politically correct and the sanctimonious; it is also his taste in lawn décor. Next time you visit Charleston, take a drive down Folly Road toward the southern end of Altman's district, and you will see what I mean. Just across from the Earth Fare supermarket, our local whole-foods Mecca where various vegans, pagans, and companion animals gather to facilitate their evolution on Sunday mornings, you will find the Altman house, where John Graham resides with his lovely wife, Charm. I say "resides," but, in fact, the place—a sort of ramshackle minimansion with peeling columns and a fake balcony plastered above the front door, situated on one of the busiest intersections in Charleston— has a desultory air of desertion about it. The only evidence that the Altmans actually *live* there are the plastic pink flamingos on the lawn. From time to time, John Graham and Charm enjoy dressing up the flamingos in cute little costumes. Reportedly, the birds were on one occasion decked out in nuptial attire. But what really riled the Earth Fare crowd was the time the Altmans painted half the flamingos black and made pointy white hats for the other half. Or so it has been rumored; I didn't personally witness the affront. One local blogger claims to have it on good authority that the event did occur. "Apparently," he writes, "[the Altmans] feel that there is nothing more festive than a mock lynching." What is truly laughable is that anyone would take such buffoonery so seriously. The costumed flamingos are really just "good ole boy" political theater. Install those same bedizened flamingos in one of our *chichi* downtown galleries, and the local art mavens would praise them as bold and provocative postmodern agitprop.

Representative Altman was involved in another piece of political theater earlier this year that brought him briefly into the national limelight. The furor erupted in April after the House Judiciary Committee considered bills intended to make both cockfighting and domestic violence felonious offenses. The Judiciary Committee passed the "gamecock" bill and tabled the domestic-violence bill—both in the same week. Rep. Gilda Cobb-Hunter (D-Orangeburg), a sponsor of the latter bill, naturally seized upon the opportunity afforded by this spectacular case of bad timing: "What we have said by the actions of the Judiciary Committee is we aren't going to create a felony if you beat your wife, partner. But now, if you've got some cockfighting going on, whoa! Wait a minute." Within hours, it seemed, a Sherman's army of women's advocacy groups had descended upon Columbia to protest. When reporter Karen Gormley of Columbia's Channel 10 News and her camera crew cornered Altman (a Judiciary Committee member) in his State House office, Gormley confronted him with the invidious comparison between cockfighting and domestic violence suggested by Cobb-Hunter. Altman's reply and the subsequent "dialogue" are savory enough to quote at length.

> Altman: "People who compare the two are not very smart and if you don't understand the difference, Ms. Gormley, between trying to ban the savage practice of watching chickens trying to kill each other and protecting people's rights in [criminal domestic violence] statutes, I'll never be able to explain it to you in a hundred years, ma'am."

> Gormley: "That's fine . . . but my question to you is: Does it show that we are valuing a gamecock's life over a woman's life?"

> Altman: "You're really not very bright and I realize you are not accustomed to this, but I'm accustomed to reporters having a better sense of the depth of things . . . "

> Gormley: "It's rude when you tell someone they [*sic*] are not very bright."

> Altman: "You're not very bright, and you'll just have to live with that."

When Gormley pointed out that South Carolina's current domestic-violence law regards such violence as a misdemeanor even on the second offense, Altman replied, "There ought not to be a second offense. The woman ought not to be around the man. I mean you women want it one way and not another. Women want to punish the men, and I do not understand why women continue to go back around the men who abuse them."

Representative Altman's "insensitivity" toward the women who "go back around the men who beat them" was, by the following day, splashed all over the cable networks and the *New York Times*. The infallibly sensitive *Miami Herald* columnist William Pitts saw the incident as proof that "plucky little South Carolina" had "shot to the head of the pack" in the competition for "Most Backward State in the Union." Of course, given the state of the Union, that's a pretty flattering distinction.

There are perfectly sound reasons to question the need for special laws for domestic violence (or "hate crimes," or "gay rights"). Unfortunately, Representative Altman failed to articulate those reasons. In the first place, domestic-violence laws rarely take into account the growing frequency of cases in which the battered woman *initiates* the violent encounter with her spouse (or "partner"). Recently, even some feminists have begun to admit that "one size fits all" domestic-violence laws fail to consider the complexity of the relationships involved. Most ominously, many such laws require that, once an incident of domestic violence has been reported, an arrest *must* be made.

In any event, in the wake of the Gormley affair and the public outcry that followed, Representative Altman came within a hair's breadth of censure by the House. To the disappointment of many, he appeared to capitulate under enormous pressure and delivered a public apology for his remarks. Whether that apology was altogether sincere is a different matter. To my ears, it sounded more like vintage Altman buffoonery. Speaking before a packed State House, he said, "I'm sorry I caused pain to those to whom I really caused pain, and I'm sorry I caused pain to anyone who might want to say 'ouch' anyway." Then he made curious reference to "some people I offended that I didn't offend . . . ," and lamented the "feeding frenzy" in the media that threatened his freedom of speech. "I don't mind dining out now and then," he added, "but I don't always like being the entrée. It's been roast pig for the last week."

Many in these parts believe that Altman's "apology" won't do him much good in 2006 when he runs for reelection. Whether Altman can do enough damage control in his own district to secure a sixth term is an open question. If he loses, the neocon Republican establishment (not to mention the Democrats) will be thrilled to be rid of a man they consider an embarrassing reminder of the bad old days when a man who battered his wife was too busy hiding from her kinfolk to worry about the law. But a victory for Altman's opponent (more than likely Charlie Smith, homosexual activist and real-estate entrepreneur, who has run against Altman twice) would be a great loss for Charleston. Representative Altman has served her interests loyally and wittily. Some would disagree about the wit, of course, but judge for yourselves. Shortly after the Massachusetts Supreme Court legalized "gay marriage," Altman was the man who coined the phrase "black robe disease" to describe the contagion afflicting judges who compulsively legislate from the bench—and that is surely a nomenclature worthy of adoption by the Centers for Disease Control over in Atlanta.

Importing Prosperity:
Out-Babbitting Babbitt

Clyde Wilson

WHEN I FIRST HEARD of the [2005 John Randolph Club] topic "Small Is Beautiful," I thought of the wonderful motto of Chilton Williamson's friend Edward Abbey: "Growth Is the Enemy of Progress." Abbey went right to the heart of the matter. The false but pervasive premise of American life is that progress and growth are the same thing and are defined and justified by increasing material wealth, which used to be called prosperity.

I would like to suggest a few contrary convictions about this matter. Not only does growth not necessarily result in progress, it does not necessarily result in prosperity, either. There is a problem with the measures we use for national and individual prosperity. Under today's conditions, the Economic Nation is an abstraction as far removed from flesh-and-blood Americans as is the Proposition Nation that supposes that anyone is an American who can sneak over the border and give lip service to a few carefully selected slogans.

Last year was the 75th anniversary of the publication of *I'll Take My Stand*, the Southern Agrarian manifesto. In a work that still commands attention, those 12 Southern gentlemen made a critique of what they called "industrialism" and its theme music, the Philosophy of Progress. They were not really opposed to progress—to things getting better. What they were condemning was what Abbey called Growth—the American commitment to the proposition that bigger is better, with no end in sight to the building of ever-more-gigantic institutions in which the real ends of human life are ever more compromised.

The picture becomes clearer when we look at *Who Owns America?*, the neglected sequel to *I'll Take My Stand*, in which Northern and British writers joined the Agrarians in pointing out, to wanderers in the economic wilderness of the 1930's, a humane path between the twin Leviathans, capitalism and socialism. They were severe critics of capitalism but, at the same time, champions of private property, which they regarded as the basis of civilization and liberty. How could that be?

They found defects of existing capitalism in two main areas: the abstractness of property and, thus, of responsibility; and a proclivity toward inhumane scale. Owning shares of stock in a corporation, which may be traded off before the end of the day, is a qualitative departure from having personal responsibility for production and payroll. As the Agrarians and Distributists saw it, ownership and work were alienated, and those who used to be our laboring fellow countrymen are now merely disposable factors of production. Capitalism had made property both abstract and too concentrated, though every sage, from the ancients to the American Founding Fathers, had taught that widespread ownership of real property was the only basis for a free and prosperous society, which inevitably was poisoned by great concentrations of wealth and the enervations of luxury.

The abstraction of ownership has proceeded much further today, when ownership has been removed several steps more from work and responsibility and is globalized—devoid of roots in any human community. In exactly what sense can we claim that a rising stock-market index signals growing prosperity for Americans, individually or nationally? What exactly does it measure? Who owns America?

The Agrarian/Distributist enemies of what they called capitalism also decried the gigantism that had accompanied its progress. Some presented hard evidence that great factories did not come into existence because they embodied economies of scale discovered by the free market. Indeed, a series of small factories scattered across the countryside could be shown in many cases to be more efficient. The overgrown, inhumane scale of workplace, living space, and mass culture that dominated American life resulted from choices—choices often made in the grip of a false assumption that bigger is always better. This assumption is not just an imposition on an unwilling people, however; it is, alas, a deeply rooted aspect of the American—or, if I may, the Yankee—national character.

The choices were made because the wielders of big capital had also wielded the biggest political influence. Alexander Hamilton's vision of government of, by, and for the wealthy had been realized. This is a central fact of American history that seldom reaches public notice. Wendell Berry has shown convincingly how big government and big business conspired to eliminate the family farm and foster agribusiness. It is equally true that the great industrial and financial fortunes of the 19th century were not created by the free market and the spirit of entrepreneurship but by the collusion of politicians and capitalists. John D. Rockefeller considered himself a public benefactor. As he saw it, he had rationalized a chaotic oil industry under his benevolent consolidated control.

He had achieved this primarily by bribing legislatures and using other slick maneuvers to gain control of the railroads, depriving independent producers of the means of distribution and forcing them into his cartel. It had little to do with the production of useful goods and services. Nobody hated Rockefeller more than the real free-market entrepreneurs who had risked and worked to get the oil out of the ground and make it useful. What kind of commonwealth is it where one Rockefeller carries more weight than any millions of us plain folk?

Rockefeller represents the American way—state capitalism. One of many strange delusions that mark American public discourse is the idea that the Republican Party is the party of free enterprise. The Republican Party is and always has been the vehicle of state capitalism—by which I mean concentrated private ownership and profit fostered and protected by government. The Republican Party initiated and fought the bloodiest war in American history to do away with free trade and free banking, to foster the mass importation of cheap foreign labor, and to guarantee that big capital would get the lion's share of the vast available natural resources in the gift of politicians. What else was the politics of Hamilton, Henry Clay, and Lincoln about? Our state capitalist economy is very far from the ideal and the spirit of free enterprise, but it is often what is meant when we hear capitalism praised or condemned.

It is true, nonetheless, that America is a great exhibit of the success of free enterprise. Because of our abundant resources and the talent and energy of our people, a vast, productive and innovative free-enterprise economy has flourished—underneath and in spite of government and big business.

WE USED TO KNOW what was meant by prosperity—a general feeling of sufficiency and ease. By that measure, we are not very prosperous. We have statistical abstractions about *per capita* income or net worth that perhaps show more prosperity than in distant times, but they also show trends that do not offer comfort to any but the tiny fraction of the very rich.

I began asking questions about progress after 40 years of viewing the condition of the people in the four Southern towns in which I have lived and others that I know about. The South has for a long time been out-Babbitting Babbitt, engaged in a desperate struggle to import prosperity by fawning over outside capital. We have flaunted our cheap resources and our cheap labor, offered special benefits of tax breaks and tax-paid infrastructure. We have even played along and flattered Yankee capitalists' pretenses of gentility and humanitarianism. One thing we actually have accomplished is to shift much of the cost of production to the local population in return for jobs with regular paychecks. It is easy to understand why we did this. Our wealth had been reduced by invasion and a century of economic exploitation by federal legislation. We were poor and without capital, and farming did not pay; and a promise of regular paychecks looked good to the local bankers and developers.

Are we more prosperous now? Perhaps we are a little more so—though, in the South, people are still paid about 75 percent of what the same job brings in the rest of the country. Perhaps the *per capita* income figures for the communities I mentioned are a little higher than they were a few decades ago. Is the community better off? There is no way of knowing, because it is no longer the same community or, indeed, any real community.

I have observed certain things about our Growth and Progress in the South. Nearly all of the best-paying and even middle-paying new jobs have been filled by people who have been imported from outside the region along with the capital, while the low-paying jobs go to the natives. Newcomers get the white-collar jobs. One does not encounter a blue-collar worker who is not a native white or, occasionally, black man. The affluent newcomers, usually calling themselves Republicans, demand public services at the munificent level to which they are accustomed and often, though not always, show contempt for all local ideas, manners, and traditions. (Let me pause in my Yankee-bashing and thank Heaven for the many good Northerners who have joined us in good faith and enriched the South throughout our history.)

The old Southern Democratic county commissioners knew of their people's hard life and were easy on taxes. The affluent newcomers have no such consideration, even though they presumably left the North to get away from the taxes their demands had imposed there. Taxation and inflation, in my observation, are literally destroying the prosperity and opportunity for upward mobility of most native working- and middle-class people.

In the county in which I live, families who have lived well off of the same land since the late 1600's have been forced to sell out because the taxes on their farmland are assessed at suburban values. In one of our South Carolina cities, carpetbagger residents of a rich gated community have demanded an undeveloped green space between themselves and the natives—supposedly for reasons of environment and civic virtue. The result has been to diminish the value of the property of hundreds of natives, property that their families settled almost three centuries ago and which is their only capital. I know also of a long-flourishing farm community that has been destroyed by pollution from one of the sought-after industries, with no compensation.

Other Southern communities that sold out for payrolls have now had the payroll (much reduced, of course) moved to Mexico. The same has happened to many Northern communities, but there is a difference: The Southern communities never had the benefit of such a long prosperous period as the North had before the plug was pulled. In some communities, Mexicans have been imported for the jobs. A seldom-noticed fact is that Hispanics are now nearly ten percent of the population in the Carolinas and Georgia, and that figure is increasing with no end in sight. I doubt that this is a sign of our economic prosperity—rather the contrary. It is certainly a disaster in every other respect.

The small is beautiful, and the big is not. In a regime in which people are interchangeable consumers and factors of production, as similar and as movable as a row of checkers, statistics about the prosperity of an individual or a community or a state or the United States have little meaning. All we can really do is protect and nourish that small and beautiful thing which is ours, if we are lucky enough to have it.

Oyster Supper

Greg Kaza

A s a nonnative from a cold-weather climate, I have observed that there are four seasons in Arkansas' Delta: warm, hot, scorching, and malarial. Another way to understand the weather in this part of the South is through the eyes of a ubiquitous inhabitant: the mosquito. They bite in February; aerial insecticide spraying commences in May; windshields are covered by July; and they breed the rest of the year. This latter point is only slight exaggeration. The weather in the Delta is so hot and humid that rice, a crop generally associated with sweltering Vietnam, is the region's main agricultural export.

The Knights of Columbus are using Delta rice oil to prepare the oysters, transported from the Gulf of Mexico, at the supper they have organized at Ss. Cyril and Methodius Catholic Church in Slovak. It is late January, and a mild breeze is blowing under a slate-gray sky. Slovak is so small that there is no traffic light, post office, or general store. The eternal debate over the relative merits of raw *versus* fried oysters has been settled. Both varieties are available to the nearly 2,500 in attendance at the all-male event. Many are dressed in outdoor gear worn to hunt duck, a popular local sport. The area is surrounded by vast farmland. There are several dozen homes and Ss. Cyril and Methodius, which includes a church, community hall, cemetery, and a building that once housed a school. A Russian Orthodox cemetery is barely visible across the horizon. Most shopping occurs 12 miles away in Stuttgart, a rice town settled by German Protestants. Catholics make up only 3.5 percent of Arkansas' population. The Delta, like much of the South, is overwhelmingly Protestant, and largely Baptist. But many non-Catholics attend the oyster supper; good food has its own special way of bringing people together.

Slovak immigrants settled this rural corner of the Delta in 1894. Recruited from Pennsylvania by a land company, they were not welcomed by all of their neighbors. One *Arkansas Gazette* headline read, "Flogging of young girls by Slavs in Pennsylvania reported" (August 7, 1894). The daily, in an editorial, warned, "Slavs welcome in Arkansas but warned to give up barbarous ways" (August 10, 1894). When measured by today's standards, the Slovaks, mostly miners and farmers, were a hardy lot. Their perseverance turned vast expanses of low-lying swamp and prairie into fertile cropland before the advent of electricity, indoor plumbing, and air conditioning. Their small community was called Slovak. It can be found on maps, 60 miles southeast of Little Rock.

Few outsiders have written about Slovak. A U.S. government document, "Slavs On Southern Farms" (1914), mentioned the community, as did Felton D. Freeman, a Ph.D. candidate at the University of North Carolina, in a 1948 article in the *Arkansas Historical Quarterly*. Freeman termed Slovak "one of the most interesting results" of promotional efforts that occurred in the 1890's. Neither article mentions the Christian faith of the Slovak immigrants. But one can observe the fruits of this faith, a legacy of five generations, by walking the parish grounds.

THE GRAVE OF MSGR. MICHAEL JUDT (born in 1876 in the old country) is at the center of the Ss. Cyril and Methodius Catholic cemetery, less than 100 meters from the church. The tombstone reads, "A zealous priest and gifted author whose works and writings are devoted to the welfare of the Slovak people in America." What manner of man was this Slovak priest who left his homeland to serve others in the name of Jesus Christ? Few clues can be found in the newspapers that reported his passing on April 23, 1942. "The Rev. Judt," the *Arkansas Democrat* wrote in its obituary, "came to Arkansas in 1926 to become priest of the church in Slovak and remained there until four years ago when ill health forced his retirement." None of the writings mentioned on Monsignor Judt's tombstone are to be found in the public libraries of Little Rock or at the University of Arkansas in Fayetteville. Apparently, the secular world barely noticed the passing of Monsignor Judt.

Yet the gifts this émigré Slovak priest left future generations are abundant in the parish's humble surroundings. Slovak has contributed a significant number of religious for a community its size. In the same cemetery are the graves of two priests (surnamed Janesko) who grew up in Slovak while Monsignor Judt served the parish. Their brother, the Rev. John A. Janesko, a priest for more than 50 years, is parish priest for Slovak and Stuttgart's Holy Rosary Catholic Church and school. It is remarkable that three members of the same family, all natives of this rural farm town, should join the Catholic priesthood and touch the lives of hundreds, if not thousands, of people who crossed their paths. Janesko sisters have also devoted their lives to Christ as nuns.

Another clue is the small wood-frame school located behind Slovak's church. It is a simple structure, utilized today for Sunday catechism. The school's cornerstone reads "1936." The Great Depression (1929-33) and a second, severe recession (1937-38) afflicted the United States in the 1930's. Unemployment was high, crop prices were generally depressed, and overall economic conditions were unfavorable. Yet a Slovak émigré priest inspired a deeply religious people to build a Catholic school under adverse economic conditions in a decade when many struggled to feed and clothe their own families. Hundreds of children attended the private school before it closed in the 1970's.

A gravel road connects the cemetery, school building, and community center. The thought of oysters is replaced for a moment by the sight of a pebble. The pebble appears insignificant to the world, yet the ripples from one tossed into the water move far beyond the initial point of impact, in concentric circles.

Southern Gastronomical Unity:
We'll Rally Round the Grits

William Murchison

WHY DON'T Y'ALL TRY to guess—go ahead—which American region, in its unofficial anthem, celebrates food. Answer? The South. Permit me, Suh:

> Dar's buckwheat cakes and Injun batter,
> Makes you fat or a little fatter,
> Look away! Look away! Look away! Dixieland.

You see? We have been in the eating business a long time down here, and even if the author of the song in question, one Daniel D. Emmett, was a damnyankee, he was not a totally unenlightened one. He sensed somehow or other what mattered in Dixieland. Food mattered then and matters now. All kinds of food, from buckwheat cakes to black-eyed peas, with stops along the way for ham hocks, cream gravy, collard greens, oysters, field corn, jambalaya, fried chicken, catfish, barbecue, pot liquor, hot buttered biscuits, rice, Tabasco sauce, spareribs, hush puppies, and she-crab soup. To imagine even a celestial portion of it is to fill the nostrils with imaginary aromas and the eyes with genuine tears. Eat away! Eat away!

Living anywhere south of the Mason-Dixon Line means eating particular things particularly well. At least that was our universal experience up to the advent of imports like the Big Mac and take-out Szechwan noodles. Even these distinctly non-Dixie products we have, to some extent, blended into our rituals. Southerners are famously adaptive. We have gone so far, if you please, as to appropriate Sauteed Escargot and Duck in Toasted Garlic Red Wine Sauce with Butternut Squash, Brie Tart, and Tarragon Horseradish Drizzle.

But I was speaking of ritual. Food is ritual everywhere, no doubt, in some sense or another. Southerners are not the sole proprietors. But oh, how we relish it at our table. (Observe the sly, typically Southern insertion of a food trope—"relish"—in this context.)

Ritual is the Way Things Are Done. It is a conservative instinct. We do things in a certain way because that is the way we do things—always making room for marginal improvements, *à la* Edmund Burke. There is piety in this manner of leading life. Piety is a Southern speciality, like grits. It would have been unnatural had feelings of reverence been chased out of the kitchen with a large rolling pin. They never were.

IT STARTED with the cultural setting, though Southerners would hardly have spoken in such a high-toned-sociology-seminar sort of way. Food in the South is/was for the gathered—the nuclear family first of all, then the cousins and aunts, then the "club," then—well, you take it from there, wide as you care to set the markers.

Edna Lewis, the cookbook author and specialist in Southern cooking, writes of food as the "bond" of her onetime rural and black community in Virginia—"gathering wild strawberries, canning, rendering lard, finding walnuts, picking persimmons, making fruitcake." It was what the people of Freetown did together.

Another small example: the ritual, practiced in my wife's family a few decades ago, of the Day After Christmas Gumbo. This dish was produced by a relatively tight circle in a large extended family in Galveston: German and Creole predominantly, by way of southern Louisiana and like exotic venues. Into an immense blue-and-white Granitewear pot, somewhere around midday, went pretty much everything left over from Christmas dinner, along with appropriate seasonings. Membership credentials in the select society of December 26 gumbo chefs were a puzzle—a matter for family speculation. A member seemed to recognize himself and the other members as well. Here again was pure, practically unspoken ritual. I might add that the ritual, duly modified, goes on. My wife procured the celebrated gumbo pot some years after death decimated the December 26 society. We use it to make our own Christmastime gumbo (albeit not on December 26). When not employing this honorable piece of equipment, we display it prominently on a kitchen shelf.

Another kind of ritual used to be performed diligently throughout the South in early and late summer, from countless kitchen or porch chairs, generally in a soft summer twilight, with crickets chirping and the first faint, cool breeze starting up. This was the ritual of the black-eyed pea shelling. Or it might be cream peas, no matter. The ultimate objective was, in due course, to gobble down the peas, boiled in bacon fat and onions. But there was a more immediate objective: conversation. A black-eyed-pea-shelling circle, so to speak, made up of about three, was ideal. There was never any shortage of family or community news—we called it news, not gossip—to dispense and digest. I cannot recall politics or religion intruding much on these refreshing occasions, unless the governor or the local Methodist pastor had exhibited notable dimness of wit. But many an errant uncle or cousin was put soundly in his place. A good black-eyed-pea shelling could take an hour, depending on the number of hands and pea pods. It could take longer. If you were going to do it at all, you might as well shell some extras for the Kraft Mayonnaise jar.

This particular ritual, I am sad to say, has ceased, done in by the high-speed pea-sheller. We now buy our peas shelled and ready to throw into the pot. What this chiefly means is that the "news" awaits the dinner hour.

SOME AMPLIFICATION of the subject of black-eyed peas seems in order. Many would call grits the distinctive gastronomic product of the Southland: a continuing bafflement to the Northern folk as these hominy dried grains slide down the breakfast plate, right into the bacon. Grits are good. Shoot, grits can be wonderful. I hold out all the same for the black-eyed pea as our fundamental contribution to gastronomy. The great James Jackson Kilpatrick, late of the *Richmond News-Leader*, seconds the motion. Kilpo is given to celebrating the black-eye with resonance and wit, going so far as to elect himself Number One Pea, Pro Tempore, of the Black-Eyed Pea Society of America. "It is impossible sufficiently to laud the Noble Legume," he wrote once in a moment of uncharacteristic restraint on the subject.

Black-eyes go agreeably with every dish known to man. Moreover, the going lasts through the entirety of summer, when peas start to arrive fresh from the fields. There is a kind of blessed assurance in the knowledge that, whatever may befall a Southerner during July and August, the black-eyed pea will be available to console and refresh.

It goes beyond that. In Texas, and likely other places as well, we single out Kilpo's Noble Legume every New Year's Day, when the eating of at least a token portion—for good luck, as we say—becomes a savory duty: a duty performed all the more pleasantly with a side of ham and a spoonful of redeye gravy. This duty I still enforce on our household, even after discovering that the New Year's black-eyed pea ritual began only during the Depression—I had imagined Adam and Eve had something to do with it—as a strategy for the promotion of black-eyed peas. Let that go. What would a Southerner wish to promote in place of the black-eyed pea? The Hoagie?

That is enough (for now, anyway) about black-eyes. Back to the larger matter—how Southerners eat.

A particular characteristic of old-fashioned Southern cuisine was heft—sheer bulk. Our food lay long and languorously on the stomach after the midday meal formerly called "dinner," now known as "lunch." Long before

obesity became the newest fixation of the professional reformers, Southerners woofed down meals that would send any self-respecting fitness expert
into a swoon. As Ben Robertson related in *Red Hills and Cotton*,

> We had red gravy in bowls and wide platters filled with thick
> slices of ham, smoked and cured and fried, and we had fried eggs
> right from the nests . . . At my grandfather's house at noontime
> we had soup and two or three kinds of meat, fried chicken, fried
> ham, or spareribs or liver pudding; and we had four or five veg-
> etables and a dessert or so and fruit.

Food of this character (leaving aside buckwheat cakes and Injun batter)
rarely went to fat. The Southerner worked or walked it off. You never met
fat—pardon me, generously proportioned—Southerners with the frequency
you encountered Upper Midwesterners of more than ordinary girth. Food,
however mouth-watering, was fuel first of all—except, of course, in Louisiana, where it early on attained religious status.

In a way, old-style eating amounted to playing catch-up ball. There had
plainly been times when food in the South was hard to come by, despite
the land's natural bounty. Humanitarians like General Sherman had taken
care of that. More than one generation of Southerners in the 30's licked dry
lips as Scarlett O'Hara uprooted and crunched down the turnip in Tara's
back garden. "As God is my witness," Katie Scarlett vowed, "I'll never be
hungry again." Ben Robertson would write: "My grandparents never forgot Lee's surrender and the days of starvation in the South, and neither
of them ever allowed any of us at their house to waste rations. 'You can
eat whatever you like and as much as you like,' my grandmother told us,
'but what you take on your plate you must finish.'" The Depression fortified this commonsensible view of life, which I myself heard propounded
as late as the 1950's.

THE SOUTH is a broad and varied land. Needless to say, experiences, memories, and gastronomic tastes have always varied to some degree. Texans love
chili, but I would not give long odds on finding a decent "bowl of red" in
Atlanta. Likely as not, if you did chance upon such a dish there, the wretch
of a cook would have mingled good meat with pinto beans. (I pause to let
the horrific thought sink in.)

Texans slice their barbecue off dead cows, North Carolinians, off dead
pigs. Nobody but nobody excels Louisianans in the preparation of gumbo.
As I have already noted, food is religion in Louisiana—thanks, no doubt,

to the French influence. A New Orleans restaurant like Galatoire's or Commander's Palace is a temple; its chefs are the high priests. Notwithstanding that Texas lies cheek to jowl with Louisiana, and that Texans love to eat, you rarely find in the Lone Star State comparable devotion to food as fine art.

For all that, the essential cultural unity of the South (a unity that transcends mere race) has provided some gastronomic unity. Grits might be less likely to turn up on breakfast plates in Texas than in Virginia, but Southerners in general appreciate the general idea of grits and rejoice to find them offered at Sunday buffets, preferably drenched in cheese. Everyone, it should suffice to say, loves barbecue with smelly onions.

All the same, I must issue a few words of caution and admonition. The gastronomic unity of which I speak is not what it used to be. All right, *nothing* is what it used to be. But I have watched the South change mightily in recent decades, along with the rest of the country. We must own up: Not even the black-eyed pea—sniff, sniff—enjoys the profound allegiance it formerly commanded.

Several changes must be noted. One is the decline of the family meal across America. We Southerners are not alone in this. The family meal—to cite just one of its achievements—focused the family's attention on the same cuisine. All ate the same thing at the same time. Not anymore, or, at any rate, not to the same extent. Too many extraneous preoccupations compete with the communal sharing of grits and peas.

Too many new foods compete likewise with grits and peas, and with ham and catfish and collard greens. Americans are caught up as never before in the Pleasures of the Table. This is partly because never before have so many pleasures been so widely available at generally affordable prices. What is new and maybe also exotic turns out to be the very thing we want tonight: come to think of it, for lunch. Much of the new food is of the "fast" variety—Domino's, Little Caesar's, Jack in the Box, Taco Bueno. Such are the lives we lead. It takes hours to cook a ham. A trip to Subway gets you ham on a sandwich bun, with dressing, provolone, and sliced onions. Not bad. But not Southern. Sigh.

More—I hope to be forgiven for putting it thus—respectable and proper cuisines also vie for our attention. Oriental is here in a big way. Vietnamese restaurants, in particular, are all over the place; so also Thai. Indian establishments serve up not fried but Tandoori chicken. Within all these various places of business, it seems safe to infer, not a single proprietor or chef or waiter or maitre d' has ever voluntarily boiled a pot of grits. Certainly, no one would think of offering them on the menu. The possibilities for going through Southern life gritless seem to expand and enlarge almost daily.

SINCE THE 60's, a large number of the Northern brothers and sisters have taken up residence in our midst, further diluting our established culinary commitments. The bagel has taken us by storm. You can slather practically anything atop it. Calories are minimal. The current Greater Dallas Yellow Pages lists no fewer than 33 bagel outlets. Nor is this counting supermarkets—virtually all of which bake their own bagels or import the chain-store varieties. What would Jeb Stuart make of the bagel? What would Thomas Nelson Page? It probably does not do to wonder.

Slack must nevertheless be cut for a non-Southern cuisine that, in fact, is demonstrably—even historically—Southern. I speak of Mexican food. Mex—the Texan shorthand for this wonderful and simple cuisine—has been with us since the memory of man runneth not to the contrary. The Mexicans, as we Celts cheerfully acknowledge, got here first. Mexico's early-20th-century revolutions and civil wars precipitated more and more Mexicans into the regions north, east, and west of San Antonio. They brought with them their food, suitably adapted to place and time. Enchiladas, tacos, frijoles, guacamole, and tostadas with salsa are a part of the environment in Texas—as fundamental to the good life as ever black-eyed peas were accounted. Tex demands his Mex several times a month. It has been confessed by some that a week without Mex is like Christmas with no bonus—bleakly unthinkable.

Mex entered the South-at-large only randomly and slowly, but it now turns up regularly from the Rio Grande to the Potomac. That is progress of a sort. Texans, when out of town, need their Mex. Hunting hard, I found it in Memphis 35 years ago. It was awful. Still, it was Mex. Same with the offerings at an out-of-the-way cafeteria in Palo Alto, California, almost 40 years ago. It, too, was awful. But it was Mex.

Texans are like that. We will defend in any gathering of Southern gourmands Mexican food's proper place in the gastronomic constellation. Whereby, perhaps, we make a key admission. Southern cuisine is that which Southerners eat. Which is to say, the commitment to eat a particular dish precedes the preparation.

What is prepared can change over time. *Has* changed, in my own longish lifetime as a Southerner. Will continue to change. Buckwheat cakes and Injun batter no longer (if they ever did) define the universe of Southern gastronomy.

Yet I think, in the main, we are adding, not subtracting; building on the past, not uprooting it. The kingdom of the black-eyed pea is shrinking, but at the Dallas farmers' market I find peas prominently displayed and hungrily sought after. Who we are now is a function of who we have been: consumers of what the Book of Common Prayer calls the "kindly fruits of the earth"—the Southern earth, in our own blessed case. If we are indeed what we eat, why, then, Suh, who would want ever to be anything but a loyal, well-fed, somewhat satiated son or daughter of the Southland?

Race Politics

John Shelton Reed

"Welcome to Darlington. The cradle of Southern stock car racing. The sport
was born near here the first time a U.S. Revenue agent figured that he could
catch a moonshiner running along a twisty back road with a car load of
booze. No way. . . . Darlington is tradition. First of the big tracks in the
Southland, the granddaddy of them all. The land of racing heroes."
—from Stand On It, *by "Stroker Ace"*

YES, I KNOW I PROMISED to write about the Georgia state flag controversy, but that prospect was too depressing. Let me address instead a
couple of more entertaining topics, namely the 43rd annual Mountain Dew
Southern 500 NASCAR Winston Cup Series Race and the recent [1992] presidential election. By the time you read this you'll know who won the election, and it's a matter of record that Darrell Waltrip won the Southern 500,
but there's a connection here that you may not be aware of. It was at the
Darlington Raceway on Sunday, last September 6, that I finally realized that
George Bush was in serious trouble.

Although I grew up twenty miles from the NASCAR track in Bristol, this
was the first race I'd ever been to. When I was a lad stock-car racing had an
image problem—and not just an image problem. A very funny novel called
Stand On It describes the drivers of my youth: "Fact of life: southern stock
car drivers are mean bastards and they have dirt under their fingernails and
chickens--t on the bottoms of their boots. The backs of their necks are red.
They race all day and drink all night. Plus a lot of interpretive fighting with
tire irons. It's their form of ballet."

And fans were cut from the same cloth: "Every other one has a wooden
match in the corner of his mouth and a bottle in a brown paper bag between
his feet. They are fine when the race starts—I suppose. By maybe the 250-
mile mark they are all liquored up and the safest place to be is upside down
out there on the g--dam track."

A chubby, bespectacled teenager survives by knowing where not to go,
so I reached mid-life familiar with racing only at second hand—from more
adventurous friends, from forgettable drive-in movies with titles like *Red Line*

7,000 and *Thunder Over Carolina*, and from Tom Wolfe's classic 1965 article about Junior Johnson, the "Last American Hero" (which, incidentally, introduced the Southern phrase "good old boy" to the rest of the world). Besides, the sport itself didn't interest me much. From time to time I ran across race coverage on the radio, but listening to it seemed about as pointless as listening to bowling. And racing wasn't much better on television: 'round and around and around and around we go, as Chubby Checker puts it.

But someone who purports to know the South needs to know the NASCAR scene, so I jumped at the chance to go to Darlington with a buddy of mine who has been going for many years and has even written about it once or twice. At the crack of dawn on race day, he and I set off for South Carolina, he pointing out such sights along the way as Eunice's Grocery ("Home of Flat Nose, the World's Only Tree Climbing Dog") and a combination house of prostitution and—well, I'd better not say, but you'd never guess.

WE PULLED INTO THE TOWN of Darlington about the time the hungover Saturday-night infield revelers were waking up and popping their first beers of the morning and went with the flow of traffic down a commercial strip, past Southland Gun Works and a crane set up for bungee-jumping, to the press office just across the road from the track. There we picked up our credentials. (Yes, I was impersonating a journalist. I told the Darlington p.r. folks that *Chronicles* is a magazine of vast readership and influence. In my defense let me say that grandstand admission ran 50 to 100 dollars.)

I drove through a tunnel under the grandstand and *across the track* (strongly tempted to hang a right and take a lap just for the hell of it) to the infield, which was a clutter of campers and trailers and converted buses, many of them with platforms on top for viewing the race. Scores of flags flapped in the breeze, enough rebel ones to give the encampment the look of a lost Confederate regiment, but also plenty of U.S. flags, plus the flags of many states, flags with the colors of favorite drivers, and flags featuring portraits of Hank Williams Jr., and Elvis.

The infield folks had paid upward of $200 to park their vehicles and hook up to utilities, plus about $30 per head. I began to figure: 95,000 fans at these prices, plus television and radio coverage and commercial sponsors' logos on everything in sight. Big bucks. And this was just one of 30 or so races in a season that started at Daytona in February and wouldn't end until November, in Atlanta.

We parked the car at the Goody's Headache Powder Media Center (free Goody's, Pepsis, Slim Jims, Winstons, Texaco ballpoint pens, sunscreen, chewing gum—this journalist business is all right), picked up a wad of press releases, and set out on a walking tour of the infield. A nearby concession area offered a mobile bank machine, booths selling T-shirts, caps, patches, pork skin, hush puppies, and $85 sunglasses, and toilets labeled "Men" and "Ladies" (think about that). For once the men's room line was longer, not surprising since by my rough count male fans outnumbered female ones by seven or eight to one. This was not because women were unwelcome or unappreciated (especially those in tight cutoffs and halter tops).

Despite the high testosterone level, however, most fans were subdued, sitting quietly by their campers and drinking beer, waiting for the race to start. Some were listening to country music, one or two to gospel. (It was Sunday morning, after all.) We saw only one halfhearted fistfight. The night before had been party time, but my buddy said that even on Saturday night things aren't what they used to be—or what they still are at, say, Talladega, where the police enter the infield only in platoon strength. "They're afraid they'll scratch their Winnebagos" was his scornful explanation.

Being journalistic, we interviewed some of the fans. Most were blue-collar guys from the South, although we talked to groups from Michigan, Pennsylvania, and upstate New York. Most wore caps and T-shirts with the logos of their favorite teams and drivers. All were white. (The only black fan I saw was a large guy in a cowboy hat who was with a couple of similarly attired white buddies; all the other black folks I saw were armed—security guards employed by the track.) We talked about where they'd come from, which drivers they were pulling for and why, and politics.

The last subject came naturally. Governor Clinton was coming in shortly to be the race's grand marshal, the first Democrat who had dared to show his face at Darlington since Jimmy Carter in 1976. Carter was well received then, but in 1992 Clinton couldn't find a driver or owner or chief mechanic willing to introduce him around the garage area. Few fans were ready to embrace the Arkansas Boy Wonder either. One fellow said he came to the races (from Pittsburgh) to get away from politics. "Politics should stay the hell out of it. Clinton, too." He was with five friends: They had five favorite drivers, but all had been for Ross Perot. Now they either were for President Bush or were planning to sit it out. I told one about how fast Arkansas women are (so fast they had to put a governor on them), and it was rather well received, if I do say so myself.

But it wasn't surprising that folks didn't like Clinton. The actual *news* was that many of those we talked to were undecided, and it looked as if Perot could have swept the field if he had stayed in. We even found a few who planned to vote Democratic—outnumbered at least two to one and a little defensive about it, but solid in their choice. Most were distressed about "the economy," especially about unemployment, but a couple were, in their own peculiar way, pro-choice. "If some old gal gets knocked up, I don't want to hear about it" is how one put it. (Incidentally, any true race fans out there will be amused to hear that the black, orange, and white colors of Dale Earnhardt, "Black #3," turned out to be an infallible political indicator. Pulling for Earnhardt is apparently like pulling for the old Oakland Raiders, and *none* of his fans were for Clinton. Not one.)

Darlington's a tough crowd for any Democrat. Among race fans, the national Democratic party is thoroughly discredited, about as popular as Honda or Toyota. Four years earlier my buddy had talked to a hundred fans at the Southern 500; in an article I swiped my title from, he reported that 99 planned to vote Republican and that only one yellow dog Democrat was for Dukakis. No, if George Bush couldn't count on this crowd, he really was in deep doo-doo.

WE DIDN'T RUN INTO ANYONE who was actually unemployed (they couldn't have afforded the steep admission), but the subject was on people's minds. What we heard too often for Bush's comfort was encapsulated as the chorus of a country song a few weeks later: "Saddam Hussein still has a job, but I don't." Since Ross Perot was temporarily not in the running, that left Bill Clinton, but there wasn't much enthusiasm for him either. In a couple of hours Clinton would serve as the Southern 500's grand marshal, facing what he must have known would be a hostile crowd, and I admit I gave him a little grudging admiration for not calling in sick.

After we finished our informal poll, we went on to the garage area, where *hoi polloi* like Clinton were not allowed. Breezing past the crowd pressed up against the chain-link fence hoping for a glimpse of the drivers, we held out our press credentials and tried to look authentically nonchalant and arrogant. It must have worked, because the guard waved us through. Inside, powerful unmuffled engines roared, and men in bright primary colors bent over and crawled under matching-colored Fords, Chevrolets, and Pontiacs, plastered with commercial sponsors' insignia. The cars looked larger than life, and certainly they were larger than the Toyotas, Hondas, and BMWs that have pretty much taken their places on the streets where I come from. My buddy took a chaw of tobacco, and we stood watching, talking with some other onlookers about the threatening weather, yelling at each other over the blats and roars of the engines. As the mechanics began to roll the cars out to their starting positions, we spied a crowd gathering and went over to see what was up. It was a chapel service, apparently a regular feature of these races, conducted by a full-time itinerant NASCAR chaplain.

We stood with the drivers and mechanics and their families as the preacher led us in song ("God is so good to me," "He saved my soul," "He's coming soon"), read a Bible passage, and delivered a little homily. (Only later, after I saw what racing looks like up close and began really to understand the danger and skill and luck it involves, did I think of bullfighters praying before a fight.)

After the service, we left the garage area, walked through a tunnel under the track, and rode an elevator to the press box beside the grandstand, where we took a couple of empty seats and helped ourselves to some of the free goodies provided for the "media." We were settling in to eat the free lunch when a NASCAR p.r. man asked to see our credentials, which turned out not to be potent enough for the press box. *Chronicles'* influence only goes so far, I guess. Asked politely to leave, we politely left, to find that in the meantime we'd missed the inferior cold cuts at the infield media center. One of the regular NASCAR reporters told us there were hot dogs at the Clinton-Gore trailer, but things were starting to happen on the stage facing the grandstand, so we scurried over to watch, pausing on the way to shake hands with Strom Thurmond, straw-hatted against the sun and working the crowd even though he wouldn't be up for reelection any time soon.

On the platform Governor Carroll Campbell of South Carolina introduced the legendary driver Richard Petty, who was driving in his last South Carolina race. The governor's every mention of Petty's name evoked cheers and applause from the otherwise thoroughly indifferent crowd. Petty stood there, lean and mean in shades and a cowboy hat, smiling beatifically as the governor proclaimed Richard Petty Day and awarded him the Order of the Palmetto.

Soon after Petty left to go get in his car there was a commotion behind us as Clinton, his handlers, go-fers, and accompanying press showed up. From 30 feet away Clinton looked much fatter than I'd thought, almost Kennedy-esque. I was startled, until it occurred to me that he probably had a bullet-proof vest on under his pullover sport shirt. For his sake, I hoped so: Despite the Secret Service men glaring from behind their shades, 20,000 of us or so had a clear shot, and nobody'd checked *me* for weapons. During the invocation and national anthem, the crowd fell silent and removed their hats for probably the only time that day. Most of the Clinton press kept right on chatting and jockeying for camera angles, but I was pleased to see the *Atlanta Journal-Constitution* reporter uncover and pay attention.

During all this, an airplane circled overhead towing a banner that read "NO DRAFT DODGER FOR PRESIDENT," and when Clinton was introduced he was roundly booed, to the obvious distress of the reporters we were standing with. I noticed, however, that the boos were more heartfelt than the chants of "Bush! Bush! Bush!" that a few people tried to start. Clinton, his glued-on smile unbroken, shouted the traditional "Gentlemen, start your engines" over the jeers and catcalls and beat a hasty retreat as the mighty machines rolled out behind the pace car, engines throbbing and growling. They circled the track at highway speed; then, at the green flag, with an unimaginable blast of engine noise, took off.

THERE ARE BETTER PLACES than here to read about racing, and better informed writers to tell you about it. I'll just say that I now begin to understand the appeal of the sport. As the author of *Stand On It* puts it, "This is so different from racing Indy-type cars you can't believe it. There are folks who wet their pants every time they hear one of these big bastard NASCAR machines roar to life." The noise, the speed, the vivid colors, the pit crews' feverish work—all of this has a visceral appeal to anyone whose inner child is an East Tennessee 16-year-old. When those mighty cars are screaming past you 20 feet away at 150 miles an hour you truly appreciate the bravery of the drivers, whose skill and preparation are the only things standing between them and death. It takes a real hero—no kidding—to go out and face that every weekend and to do it with the self-deprecating insouciance so characteristic of these men. (From *Stand On It*, again, Sam Bisby's Law: "It is useless to step on the brakes when your car is upside down.")

A couple of months later, when Petty was fixing to run the Hooters 500 in Atlanta—his last race, period—CBS television, for no apparent reason, sent a crew around to ask me to comment on his status as a Southern cultural icon. The Yankee interviewer kept asking why King Richard is so admired in the South, and I tried to tell him, but he didn't seem to like what I said. Anyway, he kept rephrasing the question. I think he wanted me to say that Southerners like Petty because we lost the Civil War and he gives us something to be proud of. But I wasn't going to say *that*. I mean, one, we're not stupid enough to believe that anyone will think better of us for having good stock-car drivers; two, Southerners who are looking for something to be proud of are found in Atlanta fern bars, not at the Darlington Raceway; and, three, I'm not sure that most race fans are aware that we lost the war. Anyway, I felt so uneasy about the interview that I didn't watch the news that night. Some of my friends say they caught me pontificating on national TV, but it's interesting that none of them can remember what I said. I hope I said that white Southern working-class folk admire Petty because he has qualities that white Southern working-class folk admire—like skill, courage, humility, and sly humor.

We watched enthralled for a time, then figured we'd better get back to work (and forage for lunch), so we nipped over to the Clinton-Gore compound to cop some hot dogs and see what the Democrats were up to. The compound consisted of a couple of trailers surrounded by chain-link fence, guarded by several burly security men in ties and gimme caps. The Clintonites, still waiting for their candidate to come shake hands, included a couple of apparent Junior Leaguers and a male sociology professor from a nearby college, and they all looked seriously out of their element. The reporters traveling with Clinton were not a down-home crowd either (unlike the sports reporters we'd been hanging out with in the Media Center). Most had beat a path straight back to the campaign's air-conditioned trailer, where someone took posterboard and markers and made a sign that said "MAKE LOVE NOT STOCKCAR RACES." Inside they pecked away on laptops and used the phone bank to file their stories about the candidate's chilly reception, which seemed to distress and puzzle most of them. My buddy and I, ever helpful, tried to explain to some that the real story was that not everybody had been booing. Sure, nobody was taking Clinton's bumper stickers or buying the ten-dollar T-shirts, but nobody was firebombing the trailer, either. We told them that was bad news for Bush, but they didn't seem to believe us.

My buddy and I gobbled our hot dogs (I guess we'll be paying for them for the next four years) and went off for one last look at the infield crowd, most of them now perched on top of their trailers and vans, studying the race intently. A complete 500-mile race would require 367 laps of the oval track, four hours or so, but the intricate Winston Cup scoring system awards points for a great many things besides where one finishes, and there is always the possibility of a collision to keep the fan attentive. I confess that we left early, after nearly three hours, with an eye on the gathering storm clouds and a desire to get away before the other 95,000 fans decided to do the same. We were headed back to North Carolina when we heard on the car radio that rain had stopped the race, at least temporarily. A couple of hours later we were drinking beer in a tavern in Wadesboro, talking with a bail bondsman and watching some of his clients play bumper pool, when the television johnnies interrupted their interviews with drivers and mechanics to announce that the race had been called for good.

The bumper-pool game stopped, and we all turned our attention to the television for the final wrap-up. Most of the discussion centered on the fact that Davey Allison had been in contention when the race was stopped. A victory for Allison would have added the "Winston Million" (a million dollars for anyone who wins three of the four most difficult races) to the $1.3 million he had already won in 1992. But Darrell Waltrip had gambled that the rain would begin and passed up a fuel stop, so he had been leading when the red flag came out and consequently won the race. Asked how much fuel he had left at the end, Waltrip grinned and said, "About a million dollars worth."

A couple of months later, as I know, Bill Clinton was ahead when that other race was called.

How to Get Along in the South:
A Guide for Yankees

John Shelton Reed

RIGHT NOW, DOWN HERE, we seem to be experiencing an influx of Northern migrants. There are so many of them, and misunderstanding is so frequent, that I fear a new wave of sectional hostility may be shaping up. I offer as evidence the fact that some of my less tolerant brethren have taken to referring to Northerners as "'rhoids"—short for hemorrhoids, from a rude joke with the punch line (approximately): "If they come down and stay down, they're a pain."

But these new invaders are friendlier than the last bunch, and some of them apparently want to fit in. So I surmise, at least, from the fact that the University of North Carolina at Charlotte sponsored a very well attended adult-education course last spring on "The South for Non-Southerners." (This goes to show how thoughtful we are down here, by the way. When I lived in Boston and New York I don't recall anyone offering a course on the North for non-Northerners, although I could have used one a few times.)

If I were running that course, I think I could boil it down to elaboration of a single theme, and I offer it to readers of this magazine at no charge. Reed's Rule for Successful Adjustment to the South is simply this: *Don't think that you know what's going on.*

William Price Fox puts the basic problem well: "No lie, the average Yankee knows about as much about the South as a hog knows about the Lord's plan for salvation." Thing about the hog, though, is that he doesn't *think* he knows. Believing that they know what's happening is probably the most common mistake Northerners make. Most other problems stem from that. Heck, half the time *Southerners* don't know what's going on here—why should someone who just unloaded his U-Haul?

Oddly, *real* foreigners often seem to have an easier time of it than folks from Wisconsin or Massachusetts or California. Brits and Germans and Japanese and Kuwaitis are likely to recognize that things in the South aren't what they're used to and can't be made that way by complaining loudly. Moreover, Northern migrants often ethnocentrically insist that we mean what they think we said instead of meaning what we mean. Choong Soon Kim, author of *An Asian Anthropologist in the South* (I'm not making this up), observes that Southerners very seldom say what they mean. He finds us, in a word, inscrutable.

Maybe Northern migrants should just accept that fact, as Kim does. But if you insist on trying to understand Southern conversation, here are a few examples that may be helpful.

Surely most of you all have been warned that "You all come see us" does not mean that you all should actually drop in. That should be Lesson #1 in any Introductory Southern course. An intermediate course, though, would teach that one thing it almost always *does* mean is "Come see us if you have to for some reason"—although that usually goes without saying. And an advanced course would teach the student that sometimes it actually does mean you all should drop in. Depending.

Similarly, "Where's your husband today?" can be, as in the North, nosiness plain and simple—or, from a male, a cautious inquiry before making some moves. In the South, though, it can also be just a polite expression of interest in your kinfolks: The questioner may not really care.

See? These things are not simple. Take the question "What church do you go to?" Many newcomers find it offensive when brand-new acquaintances ask that. They assume that it is the prelude to some serious witnessing, and it may be. On the other hand, it can also be just a conventional pleasantry, like "What do you do?" (a question Southerners sometimes find offensive) or "What's your sign?" (a question I always answer "No Trespassing"). "What church do you go to?" can also be an insult, especially if the emphasis is on the word "you." Again, it depends. Migrants should just recognize that they don't have a clue and hope for the best.

REED'S RULE has an important corollary: Since you don't know what's going on, *be very careful about offering advice.* A story going the rounds down here illustrates that point: A Northern gentleman retires to the rural South. The first morning he's sitting on his porch enjoying the scenery when a farmer comes walking down the road with a hog beside him. The newcomer greets his new neighbor and asks him where he's going with the animal. The farmer says that he's taking the hog to a fine mudhole down the road to let him wallow some.

"What's the matter?" the Yankee asks. "Don't you have water at your house?" Slightly offended, the farmer replies that of course he has water.

"Well, couldn't you make a mudhole up there?"

"I expect I could, but why would I want to do that?"

"Good Lord, man, think of the *time* it would save!"

"Yeah," says the farmer, "but what's time to a hog?"

(Watch it: Don't be so sure who that joke is on.)

I have a similar story—a true one. Last fall I hired a couple of men to tear down our old garage (a job the termites already had well in hand). While they were slamming away with crowbars and sledgehammers, my neighbor's father, visiting from Michigan, came over to where I was watching. "You know, up North we'd get a front-end loader in there and we'd have that baby down in a half-an-hour."

Well, now. Here's another rule for getting along in the South. If you must give unsolicited advice, pretend it's something that just occurred to you.

Never, under any circumstances, tell us how it's done up North.

Never mind that you think the Northern way is superior. Even if it is—*especially* if it is—we don't want to hear about it. Even the most cosmopolitan Southerner is likely to bristle at that. Atlanta columnist Lewis Grizzard puts it eloquently: "Delta is ready when you are."

Now my neighbor's father meant well, and she and her husband are nice folks, and they *are* my neighbors. So I did not say "Eat hot lead, Yank."

Neither did I say: "Well, down here we get a couple of old boys in with crowbars and save us some money and keep 'em off the welfare." But I could have. It's true that heavy machinery could have done that job in half an hour instead of the three or four it took the fellows I hired. But I paid them $60 instead of the $75 minimum it would have cost me for a machine and an operator. And my county has an unemployment rate of about three percent. What's Lansing's?

As a matter of fact, though, I didn't say much of anything at all, just mumbled something.

I did a little better last summer when a New York acquaintance, thinking of retiring to our area, asked if there had been much Klan activity lately. Now that question is about as appropriate as my asking him about the Mafia—no less, no more. It's a fact that the Klan exists. It's an unpleasant feature of our cultural landscape. But there's less activity than there used to be; it doesn't affect most of us in our daily lives (we go whole months without thinking about it); and it's unobtrusive enough that most of us are content to let the police worry about it. I guess I could have said all that, but I actually said something like: "Well, some of the boys act up now and then, but if you keep your opinions to yourself and don't let 'em hear your accent, they won't bother you none."

I'm afraid that New Yorker now thinks he knows what's going on. That's his second mistake.

U.S. Out of Dixie

John Shelton Reed

BROWSING AT A LOCAL NEWSSTAND the other day, I spied a startling comic book, issue #11 of *Captain Confederacy*. Its $1.95 price was even more startling (the last comic book I bought, back about aught-56, cost something like 15 cents), but I had to take this one home, and did. Let me tell you about it.

In the book, it is the present, in a South that won the Civil War. The protagonist is an actor who plays Captain Confederacy, a superhero in Confederate television propaganda films. His former girlfriend is the actress who plays the captain's companion, Miss Dixie. There are a dozen or so supporting characters, including "Monsieur Hex," an underground agent from Free Louisiana, and Dr. Kitsune Lee, a Japanese woman a.k.a "the White Ninja."

The story has something to do with a resistance movement against a Confederacy that looks rather like South Africa. President Lee apparently freed the slaves in the 1870's, but signs still say things like "Whites Only Beyond This Point." (The Great Emancipator was the *first* President Lee. The current president, a woman, is a Lee, too.) Coming in at issue #11 as I did leaves much to be desired, but the plot does seem confusing, not to say silly.

Nevertheless, there's much to enjoy here. In particular, the letters section offers some engaging speculation from readers. There seems to be general agreement that, in this world, the fragmentation of the United States didn't stop with the 1860 War. Texas soon split off from the Confederacy, and California became a separate country, too, along with adjoining parts of Mexico. To the north is the Commonwealth of Columbia, where (with no federal government to build dams) happy Native American salmon fishers have largely escaped history. Some of the letters are ingenious; one, for example, explains why the Girl Scouts are found in the Confederacy and Texas, and the Campfire Girls in the United States and Deseret.

Some incidental touches are nice, too. One panel shows a can of Stars and Bars Beer; the *Good Morning Dixie* television program offers an off-hand reference to "the Yucatan Territory uprising"; and there's a baseball card for Fidel Castro, power-hitting left fielder for the Havana Smokes of the Confederate League. (At $2.00 a pop, I decided against a complete set of *Captain Confederacy,* but you can get one or all of the 12 available issues from the Steel Dragon Press, at Box 7253, Powderhorn Station, Minneapolis 55407. Yes: Minneapolis.)

The authors of *Captain Confederacy* are by no means the first to wonder in print about what the world would be like if the ragged legions of the CSA had swept to victory; there seem to be almost enough books on the subject for us to call it a subgenre. But they sure are hard to track down. A friend tells me that Ward Moore's *Bring the Jubilee* (1953) is one example, and Harry Harrison's *A Rebel in Time* (1983) is another. I'm especially determined to find the latter; it's about a 20th-century sympathizer who travels back in time to show the Confederates how to make automatic weapons.

One of the best-known such treatments (and one I have read) is by MacKinlay Kantor, the author of *Andersonville.* In his unimaginatively titled *If the South Had Won the Civil War,* as I recall, the South wins after Grant is thrown from a horse and killed. When slavery proves economically unviable, naturally the slaves are freed. As in *Captain Confederacy,* the secession of Texas reveals the inherent weakness of the Confederate constitution—or, alternatively, the devotion of Southerners to their principles. Eventually, however, Texas, the Confederacy, and what is left of the United States are happily reunited after they make common cause against 20th-century totalitarianism. Kantor's book was published in 1961, and shows it.

BY NOW, five generations of white Southerners have enjoyed the counterhistorical fantasy of Confederate victory and Southern independence. In fact, that fantasy antedates the Confederacy itself. In 1860, Edmund Ruffin published *Anticipations of the Future,* a hostile response to the impending election of Abraham Lincoln in which the South endures eight years of Lincolnian tyranny before striking a successful blow for independence.

As time has passed, though, the image of an independent Confederate States of America has become droller. As in *Captain Confederacy,* the juxtaposition of Confederate imagery and the accoutrements of modern life makes for some cute effects. Here, for instance, is Will Barrett, in Walker Percy's *The Last Gentleman.* Will is 20 miles from Richmond:

> As he ate Ritz crackers and sweet butter, he imagined how Richmond might be today if the war had ended differently. Perhaps Main Street would be the Wall Street of the South, and Broad might vie with New Orleans for opera and theater. Here in the White Oak Swamp might be located the great Lee-Randolph

complex, bigger than GM and making better cars (the Lee sur-
passing both Lincoln and Cadillac, the Lil' Reb outselling even
Volkswagens). Richmond would have five million souls by now,
William and Mary be as good as Harvard and less subverted. In
Chattanooga and Mobile there would be talk of the "tough, cyni-
cal Richmonders," the Berliners of the hemisphere.

Sometimes, as here, images of an independent Southland are used only to
amuse. Other times, though, as for Edmund Ruffin, they have served contemporary political purposes.

Consider, for instance, last October's [1988] Country Music Association
awards program. Just before Hank Williams, Jr., won his second straight
Entertainer of the Year Award, he regaled the TV audience with his current
hit, "If the South Would Have Won (We'd Have Had It Made)." If you can
leave aside the grammar (my wife can't, or won't), it's quite a song.

If the South had won, Hank sang cheerfully, he'd run for president and
put the Supreme Court in Texas, so murderers would swing, "instead of writing books and going on TV." You wonder why Lloyd Bentsen and whatsisname were doomed before they started in the South?

Hank goes on. He'd have all the cars made in Carolina, and he'd "ban all
the ones made in China." (OK, so geography's not his strong point, but all
those Oriental cars do sort of look alike, don't they?) Far be it from me to
give the Democrats advice, but protectionism and xenophobia *à la* Gephardt
might have played better than what they came up with.

There's much more where this came from, but the point is that plainly the
song's subtext was a disparaging commentary on the election of 1988. Surely
it's no accident that the idea of a victorious Confederacy made it to network
television and the *Billboard* country music top ten at just the time last fall
that some of us down here were biting our tongues while old George went on
about the Pledge of Allegiance—not because we agreed with whatsisname,
but because, deep down, we're still not sure about "indivisible."

About the Authors

All articles originally appeared in Chronicles: A Magazine of American Culture. *The publication date of each article is listed in its author's biographical entry.*

DON ANDERSON was the founder of the National Association for the Southern Poor. "Reviving Self-Rule: Ward Government in the South" appeared in the March 1990 issue.

PATRICK J. BUCHANAN is a syndicated columnist, former speechwriter for Presidents Nixon and Reagan, and former presidential candidate. "Mr. Lincoln's War: An Irrepressible Conflict?" appeared in the October 1997 issue.

THOMAS FLEMING is the editor of *Chronicles: A Magazine of American Culture* and the president of The Rockford Institute. "Jefferson or Mussolini?" appeared in the November 1998 issue; "Southern Men, American Persons," in May 1994.

SAMUEL FRANCIS was a syndicated columnist and Washington editor for *Chronicles: A Magazine of American Culture.* "Witchfinder: The Strange Career of Morris Dees" appeared in the November 1997 issue.

GEORGE GARRETT, novelist, essayist, and poet, was the Henry Hoyns Professor of Creative Writing at the University of Virginia. "Tyranny by Sloth" appeared in the June 1988 issue; "A (Pardon the Expression) Baccalaureate Address," in September 1987.

MICHAEL HILL, an historian, is president of the League of the South. "The South and the New Reconstruction" appeared in the March 1997 issue.

GREG KAZA is the executive director of the Arkansas Policy Foundation. "Oyster Supper" appeared in the March 2006 issue.

TOM LANDESS, a contributing editor to *Chronicles: A Magazine of American Culture,* is a retired English professor who has published a number of books and articles. A shorter version of "Outgrowing the Past: Eminent Domain Down South" appeared in the January 2006 issue. "It's Hard Times, Cotton Mill Girls: Manufacturing, Gone With the Wind" appeared in October 2006.

DONALD W. LIVINGSTON is a professor of philosophy at Emory University and the founder of the Abbeville Institute. "One Nation Divisible" appeared in the February 1998 issue; "Losing Federalism: When Did It Begin?" in May 2003.

WILLIAM MURCHISON, a corresponding editor for *Chronicles: A Magazine of American Culture,* is a nationally syndicated columnist. "Southern Gastronomical Unity: We'll Rally Round the Grits" appeared in the August 2002 issue.

JOHN SHELTON REED, a sociologist, is the author of numerous books and essays on the South. "Bubba-cue Judgment Day" appeared in the September 1992 issue; "Race Politics" as two parts, in January and February 1993; "How to Get Along in the South: A Guide for Yankees," in January 1987; and "U.S. Out of Dixie," in January 1989.

J.O. TATE is a professor of English at Dowling College on Long Island. "Showdown at Gettysburg" appeared in the May 1994 issue; "Clip Clop, Bang Bang," in April 1997.

EGON RICHARD TAUSCH is an attorney in San Antonio, Texas. "*Gott Mit Uns*" appeared in the August 2007 issue.

JACK TROTTER writes from Charleston, South Carolina. "GOP Country: A Troubled Marriage" appeared in the October 2007 issue; "The Flamingo Kid," in October 2005.

WILLIAM J. WATKINS, a research fellow at the Independent Institute, is a legal scholar specializing in constitutional law. "*Plessy* v. *Ferguson*—One Hundred Years Later" appeared in the August 1996 issue.

CHILTON WILLIAMSON, JR., is senior editor for books for *Chronicles: A Magazine of American Culture.* "The Character of Stonewall Jackson" appeared in the July 1997 issue.

CLYDE WILSON, the editor of the papers of John C. Calhoun and a contributing editor to *Chronicles: A Magazine of American Culture*, arranged the pieces in the two volumes of *Chronicles of the South* and wrote the introductions. "What the Founders Didn't Count On" appeared in the December 1987 issue; "Calhoun and Community," in July 1985; "Reclaiming the American Story," in February 2003; "American Historians and Their History: Scratching the Fleas," in September 2005; and "Importing Prosperity: Out-Babbitting Babbitt," in April 2006.